Underst
an

William G. Egelhoff • Joachim Wolf

Understanding Matrix Structures and their Alternatives

The Key to Designing and Managing Large, Complex Organizations

palgrave
macmillan

William G. Egelhoff
Gabelli School of Business
Fordham University
New York, USA

Joachim Wolf
Institute of Business Admin.
Christian-Albrechts University of Kiel
Kiel, Germany

ISBN 978-1-349-84577-4   ISBN 978-1-137-57975-1   (eBook)
DOI 10.1057/978-1-137-57975-1

Library of Congress Control Number: 2016961068

© The Editor(s) (if applicable) and The Author(s) 2017
Softcover reprint of the hardcover 1st edition 2017 978-1-137-57974-4
The author(s) has/have asserted their right(s) to be identified as the author(s) of this work in accordance with the Copyright, Designs and Patents Act 1988.
This work is subject to copyright. All rights are solely and exclusively licensed by the Publisher, whether the whole or part of the material is concerned, specifically the rights of translation, reprinting, reuse of illustrations, recitation, broadcasting, reproduction on microfilms or in any other physical way, and transmission or information storage and retrieval, electronic adaptation, computer software, or by similar or dissimilar methodology now known or hereafter developed.
The use of general descriptive names, registered names, trademarks, service marks, etc. in this publication does not imply, even in the absence of a specific statement, that such names are exempt from the relevant protective laws and regulations and therefore free for general use.
The publisher, the authors and the editors are safe to assume that the advice and information in this book are believed to be true and accurate at the date of publication. Neither the publisher nor the authors or the editors give a warranty, express or implied, with respect to the material contained herein or for any errors or omissions that may have been made. The publisher remains neutral with regard to jurisdictional claims in published maps and institutional affiliations.

Printed on acid-free paper

This Palgrave Macmillan imprint is published by Springer Nature
The registered company is Macmillan Publishers Ltd.
The registered company address is: The Campus, 4 Crinan Street, London, N1 9XW, United Kingdom

Preface

The matrix structure is a familiar but poorly understood form of organization design. It exists when two or more elementary structures are overlaid. This can best be visualized by looking ahead to Fig. 2.1. The need for matrix structures in large, complex organizations like MNCs is growing. This growth is driven by the need to implement increasingly complex strategies.

Aside from the research described in this book, there has been little reported academic research on matrix structures in large, complex organizations over the past 30 years. This means most currently active academics have spent little time studying matrix structures. In most cases, their views about matrix structures are more likely to be based on the negative judgments of others than on their own investigation of the subject. This book represents an opportunity to personally investigate the subject with minimal time and effort. It tries to bring together the information academics would want to consider.

Next, we want to describe the book in two paragraphs. It tries to develop a more comprehensive and integrated theory about matrix structures and their relationship to strategy. The theory is based on an information-processing approach to organization design (Galbraith 1973; Tushman and Nadler 1978; Egelhoff 1991). Much of the content of the first half of the book is based on four articles we have published in referred journals. When integrated in the book, this content creates a much larger and more integrated picture of strategy–structure fit. It includes not only matrix structures, but also elementary structures (where there is a single hierarchy) and network designs. The latter are the alternatives to using a matrix structure. The book attempts to develop a contingency framework which specifies when each type of organizing should be used. One of the advantages associated with using an information-processing theory is that it provides a clearer picture of how information is processed and decisions are made within an elementary structure, a matrix structure, or some type of network design. The perspective is often that of someone inside the organization.

The second half of the book is based on exploratory research we have been conducting over the past several years in MNCs with matrix structures. It reveals that practitioners have not been idle. They have been attempting to address the problems that are frequently associated with matrix structures. In some cases they are changing the way decision-making occurs within a matrix structure. In the later chapters of the book, we have tried to reconceptualize the design of a matrix structure to accommodate this development. Instead of focusing solely on the structural configuration of a matrix structure, we now view the mode of decision-making within a matrix structure as a second dimension of a matrix structure's design. The mode of decision-making can be either balanced decision-making (where both dimensions of a matrix jointly engage in decision-making) or what we refer to as "rule-based" decision-making (where types of decisions are pre-assigned to one dimension or the other for unitary decision-making). The additional degree of freedom created by varying the mode of decision-making within a matrix structure has potentially significant consequences for the future of matrix structures. In a more speculative chapter, the book attempts to logically argue that large, complex organizations like MNCs can use the more flexible type of matrix structure to become more ambidextrous at the macro level.

While this book is primarily aimed at scholars and researchers interested in macro-level organization design, we believe it should also be of interest to managers and consultants who struggle with this same problem in the real world. We have tried to write the book in a clear, concise, and readable style that minimizes a big part of the divide that often separates academics and practitioners. What distinguishes this book from most books addressed to practitioners is the presence of a well-defined theory—and our insistence on using this information-processing theory to understand and describe most of the things we are discussing. No engineer would think of designing a large, complex bridge without using the theories of physics and engineering that are commonly associated with that task. A large, complex organization is an equally complex system. One needs some kind of overall theory to understand and describe how it functions—how it succeeds, how it fails. The information-processing theory applied throughout the book provides this kind of understanding and insight. Our intention is that matrix structures should become a better understood form of organization design, by both academics and practitioners.

William G. Egelhoff
New York, USA

Joachim Wolf
Kiel, Germany

References

Egelhoff, W. G. (1991). Information-processing theory and the multinational enterprise. *Journal of International Business Studies, 22*(3), 341–358.

Galbraith, J. R. (1973). *Designing complex organizations*. Reading, MA: Addison-Wesley.

Tushman, M. L., & Nadler, D. A. (1978). Information processing as an integrating concept in organizational design. *Academy of Management Review, 3*(3), 613–624.

Acknowledgments

The authors are indebted to many people who provided the information and understanding that made this book possible. Over the past five years, many managers in German MNCs with matrix structures have agreed to our requests for interviews. They have patiently shared their experiences and understanding of matrix structures with us. In this regard, we are especially thankful to Dr. Kurt Bock (CEO, BASF AG), Dr. Heinrich Hiesinger (CEO, Thyssen Krupp AG), and Ludger Becker (Head of Corporate Organization, Bayer AG) for allowing us to conduct a series of interviews in their firms. The information from these interviews has shaped the last half of the book and also facilitated our interpretation of the statistical analyses of data on matrix structures. Prior to the interviews, we had conducted numerous mail surveys of managers in MNCs. The data from these surveys support the extensive empirical testing of hypotheses and the development of theory that are presented in the first half of the book. None of this would have been possible without the selfless cooperation of the many managers who participated in these studies.

Finally, we acknowledge the kind permission of *Administrative Science Quarterly*, *Global Strategy Journal*, *International Business Review*, and *Management International Review* to reprint portions of articles which we previously published in those journals.

Contents

1 **Introduction** 1
  1.1 Reasons for Writing the Book 2
  1.2 Summary of the Book's Chapters 4
  Bibliography 12

2 **The Historical and Conceptual Contexts for Understanding Matrix Structures** 13
  2.1 A Brief History of the Broader Subject of Organization Design 13
  2.2 The Development of the Multidivisional Structure 16
  2.3 The Development of Matrix Structures 24
    2.3.1 Definition of a Matrix Structure 24
    2.3.2 History of Matrix Structures 27
    2.3.3 Problems with Matrix Structures 28
  2.4 Why Strategy–Structure Fit Is Important 29
  2.5 A Growing Interest in Network Designs 31
  2.6 The Development of an Information-Processing Perspective of Organizations 32
  2.7 An Information-Processing Model for Relating Strategy and Structure 36
  Bibliography 40

Contents

3 Designing Elementary Structures to Fit MNC Strategy   43
   3.1   Literature Review   44
   3.2   The Need to Better Conceptualize the Strategy–Structure Paradigm   46
   3.3   The Information-Processing Capacities of the Elementary Structures   49
   3.4   The Information-Processing Requirements of Strategy for Elementary Structures   53
       3.4.1   Foreign Product Diversity   54
       3.4.2   Product Modification Differences   55
       3.4.3   Product Change   56
       3.4.4   Size of Foreign Operations   57
       3.4.5   Size of Foreign Manufacturing   58
       3.4.6   Number of Foreign Subsidiaries   59
       3.4.7   Extent of Outside Ownership   59
       3.4.8   Extent of Acquisitions   60
   3.5   Testing the Hypotheses   61
   3.6   A Multivariate Test of Fit Between Strategy and Different Types of Elementary Structure   63
   3.7   The Coordination Capacities and Limitations of Different Types of Elementary Structure   67
   Bibliography   73

4 Designing Matrix Structures to Fit MNC Strategy   75
   4.1   Literature Review   76
   4.2   The Information-Processing Capacities of Matrix Structures   79
   4.3   The Information-Processing Requirements of Strategy for Matrix Structures   82
       4.3.1   Foreign Product Diversity   82
       4.3.2   Size of Foreign Operations   84
       4.3.3   Number of Foreign Subsidiaries   87
       4.3.4   Size of Foreign Manufacturing   88
       4.3.5   Strategic Orientation   89
   4.4   Testing the Hypotheses   91

4.5	A Multivariate Test of Fit Between Strategy and Different Types of Matrix Structure		93
4.6	Extending and Modifying the Theory for Elementary Structure Fit So That It Is Applicable to Matrix Structures		99
	4.6.1	The Combination of the Functional Division and Product Division Dimensions in a Matrix	99
	4.6.2	The Multiple Roles of a Geographical Region Dimension in a Matrix	101
	4.6.3	The Failure of the Existing Model to Adequately Specify the Strategic Domain of the Functional Division × Product Division × Geographical Region Structure	102
	4.6.4	Some Concluding Remarks	104
Bibliography			106

5 Understanding the Causes of Conflict in Matrix Structure Firms 109
  5.1 Literature Review 110
  5.2 Hypothesis Development 114
  5.3 Testing the Hypotheses 118
    5.3.1 The Study 118
    5.3.2 Results 119
  5.4 Discussion 122
    5.4.1 Overall Findings 122
    5.4.2 Limitations of the Study 125
  5.5 Implications for Future Research and Practitioners 126
  Bibliography 128

6 Decision-Making Within Matrix Structures 131
  6.1 The Modes of Decision-Making in a Matrix Structure 132
  6.2 Further Conceptualizing the Design of Matrix Structures 138
  6.3 Defining the Information-Processing Capacities of the Two Modes of Decision-Making 142

	6.3.1	Accountability During Decision-Making	144
	6.3.2	Speed of Decision-Making	144
	6.3.3	Economizing on Human and Monetary Costs During Decision-Making	145
	6.3.4	Novelty and Innovativeness of Alternatives Generated During Decision-Making	145
	6.3.5	Thoroughness with Which Alternatives Are Evaluated During Decision-Making	146
6.4		Identifying the Situations Best Addressed by the Two Different Modes of Decision-Making	147
	6.4.1	Situations that Fit a Rule-Based Mode of Decision-Making	147
	6.4.2	Situations that Fit a Balanced Mode of Decision-Making	152
6.5		Designing a More Flexible Matrix Structure	157
Bibliography			159

7 How a Flexible Matrix Structure Supports a More Ambidextrous Organization — 161

7.1	The Need for Ambidexterity in Organizations	161
7.2	How Ambidexterity Is Currently Implemented in Organizations	162
7.3	A Hypothetical Example of a Flexible Matrix Structure Contributing to Ambidexterity	165
7.4	How Ambidexterity at the Macro Level Compares to Ambidexterity at Lower Levels	169
7.5	How a Flexible Matrix Structure Supports Ambidexterity at the Macro Level of Large, Complex Organizations	174
Bibliography		179

8 The Joint Use of Matrix Structures and Network Designs to Implement Multidimensional Strategies — 181

8.1	Introduction	181
8.2	Literature Review	182
	8.2.1 Hierarchical Structures	182
	8.2.2 Network Designs	183

8.3	The Information-Processing Characteristics of Hierarchies and Networks	186
	8.3.1 Goal Structure	186
	8.3.2 Information Flows	188
	8.3.3 Motivation and Behavior	189
	8.3.4 Decision-Making	189
8.4	Situations Where Hierarchical Structures Should Outperform Network Designs	190
	8.4.1 Tight Coupling	191
	8.4.2 Significant Economies of Scale and Scope	196
	8.4.3 Significant Innovation	197
8.5	Two Alternative Conceptualizations of the Matrix Idea	202
	8.5.1 The Concept of a "Structured Network"	202
	8.5.2 The Concept of a Matrix in the Mind of the Manager	203
8.6	Expanding Information-Processing Capacity Through Matrix Structures and Network Designs	204
	8.6.1 The Problem of Simultaneously Managing Local Adaptation and Global Integration in a Firm	204
	8.6.2 The Problem of Managing Significant Innovation in a Firm	208
8.7	Conclusion	209
	Bibliography	212

9 Conclusion — 215

9.1	The Future of Matrix Structures	215
9.2	The Need for Better Theory about the Functioning of Matrix Structures	217
9.3	The Need for More Academic Research	219
	Bibliography	220

Bibliography — 221

Author Index — 231

Subject Index — 235

List of Figures

Fig. 2.1	Information-processing flows in a product division × geographical region matrix structure	25
Fig. 2.2	A model showing the role played by strategy and structure as higher-level intervening concepts	29
Fig. 2.3	An information-processing model of strategy–structure fit	36
Fig. 2.4	Four types of information processing	38
Fig. 3.1	Stopford and Wells Model showing the relationship between strategy and structure in MNCs	45
Fig. 3.2	Simplified organization charts of the elementary structures	50
Fig. 3.3	Important fits between elements of strategy and types of elementary structure	68

List of Tables

Table 2.1	Summary of Problems and Complaints Involving Matrix Structures	28
Table 3.1	Type and Level of Information-processing Capacity Provided by Different Types of Structure	51
Table 3.2	Hypotheses and Results of Bivariate ANOVA Contrasts for Elementary Structure	62
Table 3.3	Multiple Discriminant Analysis of Elements of Strategy on Type of Elementary Structure	64
Table 3.4	Predicted Type of Elementary Structure from Coefficients of Discriminant Functions	64
Table 3.5	Centroids of the Four Elementary Structural Groups Measured along the Discriminant Functions	65
Table 3.6	Quality of Relationship between Parent and Foreign Subsidiaries	66
Table 4.1	Hypotheses and Results of ANOVA Contrasts for Matrix Structures	92
Table 4.2	Multiple Discriminant Analysis of Elements of Strategy on Type of Matrix Structure	94
Table 4.3	Predicted Type of Matrix Structure from Coefficients of Discriminant Functions	94
Table 4.4	Centroids of the Four Matrix Structure Groups Measured along the Discriminant Functions	95
Table 5.1	MNC Matrix Case Studies	111

Table 5.2	T-tests between Mean Levels of Conflict in Matrix and Elementary Structure MNCs	119
Table 5.3	ANOVA Contrasts of Levels of Conflict Associated with Two-Way Matrix Structures and Relevant Elementary Structures	120
Table 5.4	ANOVA Contrasts of Levels of Conflict Associated with a PD×GR×FD Matrix Structure and Relevant Elementary Structures	121
Table 6.1	Characteristics of the Classical Balanced Mode and the New Rule-based Mode of Decision-Making	133
Table 6.2	An Information-processing Perspective of Decision-Making within Elementary and Matrix Structures	141
Table 6.3	Information-processing Capacities of the Two Modes of Decision-Making	143
Table 8.1	Characteristics of Network Designs in the MNC Literature	185
Table 8.2	Important Differences between Hierarchical Structures and Network Designs that Influence Their Information-processing Capacities	187

1

Introduction

This is a book about the design and use of matrix structures in multinational corporations (MNCs). While its content should be of interest to anyone concerned with the design and functioning of large, complex organizations, it is important to know that the underlying research for the book was done in MNCs. Since MNCs tend to be the most complex form of organization in widespread use today, this context best reveals the difficult organizing and managing challenges that matrix structures typically seek to address. Our definition of a matrix structure is an overlaying of two or more elementary structures.

Currently, many scholars and practitioners believe matrix structures are too complex an organizational form to work with. They suggest using simpler organizational forms such as elementary structures and network designs. But unless one also simplifies the strategy the firm is attempting to implement, this suggestion will not work. Generally, complex strategies will require equally complex organizational forms. The law of requisite variety requires this. So the best response to complexity is not arbitrary simplification, but better understanding the complexity. Better understanding the complexity usually requires successfully conceptualizing it in a more abstract way. After this has been accomplished, the complexity can usually be represented by a more simplified model. This simplified model describes those parts of the original complexity that the task at hand seeks to address and tends to ignore other parts of the original complexity that are not relevant to the task at hand. This is the best way to understand and deal with complexity.

1.1 Reasons for Writing the Book

One reason for writing this book at this time is that most of the existing literature on matrix structures is quite old, and there is evidence that firms employing matrix structures currently are frequently using them in ways that differ from what is described in the earlier literature. We will discuss the history of matrix structures more fully in Chap. 2, but some readers may already know that matrix structures have been out of favor among US firms since the late 1980s. This loss of interest largely explains the shortage of academic research and publication on matrix structures over the past 30 years. Currently, we believe there is a growing interest in matrix structures among practitioners—not yet among academics—largely driven by the increased complexity of the strategies that many firms are required to implement (Burton et al. 2015).

A second reason for writing this book is to provide a better conceptual model for understanding and working with matrix structures. Not only is most existing literature on matrix structures dated, it frequently reflects an early attempt to describe an emerging organizational form. As a result, many of the early publications are more optimistic than realistic, more interested in touting the new form than in critically evaluating it. Similarly, when matrix structures fell out of favor in the 1970s, another set of publications criticized matrix structures in general, without providing any useful insight into how to design successful matrix structures. We will review the literature on matrix structures more fully in Chap. 2. But, the point we want to make here is that there is a shortage of useful theory about matrix structures—theory about how matrix structures function, theory about how to design matrix structures to fit the unique characteristics of a firm's strategy and environment. What theory does exist tends to be fragmented and scattered across a number of scholarly publications. It takes time for potential contributions to a more general theory to accumulate and become reconciled, and for a more cumulative and general theory about some phenomenon to result. And for matrix structures, this never happened. The volume of research on matrix structures was too small and the period when there was a scholarly interest in matrix structures too brief for a more cumulative, general theory to emerge.

As a result of the above situation, there is a need for a deeper understanding of how matrix structures function, and how dual hierarchies of headquarters (HQs) interact and provide coordination. And, this understanding needs to reflect how matrix structures are being used in companies today, since there is evidence that this may differ from the way they were reported to function 30 years ago. The way structures and organization designs are used tends to evolve as practitioners attempt to address the problems and shortcomings they encounter. Since matrix structures have been associated with numerous problems, it is important to restudy how matrix structures are actually being used in companies today. The concluding chapters of the book will look at this issue and attempt to adjust our theory to accommodate the more recent changes that have occurred.

And this new understanding of matrix structures needs to exist within a broader context that also includes the alternatives to using a matrix structure. Most academics today would probably argue against using a matrix structure. Instead, they would recommend using an elementary structure (with a single type of hierarchy) supplemented by a heavy use of network coordination. In academic circles, adding more non-hierarchical network coordination has been the preferred way of increasing the coordination capabilities of organizations for the past three decades. Any attempt to critically evaluate the use of matrix structures clearly needs to take this alternative to a matrix structure into consideration. So the conceptual framework underlying a more general theory of matrix structures needs to reconcile and integrate the hierarchical coordination provided by a matrix with the non-hierarchical, more lateral type of coordination provided by networks. This is a richer, more encompassing view of coordination in organizations than presently exists in the academic literature.

The intended result should be a much better understanding of matrix structures and their alternatives.

1.2 Summary of the Book's Chapters

This section provides an overview of what is in each chapter. While it may be tempting to skip the earlier chapters and go immediately to Chap. 4, where the discussion turns exclusively to matrix structures, we warn against this. The earlier chapters are more than a lengthy introduction. They develop the context and important concepts that help the reader understand matrix structures in a new and much more complete way. Matrix structures are a complex form of organization, which combines simpler forms of organization. One must first understand the simpler forms of organization before one can truly understand matrix structures. Chapters 2 and 3 attempt to develop this preliminary knowledge in a cumulative, easy-to-understand way, one step at a time.

Chapter 2 develops the historical and conceptual contexts for thinking about and understanding matrix structures. It begins by briefly reviewing the extensive experience that humans have had in attempting to organize themselves to accomplish tasks and achieve goals. Two important concepts emerge. The first is "interdependency among the actors." As the strategies of organizations become more complex, there is increasing interdependency among the actors. This interdependency creates the need for coordination and organizing. Reducing or simplifying the interdependency reduces or simplifies the need for organizing. The second concept is "bounded rationality." It refers to the fact that humans are limited in terms of the information and knowledge an individual or subunit can possess. This limits their ability to make rational decisions. In order to address this limitation and be sufficiently competent, individuals and subunits tend to specialize. This isolates knowledge in different parts of an organization. It requires organizations to bring such isolated knowledge together and to coordinate the decisions of separated subunits in order to implement an organization's strategy. Organization design is the way organizations accomplish this. Both of these fundamental concepts will be illustrated and used throughout the book, so that they become a kind of subconscious framework for understanding and evaluating the problem of coordination.

The second part of Chap. 2 deals specifically with the history of matrix structures and their alternatives (some form of network design). The concept of a matrix structure probably evolved as practitioners adjusted and tweaked their organizational structures to better accomplish their organizations' goals. The growth of specialized staff functions in military organizations and later in large business firms created situations where some kind of shared decision-making involving line and staff officers arose. Given the sanctity of the principle of "unity of command" in military organizations (and probably most early business firms), this situation was generally addressed by giving line officers command authority and staff officers advisory authority over the situation (and more specifically, over the subunits that had to make decisions to address the situation). This is very close to being some kind of matrix structure. Formally, matrix structures first appeared in the US aerospace industry in the 1950s, but their antecedents and the concepts of shared responsibility and shared decision-making clearly existed well before this time.

Unfortunately, the term "matrix structure" is not used in a consistent manner throughout the existing literature. In Chap. 2 we will further discuss our definition of a matrix structure: a matrix structure combines or overlays two or more types of elementary hierarchical structure. Those who need to see a picture of this now can look ahead to Fig. 2.1. Matrix structures soon spread to other industries beyond aerospace, where they were applied in a broader way, combining different kinds of elementary structures to produce different combinations or configurations of matrix structure. This broadened the concept of a matrix structure and led to a design problem for firms. Which dimensions or types of elementary structure should a firm's matrix structure contain? The answer depends on the strategy of the firm.

The latter part of Chap. 2 introduces and describes the conceptual framework that will be used throughout the book to evaluate the coordinating potential of different types of structure and organization design. It is called an "information-processing approach" to organization design. Under this perspective, the organization is viewed as an information-processing system, and information processing between an organization's subunits is considered an important aspect of organizational performance. Information processing in organizations is generally defined as including the gathering of data, the transformation of data into information, and the communication and storage of information in the organization. Each of the various types of organization structure or organization design available to a firm can be seen as facilitating certain types of information processing between the subunits of the organization, while at the same time restricting other types of information processing. Just as structure and organization design largely define the information-processing capacities of a firm, the strategy and environment of a firm largely define the information-processing requirements that the firm must seek to satisfy. There is good fit between organization design and strategy when the information-processing requirements of a firm's strategy are satisfied by the information-processing capacities of its organization design. This is the basic model or conceptual framework that the book will use to evaluate and compare the effectiveness of matrix structures against the effectiveness of their alternatives. It will lead to a deeper and more consistent understanding of the strengths and weaknesses of the different types of matrix structure and it will provide a logic for designing matrix structures that are appropriate for implementing specific elements of a firm's strategy.

Chapter 3 discusses the fit between strategy and the various types of elementary structure. Before one can understand matrix structures, one must understand how an elementary structure functions and how it can be related to strategy. An elementary structure exists when one dominant type of hierarchy is used to organize a firm at the second hierarchical level (the level right below the firm's CEO). The most common elementary structures are a functional division structure, a product division structure, and a geographical region structure. The subject of strategy–structure fit for elementary structures is well developed in the scholarly literature. It begins with the work of Chandler (1962) and other researchers, who attempted to explain why large firms like DuPont had to change from a functional division structure to a product division structure when their strategies began to embrace higher levels of product diversity. The later and most developed part of this stream of research deals with how to structure MNCs, so that they can successfully implement strategies that are not only more diversified in terms of products, but more international. The information-processing approach discussed above was initially developed to model the fit between specific elements of an MNC's strategy (e.g., the degree of foreign product diversity, the extent of internationalization) and the specific types of elementary structure available to an MNC.

Chapter 3 describes the key fits between elements of MNC strategy and the four principle types of elementary structure used by MNCs (an international division structure, worldwide functional division structure, worldwide product division structure, geographical region structure). The focus is on describing these fits as clearly as possible in terms of the information-processing requirements posed by the strategy and the information-processing capacities provided by the structure. Using this logic, hypotheses are developed. They are empirically tested with a sample of 34 elementary structure MNCs. The strategy–structure fits developed here are the necessary foundation for being able to subsequently understand the key fits between the various configurations of matrix structure and strategy.

A matrix structure combines the information-processing capacities of the elementary structures that make up the matrix. Thus, elementary structures are the building blocks for designing matrix structures, and one needs a deep and thorough understanding of their capabilities and limitations before attempting to evaluate and design matrix structures. This idea of decomposing a matrix structure into a set of specific elementary structures (to better understand and specify its coordination capabilities) has largely been developed by the authors and supported by their own empirical research. Most articles and books on matrix structures tend to generalize across the various configurations of matrix structure. In our view, this hinders a deeper understanding of how matrix structures provide coordination. Our more detailed and explicit model of how a specific configuration of matrix structure provides coordination is unique and probably one of the most important contributions of this book.

Staying with the above issue a bit longer, we view matrix structures as a complex, high-level concept, which needs to be decomposed into a set of simpler concepts before it can be effectively understood and worked with. In our view, much of the existing literature on matrix structures attempts to address the subject without first building an adequate foundation or conceptual framework for understanding such a complex concept. Our approach is to first lay the foundation or build the conceptual framework before we attempt to work with the concept of matrix structures. While this is a longer path to take into the subject, we believe it will ultimately take one much further than the existing literature.

Chapter 4 describes the key fits between elements of MNC strategy and the four principle types of matrix structure used by MNCs: a product division × geographical region matrix, a product division × functional division matrix, a geographical region × functional division matrix, and a functional division × product division × geographical region matrix (the latter is often referred to as a Tensor structure in Germany). The approach here parallels that used in Chap. 3 for elementary structures. The same information-processing logic is used to hypothesize fit relationships between the specific dimensions of a matrix structure and specific elements of MNC strategy. The empirical testing of the hypotheses with a sample of 57 matrix structure MNCs both (1) confirms the overall information-processing logic underlying our theory, and (2) helps to refine and extend that theory in a number of areas that are unique to matrix structures.

Because we are attempting to develop a general model or theory for fitting matrix structures to strategy, the knowledge or learning developed in this chapter should not be confined to the four configurations of matrix structure that are explicitly discussed. Readers should be able to apply the logic and understanding developed here to matrix structures containing other kinds of structural dimensions (such as businesses or customers) and to strategies embracing different strategic characteristics.

Our empirical research supports using the same logic to fit the dimensions of a matrix structure to the strategy of a firm, as was previously used in Chap. 3, to fit the various types of elementary structure to a firm's strategy. The development of a common logic for designing matrix structures and elementary structures simplifies the design process and makes it easier to understand matrix structures. Naturally, some additional understanding and conceptualization is required to design matrix structures. For example, a matrix structure can contain a functional division dimension and a product division dimension. When designing an elementary structure, a functional structure fits a strategy with low product diversity while a product division structure fits a strategy with high product diversity. A matrix structure that simultaneously employs both of these dimensions obviously requires some additional understanding and conceptualization that describes how these two dimensions work together to constructively process information inside a matrix structure. Our research further explains a number of these kinds of situations that are unique to matrix structures.

Chapter 5 discusses conflict in matrix structure firms. When many MNCs abandoned matrix structures in the 1980s, one of the most frequently reported problems was high levels of interpersonal and interunit conflict. While conflict is generally regarded as a common characteristic of matrix structures, there has actually been limited empirical investigation of this issue. Most reports of conflict come from clinical research and case studies. Our own research used a survey study of conflict in matrix and elementary structure MNCs, which supports the use of statistical analysis and the generalization of the findings to a broader population of firms. This research shows that conflict may be influenced by the structural configuration of a matrix structure. Structures which matrix a product division dimension with a geographical region dimension tend to have higher levels of conflict than structures which matrix a functional division dimension with either a product division dimension or a geographical region dimension. While this finding is new and requires additional research, Chap. 5 discusses what it may be saying about the causes of conflict in matrix structures.

Chapter 6 discusses two different modes of decision-making which can exist within a matrix structure. The first is the joint or balanced mode of decision-making, where decisions are jointly made by both dimensions of a matrix. The second is a unitary or rule-based mode of decision-making, where rules pre-specify which dimension of a matrix will unilaterally make certain types of decisions. Existing matrix structure theory generally assumes the joint or balanced mode of decision-making, but our recent exploratory research in matrix structure MNCs reveals that many firms appear to be adopting the rule-based mode of decision-making for various types of decisions. The information-processing capacity associated with the rule-based mode of decision-making differs significantly from the information-processing capacity associated with the balanced mode of decision-making. As a result, we want to conceptualize mode of decision-making as an important second dimension of matrix structure design, along with the existing primary dimension of structural configuration (which is defined and addressed in Chap. 4).

This Chapter develops the information-processing capacities of the two modes of decision-making. It suggests that MNCs should be able to use both modes of decision-making on a contingency basis, the unitary or rule-based mode of decision-making and the joint or balanced mode of decision-making. Propositions are developed specifying which mode of decision-making best fits a given type of situation. The insight, that the difference between a rule-based matrix and a balanced matrix structure depends on a difference in the mode of decision-making, is an important observation. Because the mode of decision-making in a matrix structure is more changeable than its structural configuration, it provides additional potential for flexibility. The intended result is a more flexible type of matrix structure that can successfully address a wider range of situations than the existing classical balanced matrix structure, which only employs one mode of decision-making.

Chapter 7 discusses how the concept of the flexible matrix structure developed in Chap. 6 (with two modes of decision-making) can support building a more ambidextrous organization. Ambidexterity can be defined as "an organization's ability to be aligned and efficient in its management of today's business demands while simultaneously being adaptive to changes in the environment" (Raisch and Birkinshaw 2008: 375). It means simultaneously winning in the short run through more efficient exploitation and in the long run through exploration and adaptation to a changing competitive environment.

The existing literature on ambidexterity tends to address the subject at the business unit level or lower. In this chapter we discuss how ambidexterity might also be developed at the macro level of large, complex organizations like MNCs by using a flexible matrix structure. This structure can be used to selectively alter the mode of decision-making at the strategic levels of the organization for an issue such as product technology development. Rule-based decision-making, which assigns decision-making responsibility to a single dimension of the matrix, supports efficiency and exploitation. Balanced decision-making, in contrast, assigns responsibility to both dimensions of a matrix. This makes the decision-making process more exploratory and innovative as it tries to reconcile the divergent goals and knowledge associated with both dimensions of a matrix. We believe a flexible matrix structure could provide such capability to the macro levels of large, complex organizations such as MNCs, and thereby enhance their performance in both the short run and the long run.

Chapter 8 discusses the flexibility that an appropriately designed matrix structure coupled with the proper use of networks can provide to an organization. The chapter first develops and contrasts the information-processing capacities of hierarchies and networks. It then uses these capacities to identify and understand three situations where hierarchical structures should outperform network designs. The situations are developing and implementing tight coupling within an organization, identifying and defining economies of scale and scope, and identifying and incorporating significant innovation into an organization's strategy. This evaluation also identifies a number of related situations where network designs should outperform hierarchical structure. The above conceptual framework is important, since it facilitates the rational use of both hierarchical structure and networks. When more hierarchical information-processing capacity is required, the adoption of a matrix structure is the primary way to add this capacity.

The chapter then considers two alternative conceptualizations of the matrix idea. The first is the concept of a "structured network" as proposed by Goold and Campbell (2003), and the second is the concept of a matrix in the mind of a manager, as proposed by Bartlett and Ghoshal (1990). Finally, the chapter addresses two of the most common organizational design problems faced by MNCs: (1) simultaneously managing local adaptation and global integration, and (2) managing significant innovation. The contingency framework developed in this chapter illustrates how firms can use both matrix structures and network designs to address a wider variety of situations.

Chapter 9 is the concluding chapter of the book. It predicts that the use of matrix structures by large, complex organizations will increase, and it discusses the need for better theory about the functioning of matrix structures. It concludes by arguing that academic research is required to develop such theory and that it is time for academic research to reengage the subject of matrix structures.

Bibliography

Bartlett, C. A., & Ghoshal, S. (1990). Matrix management: Not a structure, a frame of mind. *Harvard Business Review, 68*(4), 138–145.

Burton, R. M., Obel, B., & Hakonsson, D. D. (2015). How to get the matrix organization to work. *Journal of Organizational Design, 4*(3), 37–45.

Chandler Jr., A. D. (1962). *Strategy and structure: Chapters in the history of industrial enterprise.* Cambridge, MA: M.I.T. Press.

Goold, M., & Campbell, A. (2003). Structured networks: Towards the well-designed matrix. *Long Range Planning, 36*(5), 427–439.

Raisch, S., & Birkinshaw, J. (2008). Organizational ambidexterity: Antecedents, outcomes, and moderators. *Journal of Management, 34*(3), 375–409.

2

The Historical and Conceptual Contexts for Understanding Matrix Structures

The first three sections of this chapter describe the history of organization design, up to and including the development of matrix structures. The fourth section discusses the more recent interest in developing non-hierarchical networks as an alternative to hierarchical structures and especially matrix structures. The fifth section discusses why strategy–structure fit is important in large, complex firms. The last two sections introduce an information-processing perspective of organizations and develop an information-processing model for relating strategy and structure.

2.1 A Brief History of the Broader Subject of Organization Design

There is a long history associated with the organization and management of human activities so that tasks are accomplished and goals are realized. What an individual acting alone can do probably hasn't changed that much over time, but what individuals acting collectively can do has changed a lot. As humans have learned how to better organize and

© The Author(s) 2017
W.G. Egelhoff, J. Wolf, *Understanding Matrix Structures and their Alternatives*, DOI 10.1057/978-1-137-57975-1_2

coordinate activities, productivity and output have soared. The advance of civilization itself can be viewed as largely an advance in organization design—in organizing people so that they are more specialized and can better transfer knowledge and information among themselves.

Early attempts to organize greater amounts of human activity at a higher level often ran into severe difficulties. In the book of Exodus in the Bible, Moses was charged by God to lead the people of Israel. In Exodus, Chap. 18, Moses complains to his father-in-law, Jethro, that he sits from morning till night listening to the problems of the people and attempting to give directions that will better coordinate their interdependent behaviors—and he can't successfully do it. This is perhaps the earliest documented description of a manager with too wide a span of control. Jethro responds with some excellent advice on how to create a hierarchical structure to manage the Israelites. He tells Moses:

> look among all the people for able and God-fearing men, trustworthy men who hate dishonest gain, and set them as officers over groups of thousands, of hundreds, of fifties, and of tens. Let these men render decisions for the people in all ordinary cases. More important cases they should refer to you, but all the lesser cases they can settle themselves. Thus, your burden will be lightened, since they will bear it with you. If you do this, when God gives you orders you will be able to stand the strain, and all these people will go home satisfied. (Exodus, Chap. 18, verses 21–23)

The above story can be used to introduce two important concepts of organizing, which we want to utilize again and again throughout the book. The first concept is *interdependency among the actors* (Thompson 1967). It explains why coordination and direction was required in the first place. Moses had just led the Israelites out of their captivity in Egypt. They were beginning their 40 years of wandering in the wilderness before they could enter the Promised Land. They were highly dependent upon each other for their defense and survival. This interdependency required the coordination that Moses and his subordinates were to provide. Thus, it is interdependency among the actors that drives the need for coordination. If one can reduce or simplify this interdependency, one can reduce or simplify the coordination. This is an obvious but often over-looked alternative for many organization design problems.

2 The Historical and Conceptual Contexts for Understanding... 15

The second concept is *bounded rationality* (Simon 1957). We see it in Moses when he informs Jethro that he isn't up to providing all of the coordination required by the Israelites. It refers to the fact that humans are extremely limited or bounded when they attempt to think and make rational decisions. They often have biases. They generally have to focus on one thing at a time. And, they are often slow in pulling information together and reaching a conclusion. As a result, most humans specialize—they are only willing to make certain kinds of decisions—and they want a suitably limited span of control. Thus, interdependency among the actors in an organization—or more specifically, interdependency among the tasks and decisions that the actors in an organization must address—drives the need for coordination, while bounded rationality makes it difficult for managers in an organization to effectively provide that coordination. It is the interaction of these two concepts that defines the organization design problem of a firm.

It is a big jump from Moses leading the Israelites to organizing the large corporations that began to emerge in the early twentieth century, but that is where we would like to go in the next paragraph. In between, the most impressive organizations from a design perspective were probably armies and the Roman Catholic Church. Fighting increasingly larger wars that employed more kinds of technology and tactics and building a globally integrated Christian Church were major undertakings that required increasing amounts of internal coordination. Both developed impressive hierarchies with many levels of decision-making and control, attached staff functions, and sets of supporting rules, regulations, and standard procedures. Weber (1947) studied both of these institutions in the early twentieth century and claimed they were good examples of the new organizational form he called a "bureaucracy." Business firms during most of this period were generally not that interesting, since most economic interdependency existed between a wide variety of small firms and was coordinated by external market coordination, not internal hierarchical coordination.

By the late nineteenth century, however, large multifunctional firms began to appear in greater numbers in the United States and Europe. They existed in industries producing steel, chemicals, and petroleum products, and in those operating railroads and department stores. While such firms realized greater economies of scale, they also benefited from greater specialization within functions. This led to rapidly improving knowledge and techniques that increased output and lowered unit costs. The time and motion studies of Frederick Taylor (1911) that led to greater efficiencies in manufacturing, the emergence of industrial research laboratories that routinely developed new products and technologies, the development of more sophisticated cost accounting, and the creation of new advertising and marketing approaches are all examples of the benefits of the greater functional specialization that occurred in the large multifunctional firms of this period. The interface between the functional areas was generally standardized to simplify the interdependency. That way it could be effectively coordinated by formal planning, rules, and standard procedures. In general, these firms were good examples of Weber's (1947) modern bureaucracy.

2.2 The Development of the Multidivisional Structure

The next major development in organization design was the multidivisional structure (also called the M-form by economists). It appeared during the 1920s and became the dominant type of structure for large firms following World War II, when both the size and complexity of firms greatly increased. The multidivisional structure is a broad category of structure. It refers to any structure that contains a number of multifunctional, relatively independent divisions or subunits. More specific examples of the multidivisional structure are a product (or business) division structure and a geographical region structure. It is important to understand how the various types of multidivisional structure emerged and why so many large firms moved from a functional division structure (also called the U-form by economists) to a product division or geographical region structure at this time. The business historian Alfred Chandler (1962) describes this transition in detail for four prominent US firms (DuPont, General Motors, Standard Oil of New Jersey, and Sears Roebuck).

The history of DuPont, which was founded in 1802, is revealing. For over a century its sole product line was explosives. The physical expansion of the United States during this period required ever-increasing amounts of explosives, and DuPont became a very large company. It had evolved a functional division structure which contained four large functional divisions (marketing, manufacturing, treasury, and development). The development division contained the research laboratories and also studied new business opportunities. This was the classical centralized functional division structure employed by nearly all large corporations during the first couple decades of the twentieth century. Since both the technical and marketing aspects of the explosives business were relatively stable, the interdependencies between the functional divisions were relatively easy to coordinate. Some routine planning and standard operating procedures were sufficient to coordinate most interdependencies, and exceptions could be referred up the hierarchy to a top management that knew the explosives business well. The functional divisions facilitated high levels of specialization that led to many improvements in the products and their production processes.

Following World War I, however, DuPont's strategy changed significantly. In order to utilize excess human and physical resources created by a sharp drop in the demand for explosives, the company added new product lines: paints, dyestuffs, plastics, and coated fabrics and films. Despite the significant increase in product/market diversity, DuPont retained its centralized functional division structure. This may appear strange to present-day managers and scholars, but one must remember that in 1920 there was no precedent for changing a structure away from the then-modern and highly regarded centralized functional division structure.

The new products and markets greatly increased and complicated (1) interdependencies between the firm and its external environment (its customers, suppliers, and competitors), and (2) interdependency between the internal functional divisions. Many of the new products and their markets were changing more rapidly than explosives. Some even represented new technologies that had to be modified in response to feedback from the marketplace. Almost all products faced a much stiffer competitive environment than the DuPont-dominated explosives business, and marketing soon became an important component of many of the product/market strategies.

18   Understanding Matrix Structures and their Alternatives

Problems soon developed which the existing organizational structure and management processes failed to successfully address:

- The marketing division, long used to "tonnage" selling, could not come to grips with what was required for effective consumer marketing.
- Raw material, work in process, and finished goods inventories could not be adequately coordinated across each of the many product lines.
- Marketing and manufacturing tended to lose contact with each other and so failed to work out product improvements and modifications to meet changing demands and competitive developments.
- Coordination between the major functional areas often broke down, since each division created its own figures and reports, and top management no longer knew how to consolidate and reconcile this information.
- It became increasingly difficult to monitor and control the performance of the functional divisions, now that they were operating in many product areas.
- Top management no longer had a total picture of a business. It became increasingly difficult to decide where to add new products or whether or not to fund an expansion.
- The company was consistently losing money on product lines where single product line competitors were making a profit. Further analysis by the company generally revealed that this was true even though the competitors had no particular cost or technological advantages.

While many in the company at first blamed these problems on the poor economy or the "newness" of the businesses, DuPont's rational data gathering and analytical approach to management steadily stripped away these arguments and led to the conclusion that "The trouble with the Company is right here in Wilmington, and the failure is the failure of administration for which we, as Directors, are responsible" (from a letter by H. Fletcher Brown, a DuPont manager, and quoted in Chandler 1962, p. 105).

Looking at the above information, one can see that the new product/market strategies radically changed both the interdependencies between the functional divisions and the interdependencies between the firm and its environment. Interdependencies among marketing, R&D, and manufacturing subunits became more complicated and changed more frequently. Where markets and technologies were new and uncertainty ran high, simultaneous or reciprocal interdependencies developed. Furthermore, as products became more dissimilar, interdependencies between various subunits of the functional divisions weakened. For example, there was only a pooled interdependency between the plant manufacturing paint and the plant manufacturing gunpowder, or the sales force selling paint and the sales force selling gunpowder. The functional structure, however, not only failed to provide the information-processing and coordination capabilities required by the new interdependencies, it continued to link subunits that shared little or no interdependency.

Similarly, the number of different interdependencies between the organization and its environment increased manyfold. Each product line interfaced with a different environmental niche or industry, which contained different customers, different competitors, and frequently different business practices. In a functional division company, top management is the only general management capable of formulating strategy and thereby planning a viable position for the organization in a competitive environment. At DuPont, the limited environmental knowledge and information-processing capabilities of the president and executive committee (whose members were also heads of the functional divisions) were quickly overloaded by demands for many new and dynamically changing business strategies. Thus, the functional division structure and its functionally centralized decision-making and control processes failed to provide adequate information processing for either strategy implementation or strategy formulation.

It took DuPont about two years to change its structure and organizational processes so that they could effectively support the new business strategies. This period was undoubtedly shortened by the economic recession of 1921, which created a much more hostile and competitive business environment that forced the company to change in order to survive. At first, DuPont attempted to provide more cross-functional coordination by establishing semi-formal "product committees," which contained those representatives from the marketing, manufacturing, and development divisions whose responsibilities dealt with the same product line. The committees proved to be the best mechanism for coordinating production and inventory levels among the divisions and often became the focal point for many of the operational decisions relating to a particular business. Clearly, these cross-functional, product-oriented committees provided the kind of lateral information processing required by the more complex interdependencies specified by the new business strategies. This decentralized information processing was much more timely, knowledgeable, and appropriate than was the previous reliance on the functional division hierarchy for coordination across functional areas and around product concerns.

The next step was DuPont's formal reorganization to a product division structure. Five semi-autonomous product divisions, each with its own functional departments, were created. The executive committee was also reconstituted to contain only non-operating executives. Henceforth, it would concentrate on the general administration of the total company and avoid becoming involved in the day-to-day implementation of specific business strategies. Nine functional staff and service departments (e.g., treasury, legal, purchasing) remained under the new structure, but their roles were primarily to advise and service the five operating line divisions. The new product division structure realigned the coordination capabilities of the organization. Instead of one highly centralized hierarchy and general management, five relatively independent or decentralized hierarchies and general managements were created, one for each product line. Each hierarchy and general management would address a different set of cross-functional interdependencies and a different set of organization–environment interdependencies. The five product division hierarchies in turn reported to a single corporate-level hierarchy and general management.

It is important to understand the DuPont example in more abstract and general terms, so that the implied lesson can be applied to other similar situations. It is apparent that the firm's strategy changed significantly. It introduced a lot more product/market diversity, which the firm now had to manage. This increased product diversity created new interdependencies between R&D, manufacturing, and marketing activities for each new product line. It also appears that there was little interdependency between the product lines. The most logical way to organize to implement this strategy is to group the R&D, manufacturing, and marketing people supporting a specific product line into a product division, under a new general manager who is responsible for the business associated with that product line. This will facilitate coordination among the R&D, manufacturing, and marketing subunits supporting a product line. It also provides a dedicated general manager who is responsible for formulating the strategy of the product line. This way of organizing respects both the high interdependency between the functional subunits supporting a product line and the bounded rationality of the general manager and people in the subunits. They only need to coordinate a single product line, which is what they were doing before DuPont adopted the new corporate-level strategy of product diversification.

When the strategy changed to include multiple product lines, the old functional division structure violated the above principles of organizing and caused the firm to perform poorly. It separated the R&D, manufacturing, and marketing subunits that supported a product line from each other in a way that seriously hindered interfunctional coordination around the product line. The subunits were each part of a different functional hierarchy. And the three functional hierarchies only came together at the level of the firm's CEO. At this level, the CEO and the management committee were incapable of formulating a reasonable strategy for each product line and providing the large amount of cross-functional coordination that was required to successfully implement each product line's strategy. It is interesting that at some point the company experimented with cross-functional committees around a product line and attempted to use this mechanism to provide the coordination that was not being provided by the hierarchical structure. This was a step in the right direction, but it was apparently insufficient to fully satisfy the requirement for more coordination around each product line. The new product division structure with a dedicated hierarchy around each product line could provide a lot more information-processing and coordination capacity than could the cross-functional committee. Perhaps more than any other company, DuPont is credited with developing the first product division or multidivisional structure.

The other type of multidivisional structure that soon evolved was the geographical region structure. Here geographical diversity rather than product diversity is the most fundamental difference or basis for specialization that the firm needs to recognize and organize around. In the 1920s, Sears Roebuck was one of the first companies to establish a nationwide chain of retail stores in the US. Prior to this it operated solely as a nationwide mail order retailer. With considerable foresight, management saw that the growth of the automobile would change the shopping behavior of customers. As a result, they decided to build a chain of stores. After a number of mishaps and an extended period of trial and error, Sears Roebuck developed a geographical region structure for the stores. It contained five regions within the US, each with its own HQ in the region and its own purchasing and marketing staffs. This allowed the regional strategies to specialize to better fit the needs of the region's customers. This was important for clothing and other seasonal products. The geographical region structure facilitated coordination between purchasing, marketing, and store operations within each geographic region. This is analogous to what occurs within each product line under a product division structure.

The defining characteristic of the multidivisional structure (a product division structure or a geographical region structure) is that it provides two levels of general management. One is at the top (the corporate or firm level) and the second is directly below it (the product or business level, the regional level). These two levels of general management facilitate formulating and implementing two levels of strategy: a corporate strategy and a product or regional strategy. When firms began to diversify, either in terms of products or in terms of geographies, two levels of strategy supported by a structure with two levels of general management became important. This was not apparent at first, but it was soon discovered by the early adopters of the new strategy. Firm-level strategy specified the product lines or geographies the firm would address, while business-level strategy specified how the responsible subunits would compete within their respective product lines or geographical regions. Corporate HQ management oversaw the performance of the product divisions or geographical regions, but typically it would not become directly involved in the formulation or implementation of their strategies. These were the responsibility of the product division or geographical region HQ management. This is a more complex system of strategy and structure than that which previously existed. The earlier functional division structure required a single or relatively uniform business strategy across the entire firm. This significantly constrained the size of firms. In such firms, there is no real difference between corporate-level and business-level strategy, and there is only one level of general management. In the earliest stage of DuPont's diversification, this single level of general management attempted to perform the duties of both corporate-level and business-level management. They failed miserably until they finally managed to develop the product division structure with two separate levels of general management, each with its own responsibilities and duties. Many scholars consider the development of the multidivisional structure to be the most significant organizational innovation of the twentieth century. Without it, none of the large, diversified firms that today dominate most industries could exist. Its discovery was akin to Moses discovering the hierarchy.

While the multidivisional structure is taken for granted today, its importance cannot be overstated. The creation of a number of semi-autonomous, multifunctional divisions, each responsible for a product line or a geographical region, meant that most of the operational decision-making could be decentralized to these divisions. This decentralization not only speeded up operational decision-making, it also freed up corporate management so that they could focus more on strategic matters and firm-level issues. The previous functional division structure always combined in a potentially confusing way the operational and strategic responsibilities of general management. This was, perhaps, less a problem when a firm's competitive environment was relatively narrow and relatively stable. But after World War I, the environments of many large firms began to change dramatically—often the result of technological change. When such change occurs, there is a much greater need to separate strategic decision-making from operational decision-making. Bounded rationality argues that the same management team cannot successfully specialize in both at the same time. The new multidivisional structure, with its two levels of general management, facilitates this kind of specialization, while the older functional division structure does not.

It is important to observe that the development of the multidivisional type of structure, along with the strategies that required it, created a new type of organizational design problem. No longer was there a single "best way" to organize a large firm (i.e., the functional division structure). Now the best way to organize varied with or was contingent on the firm's strategy. If product diversity was low, the best structure would be a functional division structure. If it was high, the best structure would be a product division structure. And, if geographical diversity was great and involved different competitive environments, the best structure would be a geographical region structure. From this point forward, one required a contingency theory to specify the appropriate strategy–structure fit.

2.3 The Development of Matrix Structures

2.3.1 Definition of a Matrix Structure

Davis and Lawrence (1977) describe a matrix structure as a "multiple command" or "two boss" structure. Matrix structures are an overlaying of two or more elementary structures. The elementary structures available to MNCs include a worldwide functional division structure, an international division structure, a geographical region structure, and a worldwide product division structure (see Fig. 3.2 for simplified organization charts). Under one of the above elementary structures, authority and communications tend to flow along a single primary hierarchy or structural dimension. Under the typical two-dimensional matrix structure, the head of a subunit in a foreign subsidiary simultaneously reports up to the parent HQ along two structural dimensions. For example, the subunit head might report to a country manager and to a lower-level manager in a worldwide product division HQ. Figure 2.1 shows a simplified portrayal of such a product division × geographical region matrix structure. The subunit is the German plastics business of a global chemical company headquartered in the US. Here the general manager of the German plastics business reports in via two hierarchies. The general manager's immediate boss in the product division hierarchy is a vice president in the plastics division. The general manager's immediate boss

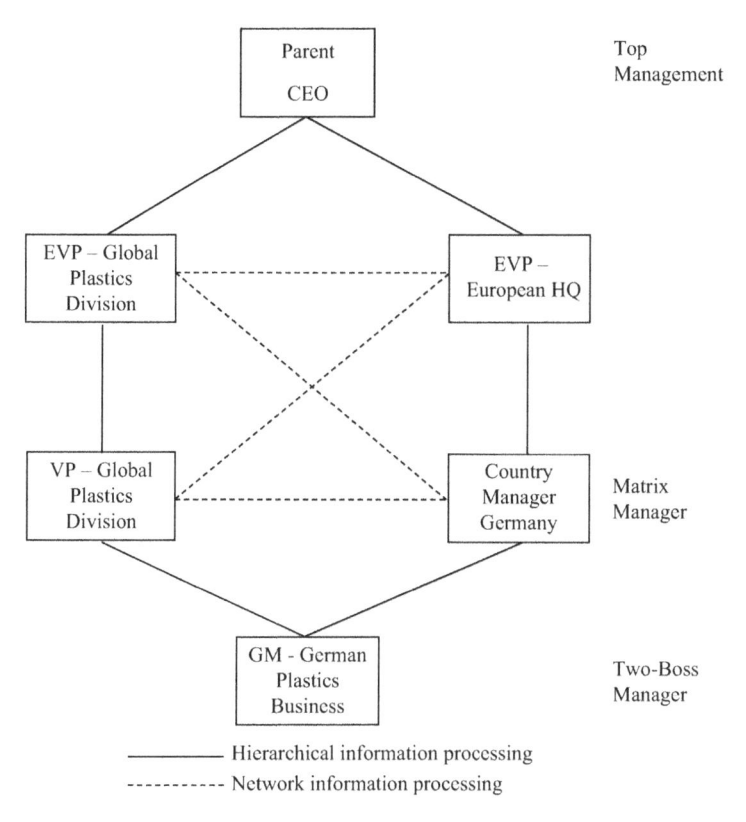

2 The Historical and Conceptual Contexts for Understanding…

```
                        ┌──────────┐
                        │  Parent  │        Top
                        │   CEO    │        Management
                        └──────────┘
                       /            \
        ┌──────────────┐            ┌──────────────┐
        │ EVP – Global │- - - - - - │    EVP –     │
        │   Plastics   │            │ European HQ  │
        │   Division   │            │              │
        └──────────────┘            └──────────────┘
              │     \  \          /  /     │
              │      \  \        /  /      │
        ┌──────────────┐            ┌──────────────┐
        │ VP – Global  │            │   Country    │
        │   Plastics   │- - - - - - │   Manager    │    Matrix
        │   Division   │            │   Germany    │    Manager
        └──────────────┘            └──────────────┘
                       \            /
                        ┌──────────┐
                        │GM - German│       Two-Boss
                        │ Plastics  │       Manager
                        │ Business  │
                        └──────────┘

     ──────────── Hierarchical information processing
     - - - - - - Network information processing
```

Fig. 2.1 Information-processing flows in a product division × geographical region matrix structure

in the geographical region hierarchy is the German country manager. These two are called "matrix managers" (Davis and Lawrence 1977), and there can be more levels of management between them and the CEO than are shown in Fig. 2.1. General managers of other business units in the German subsidiary and in other subsidiaries will also report in through a product division hierarchy and a geographical region hierarchy. Figure 2.1 shows the coordination or information-processing flows that occur within the matrix structure. We will discuss an information-processing perspective of organization design more fully later in this chapter. At this point one can simply think of the interconnected subunits exchanging and processing information with each other. The solid lines represent hierarchical information processing along each of the hierarchies. The dashed lines represent non-hierarchical network-like information processing between members and subunits of the two hierarchies.

The traditional matrix structure in MNCs and other large firms has generally been conceptualized as a balanced matrix (Davis and Lawrence 1977). That is both dimensions of the matrix have relatively equal power and influence over decision-making in the firm. While the balance of power in a matrix often shifts from one dimension to the other, reflecting changes in strategies and environments, and the personalities of the relevant managers, the underlying assumption is that there is always a meaningful level of shared power and influence between the dimensions of a matrix. In Fig. 2.1 the solid and dashed lines together represent the information-processing flows that would occur under the classical balanced mode of decision-making. To illustrate how decisions are made with this mode of decision-making, consider the information processing around important decisions associated with the annual plan of the German plastics business shown in Fig. 2.1. Such information processing occurs hierarchically along both the product and the geographic dimensions, and important inconsistencies are reconciled by network information processing between the two dimensions. Usually, the German plastics manager will be heavily involved in the reconciliation process as well.

Some scholars and practitioners have used a broader definition of a matrix structure than we do, where it includes both hierarchical and non-hierarchical dimensions of coordination. Galbraith (2009) in particular includes hierarchical and non-hierarchical dimensions of coordination in his definition of a matrix. As a result, he describes IBM having a six-dimensional matrix structure, although most of these are not formal hierarchical dimensions. Since most MNCs use non-hierarchical mechanisms to coordinate around a variety of different goals, this broader definition can result in almost all MNCs being classified as matrix structures. To maintain a meaningful distinction between a matrix structure and a non-matrix structure, our preference is to define a matrix structure as two or more hierarchies overlapping and operating at the same organizational level. This definition is consistent with the way the concept of a matrix structure has been used in the MNC strategy–structure literature

(Stopford and Wells 1972; Franko 1976; Wolf and Egelhoff 2002), and it facilitates distinguishing hierarchical coordination from non-hierarchical network coordination.

2.3.2 History of Matrix Structures

The documented history of matrix structures begins with their use in the aerospace industry in the 1950s. The need to simultaneously manage several large projects within a company led to a project management structure being overlaid onto the existing functional division structure (Galbraith 1971; Ford and Randolph 1992; Burns and Wholey 1993; Kuprenas 2003). By the 1960s, the matrix structure was also being used in MNCs (Stopford and Wells 1972; Franko 1976; Davis and Lawrence 1977). It is important to distinguish between these two broad categories of matrix structure. They differ in terms of their goals and problems, and each tends to have its own separate history and literature. Project management matrix structures are still used by aerospace companies, and they are also used by construction firms, consulting firms, public accounting firms, and other businesses where the workflow tends to be divided into a number of large, temporary projects that pull their resources from a common resource pool. This category of matrix structure only involves one kind of structural configuration: a project structure overlaid on a functional division structure. When a new project is undertaken, a new project hierarchy is created. When the project is completed, this hierarchy is dissolved, and its functional resources are reassigned to other project hierarchies. The history of such project management matrix structures has been relatively stable and successful. It avoided the boom and bust cycle that has characterized the history of matrix structures in MNCs and other large organizations.

During the 1970s, matrix structures became extremely popular among MNCs and other large, complex firms (Goggin 1974; Sayles 1976). The literature of the period often described them in glowing terms. Then, during the 1980s, they fell out of favor in the US, when numerous firms reported difficulties managing them. We are especially interested in documenting the problems associated with the traditional MNC matrix structure. Later, in Chap. 6, we intend to compare a new or emerging form of MNC matrix structure (one that employs rule-based decision-making) against the traditional form (which employs balanced decision-making). It is conceivable that the newer form will reflect and attempt to respond to the perceived deficiencies of the earlier form. The evolution of organizational design often follows such a path.

2.3.3 Problems with Matrix Structures

A summary of the problems and complaints found in the literature on matrix structures is shown in Table 2.1. The existence of two or more overlapping hierarchies in a matrix structure clearly violates the long-held principle of unity of command (Fayol 1949). A recent study in Dutch firms found that this principle still underlies the norms of most managers (Strikwerda and Stoelhorst 2009). Consistent with this norm, managers tend to associate matrix structures with unclear responsibilities and a lack of accountability. Since power is divided between the dimensions of a matrix and neither has primacy, power struggles and conflict are

Table 2.1 Summary of Problems and Complaints Involving Matrix Structures

- Unclear responsibilities that create ambiguity and conflict (Sy and D'Annunzio 2005; Strikwerda and Stoelhorst 2009)

- Difficulty in monitoring and controlling (Larson and Gobeli 1987); Degradation of performance measures (Chi and Nystrom 1998); Violates principle that authority should equal responsibility (Sy and D'Annunzio 2005); Lack of accountability (Strikwerda and Stoelhorst 2009)

- Conflict and power struggles between managers with overlapping responsibilities (Larson and Gobeli 1987); Conflict and internal lobbying activities (Chi and Nystrom 1998); Political battles over resources (Strikwerda and Stoelhorst 2009)

- Excessive time spent reaching decisions (Pitts and Daniels 1984); Slow reaction time (Larson and Gobeli 1987)

- Excessive overhead (Larson and Gobeli 1987); Increased cost (Sy and D'Annunzio 2005)

- Increased stress and anxiety among employees (Pitts and Daniels 1984; Larson and Gobeli 1987)

- Matrix degenerates into anarchy and then becomes bureaucratic and non-creative (Peters and Waterman 1982) more likely to occur in a matrix structure than in an elementary structure firm. The need for agreement between the overlapping dimensions means more time is required to reach an agreement and decision-making is slower. And a firm with two hierarchies is obviously more costly than a firm with one hierarchy. Matrix structures also tend to be associated with increased stress and anxiety among the employees. Finally, in the well-known book *In Search of Excellence*, Peters and Waterman (1982) even report that matrix structures can degenerate into anarchy and then, as a reaction, become more bureaucratic and non-creative. This is a summary of the deficiencies most often associated with the classical balanced matrix structure in the existing management literature.

2.4 Why Strategy–Structure Fit Is Important

It is important to realize that strategy and structure are not the most basic concepts that explain the survival and performance of firms in competitive environments. As Fig. 2.2 shows, both are intervening concepts that lie between the characteristics of a firm's competitive environment and the organizational behaviors emitted by a firm. For example, one

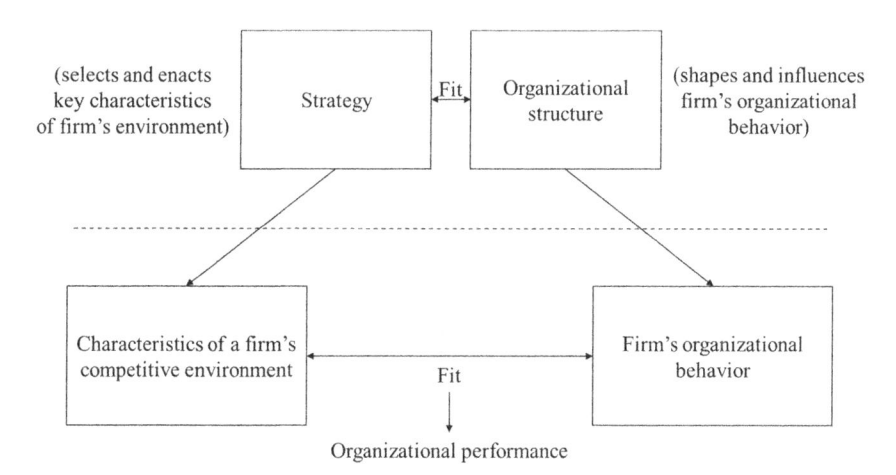

Fig. 2.2 A model showing the role played by strategy and structure as higher-level intervening concepts

characteristic of a competitive environment might be whether customers want technologically superior global products or differentiated national products. Organizational behavior, which largely consists of the decisions and actions taken by a firm, can either fit or misfit this environmental characteristic. If customers primarily want a technologically superior global product (like a microprocessor), a firm that decides to decentralize product development and proceeds to develop different national versions of a microprocessor will probably not succeed. There is a misfit between an important environmental characteristic and the behavior of the organization. As an intervening and higher-level concept, strategy selects and enacts the key characteristics of a firm's environment. It identifies the various environmental requirements that the firm intends to address, and further generalizes about how the firm will address them.[1] Similarly, organizational structure shapes and influences a firm's organizational behavior so that it too reflects some higher-level purpose and focus. Viewed this way, fitting strategy and structure on one level helps to align a myriad of individual organizational behaviors with a specific set of environmental requirements at a lower level. It is at this lower level that success and failure actually are determined in a competitive environment.

Such higher-level intervening concepts are most useful when environments are complex and organizations are large. A two- or three-person firm competing in a simple environment doesn't need a formal structure or strategy to align the small number of organizational behaviors with the obvious demands of the environment. But, as firms become large, the potential combinations of organizational behavior a firm can emit become infinite. And, as environments become complex, the range of environmental demands a firm might potentially address also becomes

---

[1] Much of the selection and enactment of a firm's environment occurs indirectly when a firm establishes its goals. Overly ambitious goals can lead to an unrealistic definition of a firm's environment and a badly focused interface between the firm and its environment. In addition to rationally selecting their environments, which implies knowledge about an environment, firms also enact parts of their environment when they lack the information to be rational (Weick 1979). For example, a firm may assume that its new product will not face any real competition for the next five years, even though there is little information supporting this assumption about the competitive environment. This assumption allows strategic planning and strategy implementation to proceed when the required information is lacking. Naturally, firms should attempt to be conscious of such assumptions or enacted parts of their environment and monitor them to ensure they subsequently conform to reality.

great. Under these conditions, aligning one with the other is extremely problematic without the aid of some higher-level intervening concepts like structure and strategy.

As Fig. 2.2 also indicates, it is not the fit between strategy and structure that directly influences organizational performance, even though this is what research has attempted to test. Rather, it is the fit between the actual organizational behaviors of a firm and the characteristics of its competitive environment that leads to organizational performance and the natural selection of the firm for survival or failure. In this case, the fit between strategy and structure is used as a proxy for the fit between the underlying characteristics of the competitive environment and organizational behaviors. Existing theory concentrates on the empirically discovered fits between strategy and structure shown above the dashed line in Fig. 2.2. What is needed to improve such theory is to conceptually understand how structure shapes and influences a firm's organizational behaviors and how these behaviors relate to (fit or misfit) the characteristics of the firm's environment. In other words, existing strategy–structure theory needs to be further conceptualized and understood in terms of the underlying concepts and relationships shown below the dashed line. The following chapter attempts to do this. It describes how the different types of elementary structure shape and influence coordination and information processing in MNCs. These are the more fundamental organizational behaviors that need to engage and fit the requirements of a firm's competitive environment. These requirements are uniquely selected and specified by a firm's strategy.

2.5 A Growing Interest in Network Designs

During the second half of the 1980s, scholarly interest in the various forms of hierarchical structure and the strategy–structure paradigm began to wane. It was largely replaced by research that took a subsidiary-level, network perspective of organization design in MNCs. This literature developed rapidly and is today the dominant organizational literature on MNCs. In this section we want to briefly describe this type of organization design and the kind of coordination it can provide, since it is the alternative to a matrix structure. As requirements for coordination within a firm increase, a firm can respond by providing more hierarchical coordination (often by adding a second dimension of hierarchy, creating a matrix structure), or it can attempt to address the requirement with non-hierarchical, network coordination. The latter involves the creation of formal and informal networks across the interdependent parties.

Some of the network literature suggests that hierarchical coordination in firms can frequently be replaced by network coordination, and that this replacement will be beneficial to the firm (Hedlund 1986; Bartlett and Ghoshal 1989; Birkinshaw and Hagstrom 2000; Forsgren et al. 2005). Our view is that hierarchical coordination and network coordination are generally not good substitutes for each other. Each has its own advantages and disadvantages, and these need to be clarified so that each type of coordination can be appropriately deployed within a firm. Before we do this, we want to fully develop the hierarchical coordination capabilities of elementary and matrix structures (which is the primary subject of the book). Then, in Chap. 8, we will contrast the coordination capabilities of hierarchies and networks, and attempt to develop guidelines for when to use each type of coordination. In the next section, we will introduce an information-processing perspective of organizations, which will facilitate making this type of comparison.

2.6 The Development of an Information-Processing Perspective of Organizations

The remaining two sections of this chapter describe an information-processing perspective of organizations. It is the conceptual framework we want to develop and use to better understand matrix structures and their relationship to strategy. It will also help us to compare the coordinating capabilities of hierarchical structures and networks. The idea that it would be useful to view organizations as information-processing systems has multiple sources. In the 1930s, when it was common to think of organization design solely in terms of formal authority structure, Barnard (1938) recommended that models of organizations should be built around the concept of intraorganizational communications.

He was the former CEO of a telephone company, and in his influential book on management, he insightfully observed that the communication and availability of information acted as important constraining factors at all levels of a large organization. Katz and Kahn (1966) also viewed the organization as a communication and information-processing system. They noted that the exchange and processing of information is the most important activity occurring within the management levels of an organization.

Another group of organization theorists focused on the decision-making processes in organizations (Simon 1957; Cyert and March 1963). They conceptualized the organization as a problem-solving system, facing an environment that does not provide all of the information required under the rules of classical decision-making. Also, the organization itself is pictured as a less than perfect decision maker, exhibiting limitations in both information-processing ability and storage capacity and influenced by the biases of its members. The major contribution of this group to an information-processing view of organizations lies in its explicit identification of some of the information-processing limitations inherent in all organizations. This is an important contribution, for if the information-processing capabilities of organizations were perfect (not limiting on organizational performance), it would make no sense to construct a contingency theory of organizations around this concept. As will be seen later, it is the differing information-processing limitations of different organization designs that make information processing such a useful contingency concept.

Still other theorists interested in viewing the organization as an information-processing system focused on environmental uncertainty and how organizations absorb uncertainty as the important contingency concept (Lawrence and Lorsch 1967; Thompson 1967; Duncan 1972). Thompson (1967) argues that the degree of uncertainty facing an organization varies with certain characteristics of its environment and technology. These differences in uncertainty lead to differences in an organization's design. For this reason, uncertainty has frequently been considered an intervening concept—intervening between the environmental and technological variables that cause uncertainty and the organizational design variables that attempt to respond to the uncertainty.

Galbraith (1969, 1973, 1977) added some additional conceptualization to Thompson's general framework and developed a much more operational model that has generally been referred to as an information-processing approach to organization design. He rigorously defined the concept of uncertainty in terms of information processing: "Uncertainty is the difference between the amount of information required to perform the task and the amount of information already possessed by the organization." A key assumption underlying this information-processing model is that organizations will attempt to close the information gap (uncertainty) by processing information (Tushman and Nadler 1978). This information-processing activity is likely to involve the gathering of additional data, transforming the data into new information, and storing or communicating the information. Effective organizations are those that fit their information-processing capacities (for gathering, transforming, storing, and communicating information) to the amount of uncertainty or the information-processing requirements that they face.

Galbraith also specified the relative information-processing capacities of different features of organization design. These features are listed below, in order of increasing information-processing capacity (Galbraith 1973: 15):

1. Rules and programs
2. Hierarchical referral
3. Goal setting
4. Vertical information systems
5. Lateral relations

Where conditions are routine and simple, rules and programs can be used to absorb the relatively small amount of uncertainty facing the organization. When uncertainty increases, exceptions must be referred up the hierarchical authority structure for decision-making. When information-processing requirements threaten to overload the management structure, goal setting and planning allow more decisions to be made at lower levels in the organization as long as they are consistent with the goal or within the plan. This relieves the information-processing load on the hierarchical structure.

When this is no longer adequate, various vertical information-processing systems can be attached to the hierarchical structure, which increase the organization's information-processing capacity. These frequently include computer-based information systems and staff groups and tend to increase the capacity for centralized information processing. When uncertainty and information-processing requirements are very great, the use of lateral relations allows more information processing to be decentralized so that the more limited information-processing capacity at higher levels of the organization is not overloaded. Lateral relations mechanisms include direct contact between individuals, liaison roles, task forces, teams, and matrix designs. Thus, Galbraith's model provides an explicit and relatively detailed framework for linking quite a number of organizational design features to the level of uncertainty or information-processing requirements facing an organization.

In summary, the information-processing perspective of organization design is a broad, loosely defined view of how organizations function. According to this view, the processing of information (its development, communication, and storage) underlies virtually everything that organizations do. While this perspective has provided a general conceptual framework for many empirical studies of organization design, generally these studies do not test a common set of hypotheses or develop a common theory. Most studies have focused on the degrees of uncertainty, change, and interdependency experienced by subunits within an organization (Galbraith 1970; Duncan 1973; Van de Ven et al. 1976; Tushman 1978; Kmetz 1984). Only a few studies have focused on these conditions at the level of the firm (Burns and Stalker 1961; Lawrence and Lorsch 1967), and generally these appear to have been relatively small, single-business firms. At this level of analysis, virtually all of these studies have been able to directly measure the type of communication (e.g., personal or impersonal, lateral or vertical) and the levels of communication between subunits associated with the workflow. While the most general finding is that higher levels of uncertainty and change are best addressed by increases in lateral relations among the interdependent subunits, the individual studies have produced many more detailed insights about successful organization design at this level of analysis. It is important to notice that the organization design problem discussed above differs significantly from the problem associated with fitting elementary and matrix structures to the strategies and environments of large, complex organizations. The latter concerns macro-level organization design, where it is difficult to directly measure the flows of information between subunits.

2.7 An Information-Processing Model for Relating Strategy and Structure

Figure 2.3 shows an information-processing model for relating strategy and structure. Information processing is conceptualized as an abstract intervening concept. Its role in the model is to help us relate strategy and structure, which are not directly comparable concepts. On the one hand, the impact of an organization's strategy and the environmental factors that it chooses to deal with can be expressed in terms of the information-processing requirements they create. On the other hand, the potential of an organization to cope with these requirements can be expressed in terms of the information-processing capacities provided by its organization design, including its structure. The boxes with solid lines are meant to indicate that strategic and environmental conditions, and organiza-

```
┌──────────────┐    ┌──────────────────┐    ┌──────────────────┐    ┌──────────────┐
│Characteristics│    │Information-processing│    │Information-processing│    │Organizational│
│of firm strategy│──▶│requirements inherent│◀──▶│capacities provided│◀──│structure     │
│and environment│    │in strategy and    │    │by structure      │    │              │
│              │    │environment        │    │                  │    │              │
└──────────────┘    └──────────────────┘    └──────────────────┘    └──────────────┘
                                    │
                          Effectiveness is a
                          function of the
                          quality of fit
```

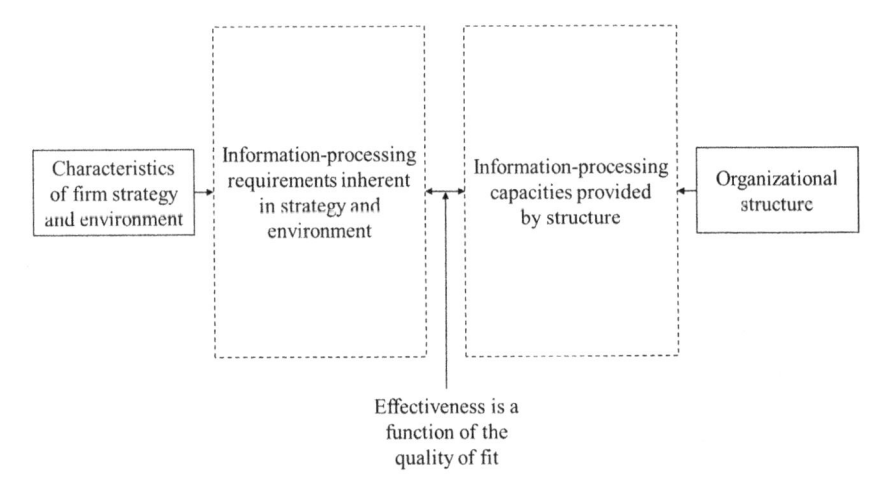

Fig. 2.3 An information-processing model of strategy–structure fit

tional structure are directly measured variables. The boxes with broken lines indicate that information-processing requirements and capacities are abstract variables, which can only be derived from measured variables.

The more micro-level studies of organizations, where the units of analysis are either individuals or small groups, have managed to measure directly such aspects of information processing as the frequency of oral communications between work groups (Tushman 1978), the extent to which policies and procedures, work plans, personal contact, and meetings are used to coordinate members of work teams (Van de Ven et al. 1976), and the structure of groups during decision-making (Duncan 1973). For more macro-level studies, such as those addressing the strategy–structure relationship, the difficulty of directly measuring such detailed information-processing phenomena between very large subunits of an organization necessitates a different approach to operationalizing the information-processing perspective. Instead of attempting to directly measure information processing, our study uses information processing more as an abstract intervening concept to aid in positing relationships between directly measured characteristics of an organization's structure and strategy, both of which have identifiable information-processing implications. How to measure fit between such dissimilar phenomena as strategic conditions and features of organization design has troubled organization theory ever since it became contingency oriented. An information-processing perspective of organization design calls for translating strategic conditions and organization design features into their respective information-processing implications. Then it will be easier to measure fit between information-processing requirements and information-processing capacities, which are more comparable phenomena.

It is important to stress that the relationship between strategy and structure expressed by the model in Fig. 2.3 is one of fit and not of causation. Consequently, it is important to remember that when structure is later referred to as the "dependent variable" and the strategic conditions are referred to as the "independent variables," we are merely applying conventional, if somewhat misleading, titles to these two sets of variables, without implying that either depends on the other in a causative sense. Under the fit model being developed here, changes in strategic conditions may cause changes in organization design, or changes in organization design may lead to changes in certain strategic conditions, or neither may have any impact on the other. What is important in the present model is the relationship or fit, and not the forces that have created it.

The above information-processing model has been specified in some detail in Egelhoff (1982, 1988, 1991), and the present chapter summarizes this earlier conceptualization. As shown in Fig. 2.4, Egelhoff identifies four dimensions of information processing in MNCs and uses these to measure and describe the information-processing capacities of the different types of international structure. The *purpose and perspective of information processing* can be defined in terms of whether it is primarily strategic or primarily tactical. Tactical information processing deals with the large volume of relatively routine day-to-day problems and situations confronting an organization. The decision-making perspective required to handle these situations tends to be relatively narrow, and it usually exists at the middle and lower levels of management. Strategic information processing attempts to deal with a much smaller volume of relatively non-routine, and usually more important, problems and situations. These problems deal with the fundamental position of the organization in its

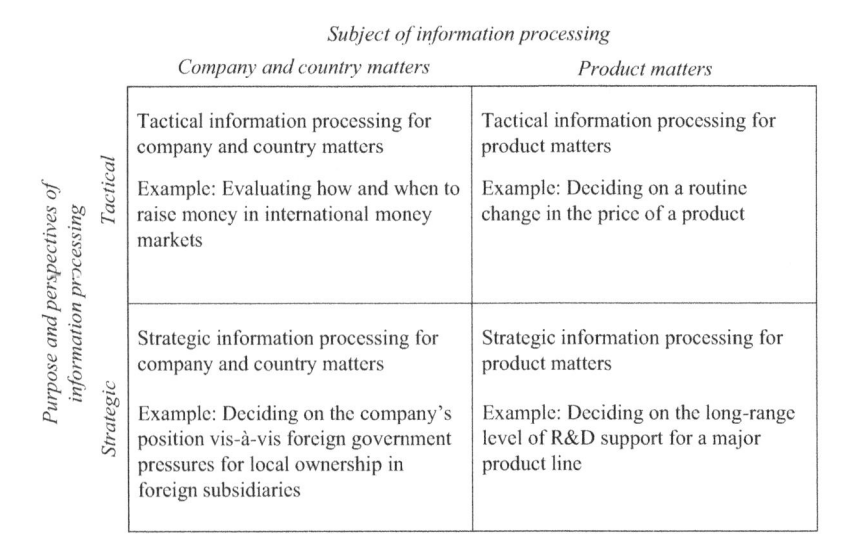

		Subject of information processing	
		Company and country matters	Product matters
Purpose and perspectives of information processing	*Tactical*	Tactical information processing for company and country matters Example: Evaluating how and when to raise money in international money markets	Tactical information processing for product matters Example: Deciding on a routine change in the price of a product
	Strategic	Strategic information processing for company and country matters Example: Deciding on the company's position vis-à-vis foreign government pressures for local ownership in foreign subsidiaries	Strategic information processing for product matters Example: Deciding on the long-range level of R&D support for a major product line

Fig. 2.4   Four types of information processing

environment and usually involve changing this position. Thus, strategic information processing has a different purpose and requires a different perspective than tactical information processing. It addresses higher-level organizational goals, is broader in scope, and usually has a longer time horizon. This perspective tends to exist at the higher levels of an organization's hierarchy.

Research suggests that different levels of an organization's hierarchy tend to process different kinds of information and have different purposes for processing information. The association of tactical and strategic perspectives with different levels of an organization presupposes that some kind of hierarchy exists in most MNCs. More recent literature suggests that some MNCs may be becoming less hierarchical (Hedlund 1986; Bartlett and Ghoshal 1989; Birkinshaw 2000; Forsgren et al. 2005; Ambos and Schlegelmilch 2007). To the extent that an MNC is less hierarchically organized, it becomes more difficult to generalize about where strategic and tactical perspectives exist in an organization.

The framework in Fig. 2.4 also reflects the *subject or content of information processing* and distinguishes between information processing for product matters (product and process technology, market information) and information processing for company and country matters (finance, tax, legal, government relations, human resources). Subject knowledge or specialization tends to vary horizontally across organizations. Different organizational structures tend to cluster it into different subunits. Using these distinctions, four types of information processing are developed, as shown in Fig. 2.4. The four types are generally not substitutes for each other, since they tend to address different problem areas that require different types of knowledge and different perspectives of the organization and its goals.

The above set of information-processing dimensions helps to distinguish where in an organization different kinds of knowledge and different kinds of decision-making capability lie. It identifies which parts of an organization need to be linked together in order to solve a given problem or address a specific decision-making situation. Thus, the dimensions are useful for measuring and understanding the influence of different types of structure on information processing. We view the above information-processing perspective and framework as complementary to many of the knowledge-based views of the firm (Kogut and Zander 1992; Jensen and Szulanski 2004), since they focus on how organization design influences the development, transfer, and utilization of knowledge.

Bibliography

Ambos, B., & Schlegelmilch, B. B. (2007). Innovation and control in the multinational firm: A comparison of political and contingency approaches. *Strategic Management Journal, 28*(5), 473–486.
Barnard, C. I. (1938). *The functions of the executive*. Cambridge, MA: Harvard University Press.
Bartlett, C. A., & Ghoshal, S. (1989). *Managing across borders: The transnational solution*. Boston, MA: Harvard Business School Press.
Birkinshaw, J. (2000). *Entrepreneurship in the global firm*. Thousand Oaks, CA: Sage.
Birkinshaw, J., & Hagstrom, P. (2000). *The flexible firm: Capability management in network organizations*. Oxford: Oxford University Press.
Burns, T., & Stalker, G. M. (1961). *The management of innovation*. London: Tavistock.
Burns, L. R., & Wholey, D. R. (1993). Adoption and abandonment of matrix management programs: Effects of organizational characteristics and interorganizational networks. *Academy of Management Journal, 36*(1), 106–138.
Chandler Jr., A. D. (1962). *Strategy and structure: Chapters in the history of industrial enterprise*. Cambridge, MA: M.I.T. Press.
Chi, T., & Nystrom, P. (1998). An economic analysis of matrix structure, using multinational corporations as an illustration. *Managerial and Decision Economics, 19*(3), 141–156.
Cyert, R. M., & March, J. G. (1963). *A behavioral theory of the firm*. Englewood Cliffs, NJ: Prentice Hall.
Davis, S. M., & Lawrence, P. R. (1977). *Matrix*. Reading, MA: Addison-Wesley.
Duncan, R. B. (1972). Characteristics of organizational environments and perceived environmental uncertainty. *Administrative Science Quarterly, 17*(3), 313–327.
Duncan, R. B. (1973). Multiple decision-making structures in adapting to environmental uncertainty: The impact of organizational effectiveness. *Human Relations, 26*(3), 273–291.

Egelhoff, W. G. (1982). Strategy and structure in multinational corporations: An information-processing approach. *Administrative Science Quarterly, 27*(3), 435–458.

Egelhoff, W. G. (1988). *Organizing the multinational enterprise: An information-processing perspective.* Cambridge, MA: Ballinger.

Egelhoff, W. G. (1991). Information-processing theory and the multinational enterprise. *Journal of International Business Studies, 22*(3), 341–358.

Fayol, H. (1949). *General and industrial management.* London: Pitman.

Ford, R. C., & Randolph, W. A. (1992). Cross-functional structures: A review and integration of matrix organization and project management. *Journal of Management, 18*(2), 267–294.

Forsgren, M., Holm, U., & Johanson, J. (2005). *Managing the embedded multinational: A business network view.* Cheltenham, UK: Edward Elgar.

Franko, L. G. (1976). *The European multinationals: A renewed challenge to American and British big business.* Stamford, CT: Greylock.

Galbraith, J. R. (1969). *Organization design: An information processing view.* Working Paper #425-69, M.I.T., Sloan School of Management.

Galbraith, J. R. (1970). Environmental and technological determinants of organizational design. In J. W. Lorsch & P. R. Lawrence (Eds.), *Studies in organization design* (pp. 113–139). Homewood, IL: Irwin.

Galbraith, J. R. (1971). Matrix organization design. *Business Horizons, 14*(1), 29–40.

Galbraith, J. R. (1973). *Designing complex organizations.* Reading, MA: Addison-Wesley.

Galbraith, J. R. (1977). *Organization design.* Reading, MA: Addison-Wesley.

Galbraith, J. R. (2009). *Designing matrix organizations that actually work.* San Francisco, CA: Jossey-Bass.

Goggin, W. C. (1974). How the multinational structure works at Dow Corning. *Harvard Business Review, 52*(1), 54–65.

Hedlund, G. (1986). The hypermodern MNC: A heterarchy. *Human Resource Management, 25*(1), 9–35.

Jensen, R., & Szulanski, G. (2004). Stickiness and the adaptation of organizational practices in cross-border knowledge transfers. *Journal of International Business Studies, 35*(6), 508–523.

Katz, D., & Kahn, R. L. (1966). *The social psychology of organizations.* New York: Wiley.

Kmetz, J. L. (1984). An information-processing study of a complex workflow in aircraft electronics repair. *Administrative Science Quarterly, 29*(2), 255–280.

Kogut, B., & Zander, U. (1992). Knowledge of the firm, combinative capabilities and the replication of technology. *Organization Science, 3*(3), 383–397.

Kuprenas, J. A. (2003). Implementation and performance of matrix organization structure. *International Journal of Project Management, 21*(1), 51–62.
Larson, E. W., & Gobeli, D. H. (1987). Matrix management: Contradictions and insights. *California Management Review, 29*(4), 126–138.
Lawrence, P. R., & Lorsch, J. W. (1967). *Organization and environment.* Homewood, IL: Irwin.
Peters, T. J., & Waterman Jr., R. U. (1982). *In search of excellence: Lessons from America's best-run companies.* New York: Warner.
Pitts, R. A., & Daniels, J. D. (1984). Aftermath of the matrix mania. *Columbia Journal of World Business, 19*(2), 48–54.
Sayles, L. R. (1976). Matrix management: The structure with a future. *Organization Dynamics, 5*(2), 2–17.
Simon, H. A. (1957). *Administrative behavior: A study of decision-making processes in administrative organization.* New York: Free Press.
Stopford, J. M., & Wells Jr., L. T. (1972). *Managing the multinational enterprise.* New York: Basic Books.
Strikwerda, J., & Stoelhorst, J. W. (2009). The emergence and evolution of the multidimensional organization. *California Management Review, 51*(4), 11–31.
Sy, T., & D'Annunzio, L. S. (2005). Challenges and strategies of matrix organizations: Top-level and mid-level managers' perspectives. *Human Resource Planning, 28*(1), 39–48.
Taylor, F. W. (1911). *The principles of scientific management.* New York: Harper.
Thompson, J. D. (1967). *Organizations in action.* New York: McGraw-Hill.
Tushman, M. L. (1978). Technical communication in research and development laboratories: Impact of project work characteristics. *Academy of Management Journal, 21*(4), 624–645.
Tushman, M. L., & Nadler, D. A. (1978). Information processing as an integrating concept in organizational design. *Academy of Management Review, 3*(3), 613–624.
Van de Ven, A. H., Delbecq, A. L., & Koenig Jr., R. (1976). Determinants of coordination modes within organizations. *American Sociological Review, 41*(2), 322–338.
Weber, M. (1947). *Essays in sociology.* London: Paul, Trench, Trubner & Co..
Weick, K. E. (1979). *The social psychology of organizing.* Reading, MA: Addison-Wesley.
Wolf, J., & Egelhoff, W. G. (2002). A reexamination and extension of international strategy-structure theory. *Strategic Management Journal, 23*(2), 181–189.

3

Designing Elementary Structures to Fit MNC Strategy

This chapter describes the Egelhoff (1982) study of strategy and structure in 34 US and European MNCs with elementary structures. In this chapter the information-processing capacities of structure are developed and used to fit four different kinds of elementary structure to eight elements of strategy. We are especially interested in the information-processing logic used to relate specific types of elementary structure to specific elements of firm strategy, since a similar logic will be used to relate specific types of matrix structure to specific elements of strategy. The chapter only reports the logic used to develop the hypotheses and the empirical results of the study. Readers who are interested in other aspects of the study are referred to the underlying publication. Next, we want to review the literature that deals with the fitting of elementary structures to MNC strategy.

Major portions of this chapter are reprinted from "Strategy and Structure in Multinational Corporations: An Information-Processing Approach" by William G. Egelhoff, published in *Administrative Science Quarterly* Volume 27, Number 3 by permission of *Administrative Science Quarterly*. Copyright 1982 by Cornell University.

© The Author(s) 2017
W.G. Egelhoff, J. Wolf, *Understanding Matrix Structures and their Alternatives*, DOI 10.1057/978-1-137-57975-1_3

3.1 Literature Review

The importance of fitting a company's organizational structure to its strategy was initially highlighted by Chandler (1962). His work subsequently motivated a series of studies of strategy and structure in domestic firms (Pavan 1972; Channon 1973; Rumelt 1974; Dyas and Thanheiser 1976), and in MNCs (Stopford and Wells 1972; Franko 1976; Daniels et al. 1984, 1985; Egelhoff 1982, 1988a). The above, along with other studies, described a reasonably consistent and seemingly important set of fits between a firm's strategy and the firm's organizational structure. These relationships and their associated interpretation and theory have come to be known as the "strategy–structure paradigm." The primary advantages provided by such strategy–structure models of the firm include (1) a clear specifying of when one type of structure is superior to another, and (2) the identification of those elements of strategy which are most important to a firm's structure. Taken together, these characteristics made strategy–structure models attractive guidelines for evaluating and designing a firm's structure and considering the implications of changes in firm strategy.

The earliest and best-known model of strategy and structure in MNCs stems from the Stopford and Wells (1972) study of 187 US MNCs. According to this model, an MNC's organizational structure needs to fit two important aspects of international strategy: the relative size of foreign sales and the degree of foreign product diversity (see Fig. 3.1). The interaction of these two contingency variables specifies four different strategic domains, each of which is associated with a different type of structure. Low foreign sales and low foreign product diversity are associated with having an international division structure, low foreign sales and high product diversity with a worldwide product division structure, high foreign sales and low foreign product diversity with a geographical region structure, and high foreign sales and high foreign product diversity with matrix or mixed structures.

Subsequent studies have both confirmed and challenged parts of the Stopford and Wells Model. Franko's (1976) study of 70 European MNCs confirmed the fits of the Stopford and Wells Model, with one

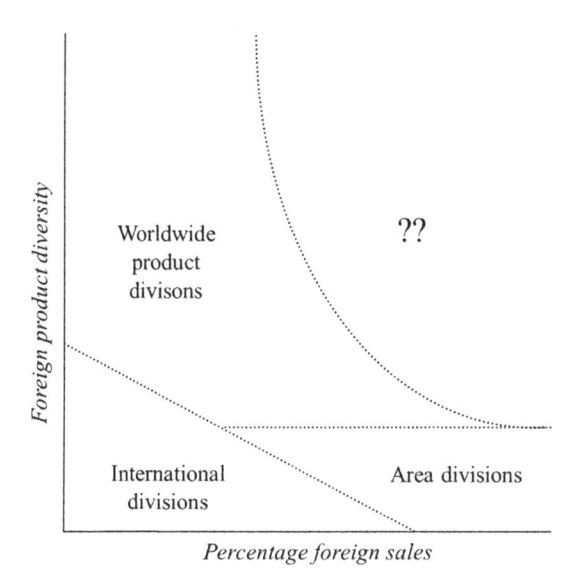

3 Designing Elementary Structures to Fit MNC Strategy

Fig. 3.1 Stopford and Wells Model showing the relationship between strategy and structure in MNCs

[Figure: Two-dimensional plot with "Foreign product diversity" on the vertical axis and "Percentage foreign sales" on the horizontal axis. Quadrants labeled: Worldwide product divisons (upper left), ?? (upper right), International divisions (lower left), Area divisions (lower right).]

major exception. European MNCs tended not to use the international division structure. Instead, when foreign sales and product diversity were relatively low, they tended to have foreign operations report directly to the parent CEO (referred to as a mother–daughter or direct report structure). As foreign sales and product diversity increased, they too followed the strategy–structure relationships specified by the Stopford and Wells Model.

Bartlett's (1979) case studies of ten US MNCs with international division structures found that this structure could successfully handle high levels of foreign sales and foreign product diversity. This contradicted the strategic domain specified by the Stopford and Wells Model. Davidson and Haspeslagh's (1982) study of strategy and structure in 57 US MNCs also supported a wider strategic domain for the international division structure. A later study of 93 US MNCs by Daniels et al. (1984, 1985) generally confirmed the relationships of the Stopford and Wells Model, except they found that when foreign sales are relatively small, MNCs tended to use a product division structure instead of an international division structure.

Egelhoff (1982, 1988a) subsequently studied strategy and structure in 50 MNCs (24 US, 26 European). Thirty-four of these MNCs had elementary structures. He used an information-processing perspective (Galbraith 1973) to specify fit relationships between MNC structure and eight elements of international strategy. This study will be more fully described in the remaining sections of this chapter. In a later study, Habib and Victor (1991) also used an information-processing perspective to study strategy–structure fit in 144 US manufacturing and service MNCs. The study confined itself to examining foreign sales and foreign product diversity as the relevant aspects of strategy, and tended to retest and confirm the key relationships of the Stopford and Wells Model. Interestingly, it found no significant differences between manufacturing and service MNCs in terms of strategy–structure relationships, thus extending the Stopford and Wells Model to cover service MNCs.

3.2 The Need to Better Conceptualize the Strategy–Structure Paradigm

While the above studies are decades old, they largely define existing strategy–structure theory as it relates to the use of elementary structures in MNCs. Perhaps the most impressive aspect of this theory, which underlies the theory for matrix structures, is the relatively consistent empirical support found for many of the strategy–structure fits. More recent studies of strategy and structure in German MNCs (Wolf and Egelhoff 2002; Egelhoff et al. 2013) reveal that most of the fits are still apparent in today's firms. The pervasiveness of such strategy–structure fit across nationalities and time suggests that it might be a fundamental condition for firm survival and organizational performance, and, indeed, when strategy–structure theory was in vogue in the 1980s, this was often how it was described (Miles and Snow 1984). But, interestingly, empirical attempts to link fit to firm performance (typically financial performance) are unconvincing. While this may be regarded as a problem by some,

3 Designing Elementary Structures to Fit MNC Strategy

Egelhoff (1988b: 265–268) has argued (1) that finding independently hypothesized strategy–structure fits in a sample of surviving and growing (i.e., successful) firms constitutes support for the hypothesized fit and its logic, and (2) that the linkage between specific aspects of organizational design and measures of financial performance is problematic for several reasons. Chief among these is the fact that it is unlikely there is any single operational fit that contributes in a consistently strong way to some broad measure of organizational performance (such as profitability or return on investment). We assume that overall fit relates strongly to overall performance, but cannot measure fit or its relationship to performance at this level.

In our opinion, the primary shortcoming of strategy–structure theory is not the failure to link different levels of fit to differing levels of organizational performance. In fact, we doubt that this is the best way to either justify or improve strategy–structure theory. Instead, we believe the route to both of the above lies through better conceptualizing the underlying meaning and implications of strategy–structure fit and misfit. Aside from the information-processing arguments put forth by Egelhoff (1982), which will be presented in the following sections of this chapter, existing strategy–structure theory is more a description of empirical findings than the presentation of a conceptual logic. It primarily describes a number of directly observed fits between strategy and structure, based on a series of survey studies. But why a fit is good and how it contributes to organizational performance are largely absent from the theory. While there may be some eclectic explanations accompanying the fits, most strategy–structure models lack a general logic that might be used to hypothesize such fits independent of their empirical discovery. This lack of a deeper conceptual understanding severely limits the value of most existing strategy–structure theory, for it gives such theory a static or historical perspective (i.e., it can't be applied to situations that are new or different and have not yet been studied).

The above situation has two major implications for theory building. First, it is difficult to generalize the empirically derived theory to a wider population of firms and situations (i.e., firms and situations that were not represented in the database used to derive the theory). For example,

Bartlett's (1979) case study of ten US MNCs with international division structures contradicts the strategic domain specified by the Stopford and Wells Model for an international division structure. For such empirically derived models, there is no way to further specify when the Stopford and Wells Model applies and when Bartlett's broader strategic domain for an international division structure applies. The second major implication is that empirically derived theories are extremely time sensitive. The specific relationships they are built upon can easily change as strategies evolve and companies become more experienced with using a given type of structure. Most survey research studies cannot control for this kind of subtle change and instability in the measured variables and their relationships.

In contrast to the above, a conceptually derived theory that is based on more fundamental principles of human and organizational behavior is likely to be more stable over time, since the fundamental principles are likely to be more stable than the measured variables. Relationships in the data that cannot be explained by the fundamental principles will tend to be ignored by such conceptual theory building. This leads to a more fundamental and stable theory about relationships. Such theory can often be extended to situations that have not previously been observed. While empirically derived theories (like the Stopford and Wells Model) are extremely useful in helping scholars and practitioners to initially understand a complex phenomenon (the strategy–structure relationship in MNCs), theory building should not stop here. To advance further, there is a strong need to push early empirically derived theory forward into more conceptually derived theory about a subject. There is no way the knowledge contained in the Stopford and Wells Model, or any of the other empirically derived models of the strategy–structure relationship, can be used to design matrix structures in today's MNCs. The Stopford and Wells Model implies that matrix structures should fit a strategy where there is both high foreign product diversity and a high percentage of foreign sales (largely because this is what the three matrix structure firms and 22 mixed structure firms in the sample had in common). As we will see in Chap. 4, there are different types of matrix structure, and a more conceptual understanding is required to design a matrix structure that fits a firm's strategy.

3.3 The Information-Processing Capacities of the Elementary Structures

Understanding matrix structures requires that one first understand the various forms of elementary structure. An elementary structure is a single hierarchical structure that connects the principal subunits of a foreign subsidiary to the parent HQ of an MNC. The primary types of elementary structure available to an MNC are a worldwide functional division structure, an international division structure, a geographical region structure, and a worldwide product division structure. A simplified organization chart for each is shown in Fig. 3.2. It should be apparent that each type of structure is named for the way it is subdivided directly below the parent CEO or HQ, regardless the way it is further subdivided.

As already described, elementary structures are the building blocks for matrix structures. A matrix structure is an overlaying of two or more elementary structures. The information-processing capacity of a matrix structure can be more than the simple sum of the information-processing capacities of the two elementary structures that are overlaid to create a matrix. But it is necessary to understand how each type of elementary structure processes information and facilitates implementing specific elements of a firm's strategy, before one can begin to access their combined capabilities within a matrix structure. It is also important to realize that the alternative to a matrix structure is an elementary structure enhanced by various types of non-hierarchical network design. Thus, a thorough understanding of elementary structures is essential to understanding and intelligently designing matrix structures.

The information-processing framework described in Chap. 2 uses relative organizational distance (or closeness) through the formal organizational structure to define where communication will be facilitated and where it will be hindered between organizational subunits. In addition to organizational distance (which specifies the interconnection among subunits), macrostructure also influences what type of information (measured in terms of subject) and what type of processing (measured in terms of purpose and perspective) can occur between interconnected subunits. Horizontal differentiation (or specialization) largely determines in which subunits certain types of knowledge reside, just as vertical differentiation largely determines at what levels tactical and strategic perspectives of the information processing between the parent and foreign subsidiaries as long as the processing can take place within a functional area. Tactical information processing across functions, however, will be low, since the structure does not facilitate communication between divisions at either the subsidiary or the tactical levels of the parent.

With an international division structure, all foreign subsidiaries report to an international division that is separate from the domestic operations. This structure tends to facilitate information processing between the parent and foreign subsidiaries, while at the same time it hinders information processing at the parent level between the international division and the domestic operations. Product knowledge tends to be centered in the domestic divisions, while knowledge about such company and country matters as international finance and foreign political conditions is centered in the international division. Consequently, parent-subsidiary information-processing capacity is relatively high for company and country matters and relatively low for product matters. There is a general management or strategic apex at both the subsidiary and international division levels. Thus, strategic as well as tactical information processing can take place between a subsidiary and the international division, but it will center around company and country matters rather than product matters.

A geographical region structure divides the world into regions, each with its own HQ. Each HQ is responsible for all of the company's products and business within its geographical area. The regional HQ is the center of the company's knowledge about company and country matters within a region. Most regional HQs also contain either product or functional staffs to provide coordination for product matters across subsidiaries in the region. There is a general management or strategic apex at both the subsidiary and regional HQ levels. As a result, this structure facilitates a high level of all four types of information processing between a subsidiary and its regional HQ. The information-processing capacity between a foreign subsidiary and domestic operations or a subsidiary in another region is low. The only hierarchical mechanism for coordinating across regions is the corporate HQ.

A worldwide product division structure extends the responsibilities of the domestic product divisions to cover their product lines on a worldwide basis. Under this structure, there is a tendency to centralize product-related decision-making at both the strategic and tactical levels in the parent product groups and decentralize all non-product decisions-making to the foreign subsidiaries. Consequently, the capacity for processing information between the parent and foreign subsidiaries for company and country matters tends to be low, since much of it has been decentralized to the local subsidiary level and parent HQ management has a product orientation. Product-related tactical and strategic information-processing capacities, in contrast, tend to be high. The foreign product divisions in the subsidiaries are connected to the centers of product knowledge in the parent. For each product line, there is a strategic apex at both the subsidiary and parent product-division levels.

The above information-processing perspective of structure has largely focused on organizational distance (or closeness) through the formal hierarchy as its key concept. This perspective can be broadened to include cognitive distance—the distance between the thoughtworlds (Dougherty 1992) of two or more subunits. Subunits that are cognitively distant (i.e., their perspectives of the same task or situation are different) will experience more difficulty processing information than subunits that are cognitively close (share a common understanding of the task or situation). Cognitive distance especially hinders the exchange of tacit knowledge or information between subunits. Physical distance between subunits can also influence their capacity to process information. Although this is not directly a characteristic of structure, certain structures imply physical distances. An international division structure implies physical distance between foreign and domestic operations. A geographical region structure implies physical distance between geographical regions. Physical distance tends to hinder informal coordination between subunits.

3.4 The Information-Processing Requirements of Strategy for Elementary Structures

Implicit in an organization's strategy are requirements for information processing between its subunits. The purpose of this section is to define these requirements for MNCs in terms of the four types of information processing identified in the previous chapter. Eight elements of company-level strategy were selected by the study as potentially important contingency variables, because conceptually they should exert a strong influence on parent-subsidiary information-processing requirements. The eight elements are foreign product diversity, product modification differences among foreign subsidiaries, rate of product change, size of foreign operations, size of foreign manufacturing, number of foreign subsidiaries, extent of outside ownership in foreign subsidiaries, and the extent of foreign acquisitions.

3.4.1 Foreign Product Diversity

Numerous studies have confirmed the importance of product diversity to the choice of appropriate macro structure (Chandler 1962; Stopford and Wells 1972; Franko 1976; Pitts 1977; Daniels et al. 1985). As product diversity increases, there is an increase in both market diversity (environmental complexity) and manufacturing and technical diversity (technological complexity). Several studies have found that, as environmental and technological complexity increase, requirements for information processing between interdependent subunits also increase (Lawrence and Lorsch 1967; Galbraith 1977). Consequently, as product diversity increases, there is a greater need for tactical and strategic information processing for product matters; for example, there will be more technical operating problems and a greater number of strategic product decisions. There is no associated increase in the complexity of non-product matters. The structure providing the most product-related information-processing capacity between the centers of product knowledge in the parent and the foreign subsidiaries is the worldwide product division structure. It utilizes several separate information-processing channels between a subsidiary and the parent, one for each product division in the subsidiary. If new product lines are introduced in a subsidiary, it is the only structure that provides for an increase in the number of information-processing channels with the parent.

Hypothesis 3.1 MNCs with product division structures will tend to have more foreign product diversity than MNCs with other structures.

The functional division structure also provides a high level of tactical information-processing capacity for product matters, but it does so along functional channels. Marketing and manufacturing matters come together and are first integrated at the parent level. This kind of centralization is manageable only if there is a narrow line of products that tend to be similar around the world. If product diversity were introduced, it would quickly overload both the limited strategic information-processing capacity at the top of the parent HQ and the limited cross-functional capacity at the tactical level of the parent HQ. Remembering the example of DuPont in Chap. 2, this is precisely the problem that occurred at DuPont, before it adopted a product division structure.

Hypothesis 3.2 MNCs with functional division structures will tend to have less foreign product diversity than MNCs with other structures.

3.4.2 Product Modification Differences

The degree to which products are locally modified or differ from one foreign subsidiary to another specifies yet another type of product complexity or heterogeneity. Although no research exists on the effects of such heterogeneity at such a macro level, it has been studied within manufacturing or operating subsystems. Woodward (1965) associated this kind of product and process heterogeneity with unit or batch production systems, Harvey (1968) with technological diffuseness, and Perrow (1967) with task variability. All found that this kind of heterogeneity led to more decentralized decision-making and communication patterns.

To the extent that a product is the same around the world, it is efficient and economical to centralize knowledge and management of the product at a single point in the parent. Under such conditions, product-related information processing can be standardized with all product subunits, and product planning can be integrated to achieve global economies of scale. To the extent that product characteristics and uses vary from subsidiary to subsidiary, opportunities to realize these advantages decline and the costs of maintaining and disseminating product knowledge from a central point increase. Consequently, as product modification differences increase, one would expect MNC s to use structures that decentralize product-related information processing. Centralization appears to be greatest in the functional and product division structures because both structures centralize all of the parent's knowledge and information-processing capacity for a product in a single parent subunit.

Hypothesis 3.3 MNCs with functional and product division structures will tend to have lower levels of product modification differences across foreign subsidiaries than will MNCs with other structures.

The geographical region structure, in contrast, has several focal points for each product line (one in each regional HQ) and provides relatively decentralized product-related information processing. Because the centers of product knowledge are relatively disconnected from foreign operations under an international division structure, there is no structural reason for hypothesizing any particular level of product modification difference for this structure.

Hypothesis 3.4 MNCs with geographical region structures will tend to have higher levels of product modification difference across foreign subsidiaries than will MNCs with other structures.

3.4.3 Product Change

Researchers have generally found that higher rates of product and process change require more information processing between interdependent subunits (Burns and Stalker 1961; Emery and Trist 1965; Lawrence and Lorsch 1967). High rates of product change require that an MNC has the ability to transfer new technology as well as the ability to reformulate product strategy on a frequent basis. Technology transfer requires product-related information-processing capacity of a tactical nature. It takes place between the centers of technical knowledge in the parent and the corresponding subunits in the subsidiary. The need to reformulate product strategy means that there is a concurrent requirement for strategic information-processing capacity.

3 Designing Elementary Structures to Fit MNC Strategy

The structure that provides both tactical and strategic information-processing capacity between the subsidiary and the centers of product technology and product planning in the parent is the product division structure. The functional division structure also provides a high level of tactical information-processing capacity for product matters (such as technology transfer), but it does not provide any strategic information processing between subsidiary and parent. The latter is centralized in the parent. Thus, a functional division structure should fit a high level of technology transfer, but not a high level of product change.

Hypothesis 3.5 MNCs with product division structures will tend to have a higher level of product change than MNCs with other structures.

3.4.4 Size of Foreign Operations

In their study of US MNCs, Stopford and Wells (1972) found that as the percentage of foreign sales in a company increased, there was a tendency for MNCs to abandon international division structures and adopt a geographical region structure. From an information-processing viewpoint, this finding makes sense. As the relative size of foreign operations increases, the opportunities for increased integration either across subsidiaries or between foreign and domestic operations increase. Thus, as the relative size of the foreign sector increases, product interdependency either within this sector or between it and the domestic sector should also increase as effective MNCs seek to realize synergies and economies of scale on either a regional or worldwide basis. This requires more product-related information-processing capacity. As developed above, all of the structures except the international division can provide a high level of product-related information-processing capacity either between foreign and domestic operations or among groups of foreign subsidiaries. Because the international division structure does not provide the kind of information processing required to realize product-related synergies and economies of scale, it tends to fit strategies with relatively small foreign operations, where these opportunities are not present. This logic contradicts Bartlett's (1979) earlier conclusion that an international division structure can support a relatively high level of foreign sales and, instead, supports the relationship found in the Stopford and Wells Model.

Hypothesis 3.6 MNCs with an international division structure will tend to have a lower percentage of foreign sales than MNCs with other structures.

3.4.5 Size of Foreign Manufacturing

A company's foreign operations can be split into the percentage of foreign sales exported from the parent and the percentage manufactured by the foreign subsidiaries. Exports from the parent to the foreign subsidiaries create numerous interdependencies that increase the requirement for product-related information processing between the two. Because geographical region structures provide relatively low information-processing capacity between foreign and domestic operations, this structure will not support a high level of parent-subsidiary exports. Instead, it supports a high level of foreign manufacture and product exchange within a region (such as Europe). Because the worldwide functional and product division structures can provide high levels of product-related information-processing capacity between domestic and foreign operations, they can support either high levels of parent exports or high levels of foreign manufacture. However, when the level of foreign manufacturing becomes very large and parent exports very small, opportunities for synergy and economies of scale will generally be more intraregional than global, and the advantages of the geographical region structure will tend to outweigh those of the functional or product division structures. Because the international division structure does not provide a high level of product-related information processing either between parent and forcign subsidiary or among foreign subsidiaries, there is no basis for associating either a high level of parent exports or a high level of foreign manufacture and intraregional exchange with this structure.

Hypothesis 3.7 MNCs with geographical region structures will tend to have higher levels of foreign manufacturing than MNCs with other structures.

3.4.6 Number of Foreign Subsidiaries

As the number of foreign subsidiaries increases, requirements for all four types of information-processing capacity at the parent level will increase. Under such conditions, decentralized structures are likely to better fit the larger number of parent-subsidiary relationships than the more centralized structures. The functional division structure centralizes information processing for both foreign and domestic operations in the same parent HQ. The international division structure also centralizes information processing for all foreign operations in a single subunit, the international division, but separates it from domestic operations. Thus, information processing is less centralized than under the worldwide functional division structure. Both the geographical region and product division structures have foreign operations reporting to several different focal points in the parent, the separate regional, or product division HQ. From the parent's point of view, parent-subsidiary information processing is less centralized under these structures. Structures with multiple focal points in the parent for parent-subsidiary information processing should be able to accommodate more parent-subsidiary relationships.

Hypothesis 3.8 MNCs with functional division structures will tend to have fewer foreign subsidiaries than firms with international division structures, which, in turn, will tend to have fewer subsidiaries than firms with geographical region or product division structures.

3.4.7 Extent of Outside Ownership

Significant outside ownership in foreign subsidiaries places additional constraints on the way that subsidiaries can be managed. Almost certainly, outside owners will oppose decisions that reduce subsidiary profits for the sake of maximizing total company profits. Because outside owners are only interested in the goals and performance of an individual subsidiary, this condition should be easiest for an MNC to accommodate when its structure favors setting goals and developing strategies for the subsidiary at the subsidiary level (i.e., strategies of subsidiaries can be relatively independent of each other). A functional division structure centralizes strategic information processing near the top of the parent HQ, and this leads to establishing goals and making decisions that are based more on optimizing total company performance than on optimizing any subunit's performance. Consequently, organizations with functional structures should find it extremely difficult to accommodate the subsidiary-level interests of outside owners.

The situation should be less severe in geographical region and product division companies because subsidiaries can participate in strategy formulation with the parent, and greater variability at the subsidiary level can be accommodated. Yet geographical region and product division structures will attempt to optimize regional or product division performance as much as subsidiary performance. The international division structure, however, does not provide the product-related information-processing capacity required to realize regional or global synergies and economies of scale across foreign subsidiaries. Because there is largely a pooled interdependency (Thompson 1967) among the individual subsidiaries, this structure should be the most consistent with setting strategy for the subsidiary at the subsidiary level.

Hypothesis 3.9 MNCs with worldwide functional division structures will have the lowest levels of outside ownership in their foreign subsidiaries, followed by firms with geographical region and product division structures. Firms with international division structures will have the highest levels of outside ownership.

3.4.8 Extent of Acquisitions

Most acquisitions are themselves multifunctional organizations. They contain subunits that already engage in manufacturing, marketing, and financial activities and possess some kind of organizational structure and information-processing system linking these subunits together. Multinational structures that can absorb a foreign acquisition while leaving the acquisition's existing structure and its associated information-processing system intact should be able to accommodate a higher rate of growth by acquisition. Macro structures that require substantial reorganization of an acquisition's structure and information-processing systems to make them consistent with those of the parent should tend to discourage acquisitions.

Worldwide functional division structures should have the most difficulty accommodating foreign acquisitions. Separate functional information-processing systems must be constructed between subsidiary and parent, and many existing interfunctional systems within the subsidiary dismantled. None of the other structures should require such significant change. In most cases, the internal structure and information-processing systems of the acquisition can remain relatively unchanged while the external, or boundary-spanning, relationships and activities absorb the change required to fit the new parent-subsidiary information-processing system.

Hypothesis 3.10 MNCs with worldwide functional division structures will tend to make fewer and smaller acquisitions than MNCs with other structures.

3.5 Testing the Hypotheses

Two types of analyses were used to examine the fit relationships between strategy and structure. First, bivariate ANOVA contrasts were used to test separately each relationship expressed by the hypotheses. Then a multivariate discriminant analysis was used to examine simultaneously the relationships between structure and all of the contingency variables (elements of strategy). Table 3.2 contains a summary of each hypothesis and the results of the associated ANOVA contrasts. Except for a few fits involving two of the elements, the sample data showed significant support for the hypotheses. Those not fully supported include Hypotheses 3.3 and 3.4, dealing with product modification differences across subsidiaries. Although all three relationships expressed in the hypotheses were directionally supported, only one, the low level of product modification differences in companies with functional division structures, was statistically significant. Hypothesis 3.9, concerning the level of outside owner-

Understanding Matrix Structures and their Alternatives

Table 3.2 Hypotheses and Results of Bivariate ANOVA Contrasts for Elementary Structure

Hypothesis	FD	ID	GR	PD	Differences
1. Product diversity greatest in PD	1.4[a]	1.7	3.4	5.8[b]	[a] Different from GR at $p<.01$ and PD at $p<.001$.
2. Lowest in FD					[b] Different from GR at $p<.01$ and FD and ID at $p<.001$.
3. Product modification differences lowest in FD and PD	1.8[a]	2.9	3.4	2.7	[a] Different from GR at $p<.05$ and from other structures at $p<.10$, based on Mann-Whitney U test.
4. Highest in GR					
5. Product change highest in PD	3.2	2.9	2.9	5.4[a]	[a] Different from other structures at $p<.05$.
6. Size of foreign operations lowest in ID	58	34[a]	47	61	[a] Different from GR at $p<.05$ and from FD and PD at $p<.01$.
7. Size of foreign manufacturing higher in GR than in FD and PD	42	76	91[a]	61	[a] Different from FD and PD at $p<.001$.
8. Number of foreign subsidiaries fewest in FD; next fewest in ID	12[a]	41[b]	55	58	[a] Different from ID and PD at $p<.001$ and from GR at $p<.01$
					[b] Different from GR at $p<.10$ and from PD at $p<.05$.
9. Level of outside ownership lowest in FD; next lowest in GR and PD; highest in ID	1.8	1.9	1.9	3.0	No difference between structures at $p<.10$, based on Mann-Whitney U test.
10. Level of foreign acquisitions lowest in FD	.8[a]	1.3	2.1	2.2	[a] Different from GR and PD at $p<.025$, based on Mann-Whitney U test.

Note: FD = Functional divisions; ID = International divisions; GR = Geographical regions; PD = Product divisions.

ship in foreign subsidiaries, also failed to receive much support from the data. Only the low level of outside ownership in the functional division companies followed the hypothesized fits.

3.6 A Multivariate Test of Fit Between Strategy and Different Types of Elementary Structure

Thus far, the study has dealt with fit between strategy and structure in a bivariate manner. This was done because it is easier to model a complex situation as a collection of independent bivariate relationships. The model is admittedly much simpler than the real situation, in which an organization must select one structure and attempt to satisfy as many of the crucial bivariate fits as it can simultaneously. Thus, while there is obvious support for the bivariate fits from central tendencies in the entire sample of MNCs, the question remains how useful the model is in a situation in which an organization must, by itself, achieve good fit between its structure and all the elements of its strategy.

While the information-processing framework has been useful for positing a series of bivariate relationships between structure and elements of strategy, it does not allow one to add up or accumulate the total information-processing requirements placed on an organization by its strategy. In order to test how well successful MNCs actually do achieve simultaneous fit between structure and the various elements of their strategy, multivariate analysis was required. Since structure was measured as a nominal variable, a stepwise multiple discriminant analysis was run using the four types of structure as the groups and the eight elements of strategy as the independent variables. The results appear in Table 3.3. Five of the independent variables had sufficient discriminating power to enter and remain in the discriminant model. The standardized discriminant coefficients indicate the relative contribution of an independent variable to the discriminant function. Only the first two discriminant functions are statistically significant.

64 Understanding Matrix Structures and their Alternatives

Table 3.3 Multiple Discriminant Analysis of Elements of Strategy on Type of Elementary Structure

Independent variable	Discriminant function 1	2	3	F-value
Product diversity	-.90[a]	-.38	.13	7.96***
Product modification differences	-.33	-.12	-.19	2.34
Product change	-.55	-.48	.75	2.12
Size of foreign operations	-.51	.20	-.73	4.45**
Size of foreign manufacturing	.26	-.99	-.01	7.98***
Canonical correlation	.86	.74	.33	
Wilks Lambda	.10***	.39**	.89	

** $p<.01$; *** $p<.001$.
Note: Type of structure is the dependent variable.
[a] All values under the three functions are standardized discriminant coefficients.

Table 3.4 Predicted Type of Elementary Structure from Coefficients of Discriminant Functions

Actual group membership	Predicted group membership FD	ID	GR	PD
Function divisions (FD)	4	1	0	0
International divisions (ID)	2	5	0	0
Geographical regions (GR)	0	3	6	1
Product divisions (PD)	0	0	1	11

Note: Structures of MNCs correctly classified = 76 percent.

Table 3.4 shows how successful the discriminant functions were in predicting the type of structure for each company, given measures of the elements of its strategy. In 76 percent of the cases, the discriminant model could predict the actual structure of a company, which is significantly better than the chance probability of predicting only 27 percent of the cases correctly. Product diversity and size of foreign manufacturing

Table 3.5 Centroids of the Four Elementary Structural Groups Measured along the Discriminant Functions

	Discriminant function		
Group	1	2	3
Functional divisions	.95	3.19	-.33
International divisions	2.05	-.13	.46
Geographical regions	.56	-.79	-.37
Product divisions	-1.85	.07	.14

provide the most discriminating power, followed by size of foreign operations. Each of these three variables was hypothesized to be an important element of strategy for type of structure to fit. The multivariate analysis confirms that companies in the sample generally realize a high level of simultaneous fit with these three pivotal elements.

Table 3.5 shows the centroids of each of the four groups (types of structure) measured along the three discriminant functions. Clearly, the first function, which largely measures product diversity, discriminates Group PD (product divisions) from the other three groups. Hypothesis 3.1 predicted that product diversity would be higher in companies with product division structures than it would in companies with other structures. The second discriminant function, which is based on the size of foreign manufacturing, discriminates Group GR (geographical regions) from Group FD (functional divisions) and to a lesser extent Group PD. Hypothesis 3.7 specified that MNCs with geographical region structures would tend to have a higher percentage of foreign manufacturing than companies with functional or product division structures. The third discriminant function, based on the size of foreign operations and product change, does a poorer job of discriminating Group ID (international divisions) from the other groups. Hypothesis 3.6 states that MNCs with international division structures would tend to have a lower percentage of foreign sales than firms with other structures. In a sense, the discriminant model has selected three of the elements of strategy and their associated fit hypotheses and used them to construct its classification scheme. This provides some evidence that successful companies do in fact achieve considerable simultaneous fit between their structures and important elements of their strategies.

Table 3.6 Quality of Relationship between Parent and Foreign Subsidiaries[a]

	Good fit cases (N = 13)	Deviant cases (N = 4)	t
Marketing matters	2.6	3.8	2.06*
Manufacturing matters	2.5	2.9	.76
Financial matters	2.2	2.6	.73

* p=.028 (single-tailed test).
[a] Lower scores denote better quality relationship.

Finally, the study attempted to check whether those companies that seemed to have poorer fit between strategy and structure (i.e., the eight misclassified cases in the discriminant analysis) also suffered from poorer quality information processing, as the framework would suggest. The instrument that Lawrence and Lorsch (1967) used for measuring the quality of integration between subunits was used to measure the quality of the parent–foreign subsidiary relationship. Although information processing was not explicitly mentioned in the instrument, at the macro level of analysis what is processed or exchanged between the parent and the foreign subsidiaries is information. Hence, the relationship can be viewed as primarily an information-processing relationship as opposed to a physical or social one. Data on quality of integration were available on 17 of the 34 companies in the sample. The reason for so many missing cases is that this was the last question asked in the interview, so that when the allotted interview time ran out the question frequently was omitted.

Table 3.6 shows the mean scores for the quality of the parent–foreign subsidiary relationship measured for marketing, manufacturing, and financial matters. The lower the score, the better the quality of the relationship. While the low N is unfortunate and hinders statistical significance, there is no reason to believe that running out of interview time (frequently a function of external interruptions) has any biasing association with the quality of the parent–foreign subsidiary relationship. Although only one of the differences approaches statistical significance, the results are consistent and provide additional support for (1) the general argument that strategy and structure can be related through their information-processing implications, and (2) the assumptions used in the model to specify this relationship operationally.

3.7 The Coordination Capacities and Limitations of Different Types of Elementary Structure

Figure 3.3 summarizes the hypothesized fits that are supported by the empirical testing. We would like to discuss each structure in turn, so that we can more fully and deeply describe its coordination capacities and limitations.

Five fits are important for firms with worldwide functional division structures: a narrow and highly consistent worldwide product line, a limited number of foreign subsidiaries, a low level of outside ownership, and few foreign acquisitions. This structure is the least flexible of the multinational structures. It requires more fits between structure and the elements of strategy than any of the other structures. The great advantage of a worldwide functional division structure is that it allows foreign operations to lean heavily on the technological and product-related strengths of the parent. A worldwide functional division structure can rapidly and efficiently move functional information up and down a functional hierarchy, because members of functional hierarchies share both organizational closeness and cognitive closeness (i.e., they share the same thoughtworlds). Functional information can be widely diffused as it travels down the hierarchy, and rapidly concentrated as it travels up the hierarchy. Because functional capabilities and expertise tend to be centralized at one point, and need not be duplicated at other locations in the organization, this structure should be the lowest cost of the high product-integration structures. (Product integration refers to the extent to which the product-related matters of foreign subsidiaries are integrated or coordinated on either a regional or global basis.) The other two high product-integration structures are geographical regions and worldwide product divisions. Offsetting the economies of highly centralized capabilities in the functional division structure are the costs of the information-processing system required to link the operating subunits to the center. Clearly, the strategic conditions that fit this structure attempt to minimize these costs by providing the organization with a relatively homogeneous and stable environment.

The great limitation of a functional division structure is its extremely limited capacity for cross-functional information processing. This means that it can't formulate complex strategies, or strategies that need to be

The primary thing a company gives up with an international division structure is the opportunity for foreign operations to take full advantage of the technological and product-related strengths of the parent. Foreign subsidiaries are not well connected to the centers of product knowledge in the parent company. Even the international division HQ, which often is co-located with the corporate HQ, tends to be organizationally and cognitively distant from the domestic subunits. When foreign operations are relatively small, this loss of synergy is more than offset by the low cost and flexibility of the structure. But, as foreign sales become more significant, the opportunities to leverage product knowledge and product strengths on a global basis typically increase. As this happens, most firms find it economically advantageous to abandon the international division structure and adopt a structure that provides a higher level of information-processing capacity for product matters. This usually involves a structure that includes either a geographical region dimension or a product division dimension.

For companies with a geographical region structure, the most important fits are a sufficiently large foreign operation and a high percentage of foreign manufacturing. The geographical region structure is a high-cost structure. It requires considerable information-processing capacity at several regional HQs for both product matters and company and country matters. Thus, from an economic viewpoint, it requires sufficient size and potential for regional optimization to offset this cost. The primary advantage associated with this structure is its ability to optimize key activities on a regional basis, as opposed to a national or global basis (Nell et al. 2011). The key activities often include manufacturing or sourcing the products and marketing or distributing the products. Some product development can also occur on a regional basis. Realizing significant synergies and economies of scale and scope on a regional basis is the primary goal for firms adopting a geographical region structure. A regional orientation is especially important when a firm's business encounters significant differences between geographical regions regarding products, customer characteristics, government regulations, or business practices. A geographical region structure can develop and implement regional strategies that retain fit with this kind of regional variation.

The primary limitation of a geographical region structure is its inability to process information between regions. If global economies of scale or scope are available or if global knowledge sharing is important, a geographical region structure cannot provide the information-processing capacity to implement these. In this case, some kind of network design (a global task force or committee) might be used to provide non-hierarchical information processing across the geographical regions. If greater capacity is required, a functional division or product division dimension might be matrixed with the geographical region structure to add this kind of information-processing capacity.

The worldwide product division structure fits strategies that are characterized by large foreign operations, high levels of foreign product diversity, and high levels of product change. It is a high cost structure, with separate marketing, manufacturing, and, frequently, research capabilities for each product division. The cost of maintaining several separate worldwide information-processing systems (one for each product division) requires sufficient size, product diversity, and product change to justify the cost associated with organizing around separate sets of product knowledge.

The primary advantage associated with a worldwide product division structure is the ability to organize around multiple products within the same company. The product division structure allows multiproduct firms to possess the same kind of information-processing capacity for each product line or business that a single product line competitor would possess. Both would possess high levels of strategic and tactical information-processing capacity for product matters. If properly managed at the corporate level, each product division in a multiproduct firm can be just as entrepreneurial and focused on its specific customers and technologies as a single product line competitor. And, the product divisions within a multiproduct firm may have some advantages that single product line competitors will lack. These largely consist of various economies of scope in marketing (brand names and reputations, shared customer information, shared advertising and distribution services), manufacturing (shared manufacturing sites and knowledge, shared purchasing and sourcing services), and R&D (shared patents and technical knowledge, shared facilities and technical staff).

Galbraith, J. R. (1977). *Organization design*. Reading, MA: Addison-Wesley.
Habib, M., & Victor, B. (1991). Strategy, structure, and performance of U.S. manufacturing and service MNCs. *Strategic Management Journal, 12*(8), 589–606.
Harvey, E. (1968). Technology and the structure of organizations. *American Sociological Review, 33*(2), 247–259.
Lawrence, P. R., & Lorsch, J. W. (1967). *Organization and environment*. Homewood, IL: Irwin.
Miles, R. E., & Snow, C. C. (1984). Fit, failure, and the hall of fame. *California Management Review, 26*(3), 10–28.
Nell, P. C., Ambos, B., & Schlegelmilch, B. B. (2011). The benefits of hierarchy: Exploring the effects of regional headquarters in multinational corporations. *Advances in International Management, 24,* 85–106.
Pavan, R. D. J. (1972). *The strategy and structure of Italian enterprise*. Unpublished doctoral dissertation, Harvard Business School, Boston, MA.
Perrow, C. (1967). A framework for the comparative analysis of organizations. *American Sociological Review, 32*(3), 194–208.
Pitts, R. A. (1977). Strategies and structures for diversification. *Academy of Management Journal, 20*(2), 197–208.
Rumelt, R. P. (1974). *Strategy, structure, and economic performance*. Boston, MA: Harvard University.
Stopford, J. M., & Wells Jr., L. T. (1972). *Managing the multinational enterprise*. New York: Basic Books.
Thompson, J. D. (1967). *Organizations in action*. New York: McGraw-Hill.
Wolf, J., & Egelhoff, W. G. (2002). A reexamination and extension of international strategy-structure theory. *Strategic Management Journal, 23*(2), 181–189.
Woodward, J. (1965). *Industrial organization: Theory and practice*. London: Oxford University Press.

4

Designing Matrix Structures to Fit MNC Strategy

As already discussed in Chap. 2, many US MNCs abandoned their matrix structures during the 1980s, when they experienced difficulties managing them (Peters and Waterman 1982; Pitts and Daniels 1984). As a result of matrix structures falling out of favor in the US, scholarly research on them largely ceased before a specified theory about how to design and use them was developed. The strategy–structure paradigm, which attempts to conceptually define fit between elements of a firm's strategy and the type of organizational structure required to successfully implement the strategy, was already well established for the elementary types of MNC structure when matrix structures fell out of favor. But, strategy–structure fit for matrix structures was still underdeveloped and not a defined part of the paradigm when research on matrix structures ceased. This is the gap or research issue the present chapter seeks to address.

Major portions of this chapter are reprinted from "Designing Matrix Structures to Fit MNC Strategy" by William G. Egelhoff, Joachim Wolf, and Mihael Adzic, published in *Global Strategy Journal* Volume 3, Number 3 by permission of *Global Strategy Journal*. Copyright 2013 by Strategic Management Society.

This chapter describes a recent study by Egelhoff et al. (2013), which addresses the above research issue. This study follows the same research design as the earlier Egelhoff (1982) study described in Chap. 3. It uses the same information-processing logic described in Chap. 2 to develop a set of hypotheses linking the structural dimensions used in matrix structures to specific elements of MNC strategy. Then it empirically tests the hypotheses using a sample of 57 German MNCs with matrix structures. As was the case with Chap. 3, the present chapter only reports the logic used to develop the hypotheses and the empirical results of the study. Readers who are interested in other aspects of the study are referred to the underlying publication. To the best of our knowledge, this is the first time that strategy–structure fit in matrix structure firms has been tested with a sample large enough to support statistical analysis. The lack of data on a sufficient number of matrix structure firms has previously impeded the development of more defined strategy–structure theory for matrix structures. Before proceeding, however, we want to review the limited scholarly research that exists on MNC matrix structures.

4.1 Literature Review

Our purpose here is to summarize the literature that is directly relevant to the design of MNC matrix structures. Davis and Lawrence (1977) developed one of the earliest conceptual frameworks for relating matrix structures to contextual factors and strategic conditions. From case studies, Davis and Lawrence identified three conditions that seem to be necessary to the adoption of matrix structures: (1) outside pressure for dual focus, (2) pressures for high information-processing capacity, and (3) pressure for shared resources. While useful as an underlying foundation, this framework is very general. Most MNC strategies today embrace all three conditions, implying matrix structures should be an alternative for most MNCs to consider. The framework says nothing about how to distinguish among the specific types of matrix structure that exist in today's MNCs.

Chi and Nystrom (1998) further conceptualized the capabilities and limitations of MNC matrix structures, emphasizing less the macro-level fit and coordination capabilities, and more the additional motivation and socialization potential provided by matrix structures. This conceptualization addresses the overall advantages and disadvantages of matrix structures and focuses more on the behaviors that are required to successfully implement matrix structures than on the criteria required to design specific matrix structures. Galbraith (2000, 2009) provides the most extensive description of matrix structures in MNCs, based on case studies and clinical research. Both design and implementation issues are addressed. While he convincingly fits specific matrix structures to specific MNC strategies, the process involves expert insight and judgment more than the employment of a specified conceptual model with hypotheses that can be subjected to large-sample empirical testing.

While the above research describes many important characteristics of matrix structures, the research which most directly addresses the matrix design problem in MNCs is the series of survey studies executed within the strategy–structure paradigm. Unfortunately, most studies included relatively few matrix structure MNCs amid larger samples of elementary structure MNCs. As a result, specifying the fit between matrix structures and strategy has generally been a secondary concern and the weakest part of these studies. The previously discussed Stopford and Wells (1972) study included three matrix and 22 mixed structure MNCs in a sample of 187 US MNCs. The study found that matrix and mixed structures (not separated) had both higher levels of foreign product diversity and larger foreign operations than firms with elementary structures. These are the two contingency variables or elements of strategy that are supposed to fit matrix structures in the well-known Stopford and Wells strategy–structure model. Another early study by Franko (1976) contained six matrix and mixed structure MNCs (not separated) in a sample of 70 European MNCs. It found the six firms had (1) higher levels of foreign product diversity and (2) manufacturing in more countries than did the elementary structure firms. Habib and Victor's (1991) study contained 16 matrix and mixed structure firms (not separated), in a sample of 144 US manufacturing and service MNCs. Like the Stopford and Wells (1972) study, it found these structures were associated with high levels of both foreign product diversity and foreign sales. Another study by Chi et al. (2004) contained 101 US MNCs. It measured the extent to which each firm possessed a product dimension and a geographic dimension, without categorizing a firm as having a specific structure. While the study confirmed the traditional relationships of the Stopford and Wells study, its principal new finding was as follows: as the product and geographic dimensions both increase (which implies a tendency toward the matrix structure), there is a tendency for a firm to be associated with higher levels of technology intensity (R&D/sales).

Empirical studies of strategy–structure relationships by Egelhoff (1988a, b) and Wolf and Egelhoff (2002) also included matrix structures and took a somewhat different approach. Egelhoff's study contained seven matrix structure firms in a sample of 50 US and European MNCs. The Wolf and Egelhoff study contained 24 matrix structure firms in a sample of 95 German MNCs. Both studies separated matrix and mixed structure firms and further distinguished among the different types of matrix structure. The first study contained three different types of matrix structure, while the second contained four different types. Both studies used an information-processing perspective to assign different information-processing capacities to a functional division dimension, a product division dimension, and a geographical region dimension in a structure. They argued that a matrix structure which combines two of these dimensions should be viewed as possessing the combined information-processing capacities of the two dimensions contained in the matrix (Egelhoff 1988b). Consistent with this, Wolf and Egelhoff (2002) developed hypotheses about the information-processing capacities of each type of structural dimension. These capacities were generally similar to those associated with the elementary structures (Egelhoff 1982), since each elementary structure contains a single structural dimension. Any structure containing a given structural dimension was hypothesized to possess the information-processing capacities of that dimension. The hypotheses were tested by combining all structures that contained a specific structural dimension (e.g., a product division dimension) to see if the information-processing capacity of this dimension and its hypothesized relationship to various elements of MNC strategy were supported. This meant that elementary and matrix structure firms were grouped to test each hypothesis. For example, elementary product division structure firms were combined with all matrix structure firms that contained a product division dimension to test the hypothesized relationships involving the product division dimension. While the results tended to support the hypotheses, much of the support was undoubtedly driven by the elementary structure firms in the sample. So these studies were only partial or incomplete tests of the proposed matrix logic.

Also employing an information-processing framework, Donaldson (2009) used data from the Wolf and Egelhoff (2002) study to demonstrate that matrix structures provide an advantage over elementary structures, when implementing complex transnational strategies that simultaneously require high levels of global integration and local responsiveness. Qui and Donaldson (2010) extended this work by developing and testing a model that further specifies under what strategic conditions each type of international structure (five types of elementary structure and four types of matrix structure) is to be preferred. The three strategic conditions are the levels of global integration, local responsiveness, and foreign product diversity. Good empirical support was found for six of the nine strategy–structure relationships, while partial support was found for three of the relationships.

In summary, the existing research that attempts to fit matrix structures to elements of MNC strategy is underdeveloped relative to the theory that exists for fitting elementary structures to MNC strategy (as discussed in Chap. 3). The latter theory is more specified, and it has been subjected to much more convincing empirical testing.

4.2 The Information-Processing Capacities of Matrix Structures

Extending our conceptual framework to matrix structures, the information-processing capacities of the elementary structures shown in Table 3.1 are combined when two of the structures are overlaid in a matrix. To better understand how this occurs within an MNC, we want to illustrate it using the matrix structure shown in Fig. 2.1. The German plastics business reports to both a subunit in the global plastics division HQ (headed by a VP) and the HQ of the German subsidiary (headed by the country manager). In terms of organizational distance, it is close to both subunits and can readily process information with each. The goals of the German plastics subunit are closely aligned with the goals of the two superior subunits, since it shares a common hierarchy with each. In contrast, the two superior subunits are more organizationally distant from each other. They do not share a common hierarchy and have goals which are not closely aligned. Coordination between the two will involve non-hierarchical network coordination. While the three subunits possess some common knowledge, they also tend to be specialized and possess substantial amounts of unique knowledge. The German plastics subunit possesses product-related knowledge that is country-specific (knowledge about the key plastics customers in Germany, the peculiarities of the German manufacturing plant). The superior subunit in the global plastics division possesses product-related knowledge that tends to be broader and more abstract (what is the global supply/demand outlook for a given type of plastic). The German subsidiary HQ, in contrast, possesses most of the country-specific company and country-related knowledge (who should we talk to in the German environmental protection agency, which German universities graduate the best chemical engineers). If more general or strategic information processing needs to occur (how will the anticipated European-level pollution standards affect our proposed project), the German subsidiary HQ will take the matter vertically up the geographical region hierarchy to the European HQ. While the German plastics subunit regularly processes information with both of its immediately superior subunits, the subject of the information processing tends to be different. This difference enriches the knowledge available to the German plastics subunit and enhances its performance. The increased level of specialized knowledge available to such subunits as the German plastics subunit is directly provided by the product division and geographical region hierarchies of the matrix structure.

Changing from one type of matrix structure to another (from a product division × geographical region matrix to a product division × functional division matrix) significantly changes the information-processing capacity of the firm. As shown in Table 3.1, each dimension of a matrix provides a different type of information-processing capacity. In the above example, the firm will lose the information-processing capacity of a geographical region dimension and gain the information-processing capacity of a functional division dimension. In practical terms this means that it will lose the capacity to coordinate across the businesses (the plastics business, the inorganic chemicals business, etc.) at the national (German) and regional (European) levels, but it will gain the capacity to coordinate globally within each functional area (R&D, manufacturing, and marketing). The potential information-processing capacity provided by the product division dimension remains the same in both the product division × geographical region and product division × functional division matrix structures, but since it combines with the information-processing capacity of the other dimension, the overall information-processing capacities of the two matrix structures are quite different.

Before leaving this section, it is useful to reflect on how the present study is modeling an MNC. The present study focuses on information-processing between the parent HQ and subsidiaries via the formal hierarchical structure. Network perspectives of the MNC tend to focus on more informal information processing between subsidiaries and between subsidiaries and the parent HQ (Hedlund 1986; Ghoshal and Nohria 1997; Birkinshaw and Hagstrom 2000; Andersson et al. 2001). Both subsystems need to be viewed as complementary parts of an MNC's overall information-processing system. Recent empirical research has found that knowledge flows between subunits in a hierarchical environment (within a firm) tend to be asymmetric, while knowledge flows in a non-hierarchical environment (between firms) tend to be more symmetric (Anand 2011). The explanation is that non-hierarchical relationships tend to be governed by norms of reciprocity (providing knowledge is accompanied by the expectation of receiving knowledge), while hierarchical authority can direct one-way or two-way flows of knowledge, whichever is required. Thus, non-hierarchical network information processing is not always a good substitute for hierarchical information processing. Within this broader framework, the present chapter focuses only on the hierarchical component, since it is directly influenced by formal structure. While hierarchical information processing is not a complete picture of information processing in an MNC, strategy–structure theory assumes that the more a formal structure can satisfy the coordination requirements of a strategy the better it will implement that strategy and contribute to the overall performance of the firm. To the extent the coordination requirements can't be satisfied by the formal structure, they must be satisfied by network coordination, or performance will suffer. So fit between strategy and formal structure is important. Misfit puts additional demands on informal networks that may already be fully utilized or may not fit a requirement for more asymmetric information processing.

4.3 The Information-Processing Requirements of Strategy for Matrix Structures

Implicit in an MNC's strategy are requirements for information processing between its subunits. The purpose of this section is to define these requirements in terms of the four types of information processing in our conceptual framework and hypothesize which structural dimension in a matrix structure fits a given requirement. This is analogous to what was done in Chap. 3 for the elementary structures. Our matrix structure study measured four elements of company-level strategy that have appeared in previous studies and were found to have important relationships to the type of elementary structure used by MNCs: foreign product diversity, size of foreign operations, number of foreign subsidiaries, and size of foreign manufacturing. In addition, the study introduced and measured the international strategic orientation of a firm as a new and potentially important contingency concept for international structure to consider.

4.3.1 Foreign Product Diversity

Many previous studies support the positive relationship between foreign product diversity and an elementary product division structure (Stopford and Wells 1972; Franko 1976; Egelhoff 1982; Daniels et al. 1984; Habib and Victor 1991; Wolf and Egelhoff 2002). Here we want to develop the information-processing logic for including a product division dimension in a matrix. As product diversity increases, so does market diversity (environmental complexity) and manufacturing and technical diversity

4 Designing Matrix Structures to Fit MNC Strategy

(technological complexity). As these increase, requirements for information processing between interdependent R&D, manufacturing, and marketing subunits in a firm also increase. Each product or business requires its own strategy and introduces its own tactical operating problems. Thus, the requirement for strategic and tactical product-related information processing between a parent and its subsidiaries should be proportionate to the level of foreign product diversity in a firm. There is no associated increase in the requirement for company- and country-related information processing. The structural dimension providing the most product-related information-processing capacity between the centers of product knowledge and the foreign subsidiaries is a worldwide product division dimension. It provides several separate information-processing channels between a subsidiary and other parts of the company, one for each product division in the subsidiary.

Hypothesis 4.1 MNCs with matrix structures containing a product division dimension will tend to have greater foreign product diversity than MNCs with matrix structures lacking such a dimension.

Historically, centers of product knowledge resided in the home country operations of an MNC and were connected to foreign subsidiaries via a worldwide product division HQ. Today, centers of product knowledge can reside in foreign subsidiaries, and a product division HQ can also lie outside of the parent country. It is important to realize that such changes in the physical location of subunits won't affect the way a product division elementary structure or a product division dimension in a matrix provides hierarchical information-processing capacity to coordinate the subunits.

As can be seen in Table 3.1, a functional division dimension in a structure also provides a high level of tactical information processing for product matters, but it does so along functional channels. In an elementary functional division structure, marketing and manufacturing matters first come together and are integrated at the corporate HQ level. This centralization is only manageable if there is a narrow line of products (Egelhoff 1982). If significant product diversity were introduced, it would quickly overload the limited cross-functional information-processing capacity of the corporate HQ. An interesting question is the extent to which this constraint applies when the functional division dimension is used in a matrix. Wolf and Egelhoff (2002) reasoned that the presence of a functional division dimension in a matrix would best fit situations where product diversity was relatively low, so that more similarity in information-processing requirements would exist within a functional area and it would be easier to realize synergy within the worldwide functional divisions. They found empirical support for this view.

Based on our own recent exploratory research in MNCs with matrix structures, we question the above view. We found a number of MNCs with strong global functional hierarchies for R&D, purchasing, and manufacturing cutting across the product divisions and/or geographical regions of MNC matrix structures. Their purpose was to better coordinate and realize global economies of scale and scope in these functional areas, sometimes across what appeared to be considerable product and market diversity. These firms appear to contradict the earlier Wolf and Egelhoff (2002) finding. In order to explore this issue further, we will retest the earlier Wolf and Egelhoff hypothesis.

Hypothesis 4.2 MNCs with matrix structures containing a functional division dimension will tend to have lower foreign product diversity than MNCs with matrix structures lacking such a dimension.

4.3.2 Size of Foreign Operations

Egelhoff (1982) conceptualized and found that a relatively low percentage of foreign sales was the defining strategic condition for an international division structure. Unfortunately, our sample of 57 German MNCs with matrix structures does not include any matrix structures with an international division dimension. As discussed in Chap. 3, international division structures have largely been used by US MNCs. Despite our inability to empirically test the relationship, we would like to hypothesize a relationship between the size of foreign operations and the use of an international division dimension in a matrix structure. Our primary motive for developing this hypothesis is to demonstrate that our theory can logically predict relationships between strategy and matrix structures that we have not yet studied or observed. In previous research, we have seen a couple examples of US MNCs with an international division × product division matrix structure, but we were unable to meaningfully observe their relationship to strategy. It makes no sense to matrix an international division dimension with a geographical region dimension, since both have a geographical focus. Conceptually, it could make sense to matrix an international division dimension with a domestic functional division structure, but we have never actually seen an MNC with such a structure.

The logic for relating a relatively low percentage of foreign sales to an international division structure is straightforward. When international operations in a firm are relatively small, it is efficient to concentrate the limited international knowledge within a firm in a single international division. This creates sufficient international specialization and facilitates information processing within the international division. The latter allows the limited international expertise to be readily accessed by the international operations that require it. The downside of an international division structure is that it hinders information processing between the international and domestic subunits of the firm. The latter generally possess the best product-related knowledge, while the former tend to possess most of the international- and foreign country-specific knowledge within the company. When foreign operations are relatively small, the loss of economies of scale and scope within the foreign operations of a firm is less important than when foreign operations grow and become relatively large. As this occurs, firms will want to convert domestic economies of scale and scope into global economies of scale and scope. This strategic thrust requires a high level of product-related information processing between the foreign and domestic operations of a firm. Unfortunately, an international division structure cannot provide this kind of information-processing capacity between the international and domestic operations. The most logical way to provide this kind of information-processing is to matrix the existing international division structure with the existing product division (or functional division) structure of the domestic operations. Under such a matrix structure, the product dimension will now provide the product-related information-processing capacity required to realize global economies of scale and scope across the various product lines, while the international division dimension continues to manage the more country-specific day-to-day operations of the foreign subsidiaries. Since the product divisions are entirely domestic organizations, they lack the international expertise required to manage the foreign subsidiaries. But, an international division × product division matrix structure should be able to provide both the company and country specific information-processing capacity and the product-related information-processing capacity required to implement the above strategy.

As the relative size of foreign operations continues to increase, the product divisions will typically become internationalized and ultimately capable of directly managing foreign operations. When this occurs, such firms might move away from the matrix structure and adopt a worldwide product division structure. In other words, there is no longer any need for the kind of information-processing capacity provided by the international division structure, since this kind of knowledge and expertise now resides inside the product divisions. Thus, matrix structures which contain an international division dimension have often been seen as a transitional structure, useful as firms move from an international division structure to one of the more global structures. This line of reasoning suggests that an international division dimension in a matrix structure will be most appropriate when the size of foreign operations are still relatively small, but greater than the size of foreign operations typically associated with an elementary international division structure. This leads to the following hypothesis:

Untested Hypothesis MNCs with matrix structures containing an international division dimension will tend to have a greater percentage of foreign sales than MNCs with an elementary international division structure, and a lower percentage of foreign sales than MNCs with any other elementary or matrix structure.

Aside from the above relationship between size of foreign operations and an international division structure, which is based on Egelhoff's (1982) earlier model for elementary structures, we would like to develop a new structural logic that conceptually distinguishes among the functional division, product division, and geographical region dimensions of a matrix structure.

When compared to the functional division and product division dimensions, a geographical region dimension reduces the geographic scope that HQ managers have to deal with. Within a region, this dimension provides high levels of both strategic and tactical information processing for product matters as well as company and country matters. This allows managers to specialize on a regional basis to develop regional synergies, economies of scale, and knowledge. But, unless the size of each region is relatively large, these synergies and economies of scale won't exceed the considerable cost of maintaining multiple regional HQs. Thus, using a geographical region dimension requires a high percentage of foreign sales. Neither the functional division nor the product division dimension shares this requirement, since the synergies and economies of scale realized within each functional or product division are global, and not dependent on the relative size of a firm's foreign and domestic operations. This logic differs from that used in the existing theory about elementary structures and leads to the following hypothesis:

Hypothesis 4.3 MNCs with matrix structures containing a geographical region dimension will tend to have a greater percentage of foreign sales than MNCs with matrix structures lacking such a dimension.

4.3.3 Number of Foreign Subsidiaries

Requirements for information processing between foreign subsidiaries and parent HQ increase with the number of foreign subsidiaries. This threatens to overload the information-processing capacities of the HQ. The structural dimension that best guards against this is the geographical region dimension, since it divides the number of foreign subsidiaries reporting in to a HQ into regional groupings. Since the functional division and product division dimensions are global, all subsidiaries containing a given functional or product area must report in to the given functional or product division HQ. A large number of foreign subsidiaries threaten to overload these HQs. Regional HQs are ideal for managing the high levels of routine day-to-day coordination that occur in most large MNCs. They reduce the geographic scope and span of control that a HQ must deal with. When matrixed with either a functional division or product division dimension, the geographical region HQ should provide a large part of the tactical information processing required to manage routine matters, while the global functional division or product division HQ largely addresses less frequent strategic and other non-routine information-processing requirements. This logic complements that developed for Hypothesis 4.3 and leads to the following relationship:

Hypothesis 4.4 MNCs with matrix structures containing a geographical region dimension will tend to have a larger number of foreign subsidiaries than MNCs with matrix structures lacking such a dimension.

4.3.4 Size of Foreign Manufacturing

Egelhoff (1982) argued that a geographical region structure provides good information processing among subsidiaries within a region, but poor information processing with subsidiaries in another region or with the home country. As a result, it fits a regional manufacturing or sourcing strategy, and not a sourcing strategy based on exports from the home country or another region. Since the functional division and product division structures provide high levels of information processing between home country and foreign operations, they can support either high levels of parent exports or high levels of foreign manufacture. When foreign manufacturing becomes relatively large and parent exports relatively small, Egelhoff (1982) argued that opportunities for synergy and economies of scale will tend to be more intraregional than global, and the advantages of the geographical region structure will tend to outweigh those of the functional division or product division structures. Egelhoff's (1982) data supported this argument, and 20 years later Wolf and Egelhoff's (2002) data again supported this argument, that international manufacturing strategies tend to be more concerned with implementing regional integration than global integration. Using an internalization theory perspective,

Rugman and Verbeke (2005) have consistently argued this as well. This leads to the following hypothesis:

Hypothesis 4.5 MNCs with matrix structures containing a geographical region dimension will tend to have a greater percentage of foreign manufacturing than MNCs with matrix structures lacking such a dimension.

4.3.5 Strategic Orientation

All of the above contingency variables have appeared in earlier research studies of the strategy–structure relationship, although new logic has been used to link some variables to specific dimensions of a matrix structure. In addition to these variables, the present study sought to include the international strategic orientation of a firm as a new and potentially important contingency concept for international structure. Different strategic orientations create different interdependencies and, consequently, different information-processing requirements.

Based largely on the work of Perlmutter (1969), Porter (1986), and Bartlett and Ghoshal (1989), four different international strategic orientations have been defined:

Multidomestic strategy—products are developed for each local market and respond to local market conditions; each foreign subsidiary possesses its own unique domestic strategy; subsidiaries tend to possess a full value chain of activities and to be relatively independent.

International strategy—products are developed for the home country market and are moved into international markets with little or no adaptation.

Global strategy—products are developed to fit the common demands of global markets; standardization of products and processes attempts to realize global economies of scale; value chain activities are located to optimize factor cost differentials and economies of scale.

Transnational strategy—attempts to simultaneously realize the local responsiveness advantages of the multidomestic strategy and the efficiency advantages of the global strategy.

Respondents in the study were asked to estimate what percentage of their firm's sales fell under each of the four strategic orientations, providing a strategic orientation profile for each firm. While this measurement of the concept is admittedly simple, the intention here is to explore whether strategic orientation should be considered when evaluating strategy–structure fit.

Several distinctions among the strategic orientations appear to have implications for structure. An international strategy orientation tends to be ethnocentric (Perlmutter 1969). Products are developed for the home country market and sold with little or no adaptation into international markets. The firm largely views foreign markets as similar to and an extension of the domestic market. The interdependencies and information-processing requirements associated with this strategy largely exist between the parent HQ and each foreign subsidiary, not between the subsidiaries. There is no reason to employ a geographical region dimension in the structure, since it facilitates information processing between subsidiaries in a region and hinders information processing between most subsidiaries and the home country. If such a firm has a matrix structure, it should logically be a functional division × product division matrix (with no geographical region dimension).

Hypothesis 4.6 MNCs with a functional division × product division matrix structure will tend to have higher levels of international strategy orientation than other types of matrix structure.

A geographical region dimension in a matrix facilitates information processing across the subsidiaries in a region, coordinating the various functional and product subunits in the region. The functional division or product division dimension that is matrixed with the geographical region dimension provides coordination between these subunits and a global product (or functional) HQ. When both types of coordination are combined in a matrix structure, it facilitates implementing a transnational strategy. The functional division or product division dimension provides the standardization and centralized coordination required to implement the global efficiencies associated with a global strategy. The geographical region dimension provides information processing that helps to reconcile these global requirements with the regional and local requirements associated with a multidomestic strategy. This leads to the following hypothesis:

Hypothesis 4.7 MNCs with matrix structures containing a geographical region dimension will tend to have a higher level of transnational strategy orientation than MNCs with matrix structures lacking such a dimension.

4.4 Testing the Hypotheses

This section parallels what was done in Sect. 3.5 for elementary structures. Table 4.1 contains a summary of each hypothesis and the results of the associated ANOVA contrasts. The data strongly support Hypothesis 4.1, linking high foreign product diversity to matrix structures containing a product division dimension. While the three relationships hypothesized by Hypothesis 4.2 are all directionally supported, the levels of foreign product diversity associated with the two structures containing both a functional division and a product division dimension are quite high (3.39 for functional division × product division, and 3.33 for functional division × product division × geographical region). For these two structures, Hypothesis 4.1 and Hypothesis 4.2 are contradictory (the product division dimension fits high product diversity, and the functional division dimension fits low product diversity). It is interesting to observe that when both dimensions are present in a matrix structure, the product division dimension apparently allows the structure to successfully manage a strategy with relatively high foreign product diversity, which contradicts Hypothesis 4.2. More will be said about this in Sect. 4.6.

Hypothesis 4.3, involving the size of foreign operations, is supported by the findings. It argues that a geographical region dimension in a matrix requires relatively large foreign operations to provide adequate regional economies of scale. Hypothesis 4.4, involving the number of foreign subsidiaries, deals with a similar concept, and it is also supported by the data. It argues that the geographical region dimension also fits a high number of foreign subsidiaries because it reduces the geographic scope and span of control that a HQ must deal with, and thus prevents

Table 4.2 Multiple Discriminant Analysis of Elements of Strategy on Type of Matrix Structure

	Discriminant function			
Independent variable	1	2	3	*F*-value
Product diversity	-.15	<u>.85</u>	.78	2.5*
Size of foreign operations	<u>.62</u>	.46	-.38	4.3**
Number of foreign subsidiaries	<u>.54</u>	-.22	-.44	2.8*
Size of foreign manufacturing	.23	-.70	<u>.83</u>	3.2**
Canonical correlation	.56	.47	.27	
Wilks Lambda	.50**	.73*	.93	

* <.10, ** < .05, *n* = 42.
Note: Type of matrix structure is the dependent variable.
All values under the three functions are standardized discriminant coefficients.

The results of the discriminant analysis are presented in Table 4.2. The standardized discriminant coefficients indicate the relative contribution of an independent variable to a discriminant function. Only the first two discriminant functions are statistically significant. Table 4.3 shows how successful the discriminant functions were in predicting the type of matrix structure for each company, given the measures of its strategy elements. In 60 percent of the cases the discriminant model could predict the actual structure of a company, which is significantly better than the chance probability of 28 percent. Size of foreign operations and size of foreign manufacturing provide the most discriminating power,

Table 4.3 Predicted Type of Matrix Structure from Coefficients of Discriminant Functions

	Predicted group membership			
Actual group membership	FDxPD	FDxGR	PDxGR	FDxPDxGR
FDxPD matrix	<u>14</u>	0	1	1
FDxGR matrix	2	<u>3</u>	2	0
PDxGR matrix	3	1	<u>7</u>	1
FDxPDxGR structure	4	1	1	<u>1</u>

Note: Structures of MNCs correctly classified = 60 percent.

Table 4.4 Centroids of the Four Matrix Structure Groups Measured along the Discriminant Functions

Group	Discriminant function 1	2	3
FDxPD matrix	-.78	.18	.01
FDxGR matrix	.22	-.72	-.44
PDxGR matrix	.72	.55	-.03
FDxPDxGR structure	.31	-.64	.47

followed by number of foreign subsidiaries and product diversity. Each of these variables was hypothesized to be an important element of strategy for type of structure to fit. While the analysis confirms that companies tend to realize a significantly higher level of simultaneous fit than might be attributed to chance, it is useful to analyze in more detail where the model succeeds and where it fails.

Table 4.4 shows the centroids of each of the four groups (types of matrix structure) measured along the three discriminant functions. The first function in Table 4.4 clearly discriminates the functional division × product division structure (which contains no geographical region dimension) from the other three types (all of which contain a geographical region dimension). From Table 4.2 one can see that the first discriminant function largely measures the size of foreign operations and number of foreign subsidiaries. So size of foreign operations largely discriminates between matrix structures which possess a geographical region dimension and those which don't. This is consistent with the conceptual logic underlying Hypothesis 4.3 and Hypothesis 4.4. Large foreign operations increase information-processing requirements and threaten to overload the limited information-processing capacity of HQ. The geographical region dimension creates multiple geographical region HQs to address this requirement and buffer the MNC from information-processing overload at the top.

The second discriminant function most strongly represents product diversity. In Table 4.4 it largely separates the functional division × geographical region structure (which lacks a product division dimension) from the functional division × product division and product division × geographical region structures (which contain a product division dimension).

This discrimination is consistent with the logic in Hypothesis 4.1, that high levels of foreign product diversity create the information-processing requirements that call for a product division dimension in an MNC's structure. Unfortunately, the second discriminant function also separates the functional division × product division × geographical region structure (which contains a product division dimension) from the other two types of structure that contain a product division dimension. This is confusing and an area where the model starts to fail. The third discriminant function, which is not statistically significant, is also not conceptually meaningful.

It is apparent from Table 4.3 that the discriminant model cannot properly discriminate the functional division × product division × geographical region structure from the other three types of matrix structure (it misclassifies six of the seven functional division × product division × geographical region structures). When the discriminant analysis is run omitting the functional division × product division × geographical region structure group, (1) the valid logic and relationships associated with the first two discriminant functions are retained, (2) the percentage of correctly classified cases increases to 71 percent (against a chance probability of 31 percent), and (3) the case classifications remain the same, except one more product division × geographical region structure case is correctly classified. Thus, the existing multivariate discriminant model (which represents or operationalizes Hypotheses 4.1, 4.2, 4.3, and 4.4) does a good job of distinguishing among the three types of two-dimensional matrix structure. Where it fails is in distinguishing the three-dimensional functional division × product division × geographical region structure from the two-dimensional matrix structures. More will be said about this in the next section.

The multivariate discriminant model strongly supports the importance of size of foreign operations as the primary driver of a geographical region dimension in a matrix and to a lesser extent the influence of foreign product diversity as the driver of a product division dimension. Both strategic fits have been found to exist separately in elementary or non-matrix structure MNCs (Stopford and Wells 1972; Egelhoff 1982). But, this is the first time they are so convincingly confirmed to also exist in matrix structures (using multivariate analysis and multiple types of matrix structure).

Next, we want to consider what happens when the three control variables (firm size, industry group, sample) are entered into the four-group and three-group discriminant models. "Sample" refers to the fact that the database for this study was created by merging two separately collected samples of data. The three-group model, which omits the functional division × product division × geographical region structure, does not change in any meaningful way. But the four-group model, which includes the functional division × product division × geographical region structure, reveals a significant relationship between the auto industry group and the functional division × product division × geographical region structure. The number of functional division × product division × geographical region structure firms correctly classified goes from one to four, with only minor changes to the other structure classifications. The logic of the existing model remains largely intact, with the new contingency variable simply adding a more direct predictor of the functional division × product division × geographical region structure. Further investigation reveals that four of the seven auto group MNCs have a functional division × product division × geographical region structure.

Our view is that the above relationship is not relevant to our model. While firms in an industry may prefer certain international structures over others, there is no information-processing logic supporting this relationship. The information-processing perspective argues that the information-processing capacity of a given structure remains basically the same regardless the industry in which it is employed. Previous MNC strategy–structure studies confirm the lack of relationship between types of industry and the structure of international operations once strategy has been adequately specified (Stopford and Wells 1972; Egelhoff 1982; Habib and Victor 1991). In the following section we will discuss what type of strategic contingency variable needs to be added to the model to adequately discriminate the functional division × product division × geographical region structure from other types of matrix structure. When this is implemented, we believe industry preferences for specific types of structure will no longer be a significant contingency variable.

Finally, we want to consider the strategy–structure–performance relationship, since the discriminant analysis specifically identifies firms with strategy–structure fit (correctly categorized MNCs) and misfit (incorrectly categorized MNCs). When we used available financial measures to compare the 25 fits against the 10 misfits from the three-group discriminant model, there were no meaningful differences in terms of profitability or sales growth (both commonly used measures of overall firm performance). For half of the 35 firms in the discriminant model, we had additional variables that measured the consequences of five different types of intrafirm conflict (conflict over goals, evaluation/interpretation, resources, interpersonal differences, limits of authority), each of which can occur between three different dyads of managers (functional and product managers, functional and geographical managers, product and geographical managers). This produced 15 variables, each measuring how constructive a firm's respondent thought the particular type of conflict was on a five-point scale, varying from 'very negative' to 'very positive.' Using this data we conducted 15 t-tests comparing the strategy–structure fits with the misfits. Eleven tests found the fits to score higher than the misfits (two at 0.01, two at 0.05, and one at 0.10 levels of significance). Three tests found the means of the two samples to be equal. One test found the misfits to score higher than the fits, but not significantly. Since intraorganizational conflict is an important outcome of matrix structures (Davis and Lawrence 1977; Galbraith 2009), it is reasonable to expect that it should be more positive or constructive in well-designed firms than in poorly designed firms. The above results are consistent with this view and confirm that strategy–structure fit is important to effective coordination in MNCs. This specific measurement of fit and effectiveness further supports the more general test of fit and performance used by most contingency theory studies of macro structure.

Once again, the logic for the more general test of fit and performance is as follows. The study has sampled the population of surviving MNCs operating in competitive environments. Yuchtman and Seashore (1967) have argued that the only area in which the effectiveness of dissimilar organizations can be compared is on their success in acquiring scarce and valued resources from their environments. For our MNCs, the "scarce and valued" resources are the sales, profits, investments, and legitimacy required to survive and grow into significant MNCs. From a population ecology perspective (Aldrich and Pfeffer 1976; Hannan and Freeman 1977), one would expect to find strategy–structure fits (which contribute to performance) instead of misfits (which detract from performance) in such a sample of surviving and successful firms. Contingency theory studies that rely on this argument to link fit to performance must be able to define fit in a logically convincing way that is independent of the fact that such fit has already been observed in samples of surviving MNCs. The present study used an information-processing model of strategy–structure fit to accomplish this.

4.6 Extending and Modifying the Theory for Elementary Structure Fit So That It Is Applicable to Matrix Structures

The empirical testing supports most of the hypotheses linking specific dimensions of a matrix structure to specific elements of international strategy. Indirectly, this testing also supports the conceptual framework used to develop the hypotheses. This framework includes the information-processing capacities assigned to the different types of elementary structure in Table 3.1, as well as the assumption that the information-processing capacities of a structural dimension tend to be similar when the dimension is used as an elementary structure and when it is used in a matrix structure. The empirical results also suggest three specific areas where additional discussion is warranted: (1) the combination of the functional division and product division dimensions in a matrix, (2) the multiple roles of the geographical region dimension in a matrix, and (3) the failure of the existing model to adequately specify the strategic domain of the functional division × product division × geographical region structure.

4.6.1 The Combination of the Functional Division and Product Division Dimensions in a Matrix

As already discussed, the functional division elementary structure fits low product diversity, and the product division elementary structure fits high product diversity. On the surface, it might appear that these two dimensions should not be used together at the same level in a structure. But of course they are used together, and it is important to better understand the logic for combining them in a matrix. The reason an elementary functional division structure requires low product diversity is because it can't handle high requirements for cross-functional information processing. Information processing in a functional division structure largely occurs within functional channels. These functional channels only come together at the top of the structure, where cross-functional information-processing capacity is extremely limited. Since R&D, manufacturing, and marketing information must be integrated for each product line, increasing product diversity creates increasing requirements for cross-functional information processing. This would overload the limited information-processing capacity of the HQ in a functional division structure.

The earlier Wolf and Egelhoff (2002) study concluded that when the functional division and product division dimensions appear together in a matrix, the functional division fit with product diversity will tend to dominate over the product division fit and there will be low product diversity. This relationship was reflected in Hypothesis 4.2. Contradicting Hypothesis 4.2, the mean levels of foreign product diversity associated with the relevant matrix structures in our sample are functional division × product division (3.4) and functional division × product division × geographical region (3.3). As a reference point, the elementary functional division structure firms in the broader sample, from which our sample of matrix structure MNCs was taken, have mean product diversity of 2.2. Given the significant levels of product diversity associated with the functional division × product division and functional division × product division × geographical region structures relative to the elementary functional division structure, it is apparent that the cross-functional information processing required to coordinate such product diversity is being provided by the product division dimension in both matrix structures, not the functional division dimension. The multiple product division HQs provide cross-functional information processing for each product area, and this reduces the requirements for such information processing at the corporate HQ level where the separate functional channels come together. Thus, when a functional division dimension is used in a matrix with the product division dimension, it only provides vertical information processing within functional channels, while the product division dimension provides the cross-functional information-processing capacity. This is why the presence of a functional division dimension in a matrix does not necessarily require low product diversity, while its presence in an elementary structure does require it.

We believe this interpretation is correct, since we recently witnessed it at work in several MNCs where we conducted exploratory research. For example, in a large healthcare MNC with separate product divisions for pharmaceuticals, branded drugs, and animal health products, we found a global sourcing activity or functional division (responsible for managing manufacturing, purchasing, and outsourcing) matrixed across the three product divisions. There was no global marketing function, so marketing and sourcing are coordinated through the product division HQs, not through the corporate HQ as in an elementary functional division structure. This kind of functional division × product division matrix structure can handle a high level of product diversity, since it provides a separate product division HQ for each product line or business. These multiple product division HQs provide the high tactical and strategic product-related information-processing capacity required by the high product diversity of the strategy.

4.6.2 The Multiple Roles of a Geographical Region Dimension in a Matrix

The study also provides substantial new insight into the use of the geographical region dimension in matrix structures. The previous conceptualization of an elementary geographical region structure was that it requires relatively large international operations to justify the overhead costs of the regional HQs and that its primary purpose is to coordinate regional manufacturing and marketing (Egelhoff 1982). To this existing conceptualization, the conceptualization of the geographical region dimension as a component of a matrix structure adds the following:

1. When international operations become very large, the geographical region dimension reduces the geographic scope and span of control of the HQ and prevents information-processing overload at the HQ level.

2. Adding a geographical region dimension to a matrix is the primary way of fitting a structure to a transnational strategy. It provides the bridge between globally managed functional and/or product activities and the demands of local environments.

Thus, the geographical region dimension plays a somewhat different role in matrix structures than it played in an elementary stand-alone geographical region structure. While the information-processing capacities of the dimension are similar in both cases, the purpose of such information processing seems to change with the structural context. As the second dimension in a matrix, the geographical region dimension is buffering the global HQ of the other dimension from information-processing overload (by managing most of the routine day-to-day operations at a regional level) and reconciling global goals and information processing with information-processing requirements stemming from the local environment. The geographical region dimension's positive association with a transnational strategic orientation and negative association with home country-dominated strategies are consistent with this interpretation. This new insight is an important addition to strategy–structure conceptualization, since today the geographical region dimension is more likely to be used in matrix structures than as a stand-alone elementary structure.

4.6.3 The Failure of the Existing Model to Adequately Specify the Strategic Domain of the Functional Division × Product Division × Geographical Region Structure

The other significant issue raised by the empirical analysis is the failure of the discriminant model to distinguish the functional division × product division × geographical region structure from the two-way matrix structures. This problem was not apparent from the bivariate analyses. The most useful way to state this problem is as follows. Given the presence of product division and geographical region dimensions in a matrix, what is the logic for adding a functional division dimension to create a functional division × product division × geographical region structure? The logic for the product division and geographical region dimensions in a matrix has already been discussed, and it is adequately represented by the three contingency variables (elements of strategy) used by the discriminant model. What is not represented by these variables is the logic for combining the functional division and product division dimensions in the same structure. This combination occurs in the functional division × product division and functional division × product division × geographical region structures. The discriminant model distinguished the functional division × product division structure by its relatively smaller foreign operations, which fits the absence of a geographical region dimension. It needs a different logic for distinguishing the functional division × product division × geographical region structure, and this logic must explain why functional division and product division dimensions are used in the same structure. This is still the missing part of an information-processing theory of strategy–structure fit.

What still needs to be explained is why an MNC would want to process information within functional channels when it already has a product division and/or geographical region dimension in its structure. Once again, our recent exploratory research in matrix MNCs provides some useful insight into this issue. In the previous section we described a healthcare MNC that had added a global functional division dimension for sourcing to its existing product division structure. The reason was to reduce the firm's product costs. This suggests that interdependency within the sourcing activities stems from technological similarities, which facilitate developing economies of scope and a common experience curve across the three product divisions. Centralizing information processing under a global sourcing function provides the information-processing capacity necessary to realize both of these economies. Matrixing this dimension with the product divisions allows the sourcing information to be combined with the relevant product and business information.

In the global telecommunications service industry and the global power generation and distribution industries we saw analogous examples, this time involving the functional division × geographical region matrix structure. Both industries are capital-intensive, and the primary global advantage available to firms is economies of scale in purchasing and deploying new technology and equipment. To realize such economies of scale, standardization and knowledge sharing across the geographical regions are required. In both firms this was being implemented by a number of global functional divisions that were matrixed with the geographical regions. Once again, this suggests that interdependency across the geographical regions stems from technological similarities that the functional divisions are both creating and coordinating.

None of the contingency variables associated with the existing strategy–structure framework adequately measures the kind of technological similarity that is referred to in both of the preceding examples. Realizing technological economies of scale and scope across regions and businesses is undoubtedly a growing phenomenon in many international strategies. Its absence from the present conceptual framework explains why the present framework and discriminant model can't adequately specify the strategic domain that fits the functional division × product division × geographical region structure. It is interesting that the multivariate analysis exposed this gap in existing theory, which heretofore has not been identified in the literature.

4.6.4 Some Concluding Remarks

The present study has sought to develop a more complete model of the strategy–structure relationship in matrix MNCs, just as the earlier study described in Chap. 3 attempted to do this for elementary structure MNCs. One way it does this is by employing a better conceptual framework for modeling and understanding the relationship. The argument presented here is that fit between strategy and structure can be accurately represented by the fit between the information-processing capacities of an organization's structure and the information processing required to implement its strategy. This argument was previously used by Egelhoff (1982) to model and explain the strategy–structure relationship for elementary structure MNCs, but the present study is the first to adapt it to model and empirically investigate this relationship in a sample of matrix structure MNCs that is large enough to support statistical testing. There are several advantages to using the proposed model. Since one can never empirically relate all of the variants of strategy and structure, the model provides a basis for predicting *a priori* the probable impact on the organization of new elements of strategy or new forms of structure and design by simply describing their impact on information processing. Another advantage is that one can predict when the general fits described in the study might have to be modified. It is important to observe that the hypotheses were formulated and fit was evaluated at the population and not the individual organization level. At the individual level, organizations may violate some of the structural fits identified by the study and compensate for this by using other information-processing mechanisms, such as non-hierarchical networks.

A second way the study has attempted to extend existing understanding is by adding more contingency variables to the explanation. The most prominent model of the strategy–structure relationship for matrix MNCs is the Stopford and Wells (1972) Model. It contains two contingency variables, foreign product diversity and the size of foreign operations. To these the present study adds the number of foreign subsidiaries and the size of foreign manufacturing. Both have previously been used to specify strategy–structure fit for elementary structures, but not for matrix structures. In a more exploratory way, the study also introduces a potential new contingency variable, the strategic orientation of an MNC. And, the multivariate analysis suggests that a key element of international strategy, the technological similarity of products across businesses, is still missing from both the proposed model and the broader strategy–structure literature.

Since the present study is the first to so specifically define and empirically test strategy–structure fit for matrix structure MNCs, it is associated with a number of limitations that future research should improve upon. The first is a more complete and robust measurement of the strategic orientation concept, since our preliminary analysis indicates it could be a meaningful new contingency variable with important implications for structure. Future research also needs to measure technological similarity across businesses in an MNC, since this appears to be the missing component of the present model. It would also be important to investigate the generalizability of the proposed model by retesting it, preferably in non-German MNCs.

Finally, it is interesting that the traditional fits of international strategy–structure theory, first established for elementary structure MNCs some 30 years ago, can, with some modification and extension, be used to explain strategy–structure fit in today's matrix structure MNCs. This continuity of logic is impressive in two ways. First, there is continuity across types of structure. The fundamental information-processing capacities of the four structural dimensions shown in Table 3.1 underlie the information-processing capacities of both elementary structures and matrix structures. This provides a more common theory for understanding and designing both types of structure. Second, there is continuity across time. Despite the many changes to MNC strategy and organization design over the last 30 years, the study shows that strategy–structure fit is not some past or vestigial property of firms that can be ignored, but an important attribute of all large firms that is continually being determined by the decisions of managers and the selection process of competitive environments.

Bibliography

Aldrich, H. E., & Pfeffer, J. (1976). Environments of organizations. *Annual review of sociology, 82*, 929–964.

Anand, J. (2011). Permeability to inter- and intrafirm knowledge flows: The role of coordination and hierarchy in MNEs. *Global Strategy Journal, 1*(3–4), 283–300.

Andersson, U., Forsgren, M., & Holm, U. (2001). Subsidiary embeddedness and competence development in MNCs: A multi-level analysis. *Organization Studies, 22*(6), 1013–1034.

Bartlett, C. A., & Ghoshal, S. (1989). *Managing across borders: The transnational solution.* Boston, MA: Harvard Business School Press.

Birkinshaw, J., & Hagstrom, P. (2000). *The flexible firm: Capability management in network organizations.* Oxford: Oxford University Press.

Chi, T., & Nystrom, P. (1998). An economic analysis of matrix structure, using multinational corporations as an illustration. *Managerial and Decision Economics, 19*(3), 141–156.

Chi, T., Nystrom, P. C., & Kircher, P. (2004). Knowledge-based resources as determinants of MNC structure: Tests of an integrative model. *Journal of International Management, 10*(2), 219–238.

Daniels, J. D., Pitts, R. A., & Tretter, M. J. (1984). Strategy and structure of U.S. multinationals: An exploratory study. *Academy of Management Journal, 27*(2), 292–307.
Davis, S. M., & Lawrence, P. R. (1977). *Matrix*. Reading, MA: Addison-Wesley.
Donaldson, L. (2009). In search of the matrix advantage: A re-examination of the fit of matrix structures to transnational strategy. In J. Cheng, E. Maitland, & S. Nicholas (Eds.), *Managing subsidiary dynamics: Headquarters role, capability development, and China strategy, advances in international management series* (pp. 3–26). Bingley, UK: Emerald Publishing.
Egelhoff, W. G. (1982). Strategy and structure in multinational corporations: An information-processing approach. *Administrative Science Quarterly, 27*(3), 435–458.
Egelhoff, W. G. (1988a). Strategy and structure in multinational corporations: A revision of the Stopford and Wells model. *Strategic Management Journal, 9*(1), 1–14.
Egelhoff, W. G. (1988b). *Organizing the multinational enterprise: An information-processing perspective*. Cambridge, MA: Ballinger.
Egelhoff, W. G., Wolf, J., & Adzic, M. (2013). Designing matrix structures to fit MNC strategy. *Global Strategy Journal, 3*(3), 205–226.
Franko, L. G. (1976). *The European multinationals: A renewed challenge to American and British big business*. Stamford, CT: Greylock.
Galbraith, J. R. (2000). *Designing the global corporation*. San Francisco, CA: Jossey-Bass.
Galbraith, J. R. (2009). *Designing matrix organizations that actually work*. San Francisco, CA: Jossey-Bass.
Ghoshal, S., & Nohria, N. (1997). *The differentiated MNC: Organizing the multinational corporation for value creation*. San Francisco, CA: Jossey-Bass.
Habib, M., & Victor, B. (1991). Strategy, structure, and performance of U.S. manufacturing and service MNCs. *Strategic Management Journal, 12*(8), 589–606.
Hannan, M. T., & Freeman, J. (1977). The population ecology of organizations. *American Journal of Sociology, 82*(5), 929–964.
Hedlund, G. (1986). The hypermodern MNC: A heterarchy. *Human Resource Management, 25*(1), 9–35.
Perlmutter, H. V. (1969). The tortuous evolution of the multinational corporation. *Columbia Journal of World Business, 4*(1), 9–18.

Peters, T. J., & Waterman Jr., R. U. (1982). *In search of excellence: Lessons from America's best-run companies.* New York: Warner.

Pitts, R. A., & Daniels, J. D. (1984). Aftermath of the matrix mania. *Columbia Journal of World Business, 19*(2), 48–54.

Porter, M. E. (1986). *Competition in global industries.* Boston, MA: Harvard Business School Press.

Qui, J. X., & Donaldson, L. (2010). The cubic contingency model: Towards a more comprehensive international strategy-structure model. *Journal of General Management, 36*(1), 81–100.

Rugman, A. M., & Verbeke, A. (2005). Towards a theory of regional multinationals: A transaction cost economics approach. *Management International Review, 45*(1), 5–17.

Stopford, J. M., & Wells Jr., L. T. (1972). *Managing the multinational enterprise.* New York: Basic Books.

Wolf, J., & Egelhoff, W. G. (2002). A reexamination and extension of international strategy-structure theory. *Strategic Management Journal, 23*(2), 181–189.

Yuchtman, E., & Seashore, S. E. (1967). A system resource approach to organizational effectiveness. *American Sociological Review, 32*(6), 891–903.

5

Understanding the Causes of Conflict in Matrix Structure Firms

When many MNCs abandoned matrix structures in the 1980s, one of the most frequently reported problems was higher levels of interpersonal and interunit conflict than existed in non-matrix structure firms (Peters 1979; Janger 1983). While MNC scholars tend to view increased conflict as an inevitable outcome of using formal matrix structures, there has actually been limited empirical investigation of the issue. The widespread view that matrix structures always lead to higher levels of intraorganizational conflict seems to be supported by (1) the reported findings of clinical research and case studies, and (2) the appealing logic that attempting to simultaneously organize around contrasting goals is bound to increase conflict between the parties representing those goals. To date, such support has sufficed, and instead of further investigating the source and extent of conflict in matrix MNCs, scholars have instead focused their attention on how to either minimize conflict or make it more constructive (Davis and Lawrence 1977; Chi and Nystrom 1998; Galbraith

---

Major portions of this chapter are reprinted from "An Empirical Evaluation of Conflict in MNC Matrix Structure Firms" by Joachim Wolf and William G. Egelhoff, published in *International Business Review* Volume 22, Issue 3 by permission of *International Business Review*. Copyright 2013 by Elsevier Ltd.

© The Author(s) 2017
W.G. Egelhoff, J. Wolf, *Understanding Matrix Structures and their Alternatives*, DOI 10.1057/978-1-137-57975-1_5

2009). As a result, there has been no prior empirical evaluation of conflict in matrix MNCs using large-sample survey research with the systematic measurement of variables across the cases.

Since increased conflict is an important consideration when firms weigh the costs and benefits of using a matrix structure, a deeper, more empirically supported understanding of intraorganizational conflict in matrix MNCs is required. To address this requirement, a recent study by Wolf and Egelhoff (2013) sought to address the following research questions:

1. Are levels of conflict in matrix structure firms higher than in non-matrix structure firms?
2. Does the type of matrix structure influence the answer to question 1?
3. Does the issue underlying the conflict influence the answer to question 1?

These questions underlie a deeper understanding of conflict in matrix MNCs, an understanding that firms considering a matrix structure need to possess. The next section reviews the relevant literature on conflict in matrix structure MNCs. The following section develops hypotheses that address the above research questions. Subsequent sections present the empirical findings, and discuss the results and their implications for researchers and practitioners.

5.1 Literature Review

Much of the empirical research on matrix structures in MNCs tends to be clinical research and case studies. Table 5.1 lists the seven MNC case studies available through the Harvard case system which involve matrix structures. The table identifies the type of matrix structure employed and summarizes what the case says about intraorganizational conflict and the role of culture and shared vision in the matrix. Four of the cases report significant matrix conflict, while three of the cases report either limited conflict or conflict that improves over time. A relatively strong company culture and shared vision seem to exist in the companies with limited

5 Understanding the Causes of Conflict in Matrix Structure Firms 111

Table 5.1 MNC Matrix Case Studies

Company	Type of matrix	Characteristics of conflict in the matrix	Role of culture and shared vision in matrix
Philips (Aguilar and Yoshino 1987; Ghemawat and Nueno 2004)	PDxGR	There is considerable friction and wasted energy in making joint decisions. A power struggle develops between dimensions when top management attempts to shift power.	Very significant, facilitated by life-time employment and the development of strong interpersonal networks among managers.
ABB (Simons and Bartlett 1992)	PDxGR	Conflict appears limited and constructive, moderated by common culture and shared vision.	High, with the adoption of the matrix they attempt to build a new company-wide culture that stresses decentralization, accountability, and decisiveness.
Bosch (Ojha 2010)	PDxGR	Perspectives and goals of the regional and global product dimensions differ and lead to conflict. A regional head can go direct to top management to escalate an issue if necessary.	Not discussed.
General Motors (Garvin 2006)	GRxFD	Conflict appears to be minimized by the rapid escalating of key decisions to the top management level.	Common culture is initially lacking, but it develops over time, assisted by the assigning of two hats (one from each dimension) to matrix managers.
Serono (Carr 2003)	PDxFD	Goal conflict occurs between the functional and business dimensions.	Not discussed.
Dow Corning (Goggin 1974)	PDxFD	Early tensions decline with experience.	High, they have established an environment of mutual trust and confidence.
Proctor & Gamble (Piskorski and Spadini 2007)	GRxPD for product development; GRxFD for product supply and sales	There are global functional conflicts, and tensions between regional and product-category managements.	Common culture appears to lie at level of functional areas and regional subunits rather than at global level.

or improving levels of matrix conflict. But overall, conflict is not richly described or analyzed in any of these case studies. Other characteristics of a matrix structure, such as its relationship to strategy and the way decisions are made, tend to be the focus of the case studies.

While most researchers report that matrix structures are associated with high levels of intraorganizational conflict, there is only limited conceptualization of the conflict issue in the matrix literature. Davis and

Lawrence (1977) state that the large number of interdependencies in a matrix structure leads to more contacts and more communications between parties, and this increases the chances for conflicts to develop. In addition to the increased frequency of contact, they further point out that matrix conflicts are more likely to occur between "people from different functions who often have different attitudes and orientations" (Davis and Lawrence 1977: 104). In a subsequent conceptual article, Chi and Nystrom link conflict in an MNC matrix structure to the fact "that the managers of two units organized along different dimensions of the organization have overlapping jurisdictions and are both evaluated partly on the economic outcomes of their respective units that partially coincide" (Chi and Nystrom 1998: 147). Thus, intraorganizational conflict in matrix MNCs tends to occur when differentiation and different goals among subunits are combined with interdependency and shared responsibilities among the same subunits. This perspective is consistent with the broader literature on intraorganizational conflict (Rahim and Bonoma 1979).

Galbraith (2009) takes a somewhat different view of matrix conflict, which he sees as normal and natural in matrix firms: "When conflict arises, it indicates that the structure is working. It should surface differences between the two or three sides of the matrix ... Absence means that the natural conflicts are being hidden and acted out in dysfunctional ways" (Galbraith 2009: 202). Galbraith then focuses on resolving matrix conflicts through participative problem solving. He seems to view conflict resolution as an integral part of the coordination that matrix structures provide. The three works just discussed are the most important attempts to conceptualize the role of conflict in matrix MNCs. It is important to remember that there are no large-sample research studies that have compared conflict in matrix MNCs against conflict in non-matrix MNCs. The above conceptualization is based on clinical research and case studies. Such research does not facilitate distinguishing between different types of matrix structure and different types of conflict issues when conceptualizing the influence of a matrix structure on intraorganizational conflict. A more comparative type of research is required to address these issues.

There is also some discussion of matrix conflict in the project management matrix literature (Barker et al. 1988; Ford and Randolph 1992;

5 Understanding the Causes of Conflict in Matrix Structure Firms

Burns and Wholey 1993; Laslo and Goldberg 2001; Kuprenas 2003). Project matrix structures are widely used in aerospace companies, R&D labs, CPA and consulting firms, and other organizations where work needs to be organized under large, temporary projects. Like the MNC matrix literature, this literature largely views conflict as an inevitable consequence of a matrix structure that needs to be managed through the organizational culture and deliberate training of employees on how to work in matrix structures (Joyce 1986; Bernasco et al. 1999). Our view is that the project matrix literature has limited relevance to the issue of better understanding what underlies conflict in MNC matrix structures. The project matrix structure is always a functional division × project structure (where each project can be seen as a temporary product division), while the organizational dimensions in an MNC matrix structure vary and lead to a variety of different types of matrix structure. As a result, our primary research question, the relationship between type of matrix structure and conflict, is not even relevant to the project management literature.

Being an MNC generally adds a significant geographic dimension to a company's strategy and structure that is typically absent from a domestic company. This additional dimension complicates the organizational design of MNCs by creating new interdependencies between geographic subunits and product or functional subunits. These interdependencies lead to new types of intraorganizational conflict that typically do not exist outside of an MNC. We will return to this issue in the Discussion section.

Finally, it is useful to link our study of conflict in matrix structure MNCs to more recent work on MNC organization design. It is important to recognize that a matrix structure formally reflects the same kind of multidimensionality that is more informally inherent in all of the more recent conceptualizations of MNC organization design. More recent designs include the heterarchical MNC (Hedlund 1986), the transnational MNC (Bartlett and Ghoshal 1989; Ghoshal et al. 1994; Ghoshal and Nohria 1997), and a variety of additional network-like conceptualizations of the MNC (Birkinshaw 2000; Andersson et al. 2001; Forsgren et al. 2005; Ambos and Birkinshaw 2010; Ciabuschi et al. 2010; Piekkari et al. 2010). What the matrix structure and the network conceptualizations of MNC design have in common is that they both try to create a more multidimensional organization design, a design capable of simultaneously coordinating along two or more dimensions, without subordinating one dimension to the other. Such a design can better respond to more complex, multidimensional problems. The formal matrix structure does this by incorporating two or three different hierarchical dimensions into its design. The network designs all emphasize non-hierarchical, network-like ways of providing a wider variety of coordination capabilities. For example, subunits under both designs attempt to simultaneously coordinate and realize geographic region goals and product division goals without consistently subordinating one to the other, as an elementary structure would do. Since the matrix structure and network designs both involve multidimensional coordination, and multidimensional coordination and information processing contribute to intraorganizational conflict, it is possible that additional insight into conflict in matrix structure MNCs will also contribute to a better understanding of such conflict in network MNCs.

5.2 Hypothesis Development

While Davis and Lawrence (1977), Chi and Nystrom (1998), and Galbraith (2009) may differ somewhat in the way they conceptualize matrix conflict and its implications, they all agree that matrix structures involve higher levels of conflict than non-matrix structures. Additional research supports this view. An early empirical study conducted in German companies with matrix structures found that conflict between the two matrix managers was one of the most important problems associated with using a matrix structure (Brings 1976). Studies have also found that most matrix structures are not balanced matrix structures, but that one organizational dimension usually has more power and influence than the other (Wagner 1978; Buehner 1993). This imbalance is generally regarded as a potential source of conflict between the two dimensions. Thus, the existing conceptualization and empirical research on matrix structure firms support the following general hypothesis:

Hypothesis 5.1 Matrix structure MNCs will tend to be associated with higher levels of intraorganizational conflict than non-matrix structure MNCs.

5 Understanding the Causes of Conflict in Matrix Structure Firms

In addition to the general hypothesis, the existing literature also suggests where in the organization conflict is most likely to occur. From the case studies discussed in Davis and Lawrence (1977) and Galbraith (2009), one can infer that matrix conflict seems to largely occur at the interface of the two organizational dimensions that are included in the matrix structure. This view is confirmed by the discussion of matrix structures in Janger (1983). If the structure is a product division × geographical region matrix, the interface begins at the second level of an MNC's hierarchy, where managers in product division HQs and in geographical region HQs share responsibility and authority over those in foreign subsidiaries. This can be seen in Fig. 2.1 (Chap. 2). Here the German plastics business reports to both a product division HQ and a geographical region HQ. Both of these HQs share the second hierarchical level in the MNC. Since they have different goals and missions, which have to be realized through the same German subsidiary, there will be significant opportunity for conflict to occur between the product division managers and the geographical region managers at the second hierarchical level and below. They attempt to resolve these differences through horizontal communication.

In the related elementary or non-matrix structures (the product division and the geographical region structures), the potential for conflict between product division managers and geographical region managers should be reduced, since they do not occupy the same hierarchical level. Since one dimension will always be under the other in the MNC hierarchy, its goals and authority will tend to be more consistent with the goals and authority of the superior dimension, and there should be less opportunity for conflict to occur. This logic leads to the following hypothesis:

Hypothesis 5.2a A product division × geographical region (PD × GR) matrix structure will tend to be associated with higher levels of conflict between product division and geographical region managers than an elementary product division (PD) or geographical region (GR) structure.

The above logic can also be extended to the other two-way matrix structures that can exist in an MNC. These are a functional division × product division matrix (FD × PD) and a functional division × geographical region matrix (FD × GR). From this we derive the following hypotheses:

Hypothesis 5.2b A functional division × product division (FD × PD) matrix structure will tend to be associated with higher levels of conflict between functional division and product division managers than an elementary functional division (FD) or product division (PD) structure.

Hypothesis 5.2c A functional division × geographical region (FD × GR) matrix structure will tend to be associated with higher levels of conflict between functional division and geographical region managers than an elementary functional division (FD) or geographical region (GR) structure.

Our empirical study of German MNCs also included a three-way matrix structure, product division × geographical region × functional division (PD × GR × FD), which in Germany is referred to as a "tensor" structure. The above logic can also be used to develop a more specified hypothesis for evaluating the levels of conflict associated with this structure:

Hypothesis 5.3 A product division × geographical region × functional division (PD × GR × FD) matrix structure will tend to be associated with higher levels of conflict between:

1. product division and geographical region managers than an elementary product division (PD) or geographical region (GR) structure,
2. functional division and product division managers than an elementary functional division (FD) or product division (PD) structure, and
3. functional division and geographical region managers than an elementary functional division (FD) or geographical region (GR) structure.

Empirically testing the above hypotheses addresses the first two of our three research questions. The third research question deals with whether matrix conflict varies with the type of issue underlying the conflict. The general conflict literature frequently distinguishes between task-related conflict and relationship or person-related conflict (Simons and Peterson 2000). Since we are interested in the influence of structure on conflict, and structure influences the way tasks are accomplished and the conflict that results, we chose to focus on three different types of task-related conflict. Case studies and clinical research on matrix firms frequently identify the differing goals of the organizational dimensions as a source of conflict (Davis and Lawrence 1977; Janger 1983; Galbraith 2009). This is a logical argument, since one of the reasons for adopting a matrix structure is to give equal priority to multiple goals. The same studies also report frequent disagreements between the organizational dimensions over which manager or subunit has authority over specific decisions. Drumm (1974) argues that it is not possible to clearly assign authority to the two hierarchies that comprise a matrix structure. Instead, it is likely that authority will tend to shift between the two hierarchies. Peters (1979) also sees conflict over authority as a frequent problem for matrix structures, since authority is shared and neither dimension has primacy.

In addition to goal conflict and authority conflict, we also chose to measure a third type of conflict, which we label evaluation conflict. It measures the conflict which can develop when individuals use different perspectives or approaches to evaluate a situation, similar to the differentiation concept of Lawrence and Lorsch (1967) and the different thoughtworlds concept of Dougherty (1992). This is likely to exist when individuals from different organizational dimensions interact over a problem or decision. Since the organizational dimensions represent different backgrounds and experiences, their members are likely to use different perspectives and conceptual frameworks. Distinguishing among these three different types of conflict will allow the study to observe whether the above hypotheses hold across these different types of conflict issue.

managers than the elementary product division (PD) structure. This supports Hypothesis 5.3. But the levels of conflict between functional division (FD) and product division (PD), and functional division (FD) and geographical region (GR) managers are not significantly greater in the three-way matrix structure than they are in the relevant functional division (FD) and product division (PD) elementary structures. This finding is similar to the previous one for two-way matrix structures.

Thus, a consistent pattern emerges from the detailed comparisons evaluated in Tables 5.3 and 5.4. Conflict between product division and geographical region managers follows the hypothesized relationship and tends to be greater in the two-dimensional and three-dimensional matrix structures than in the relevant elementary structures. But conflict between functional division and product division managers, and between functional division and geographical region managers fails to support the hypothesized relationship. Here conflict tends to be similar or not significantly different between matrix structures and the relevant elementary structures. One should remember that we can't adequately represent or test conflict in the elementary geographical region structure.

It should also be noted that the study deliberately measured three different types of task-related conflict across each relationship. The correlation among the three types of task-related conflict varies from 0.30 to 0.66, so there is sufficient independency to make this a meaningful test. The intent was to investigate whether the issue underlying conflict might influence the level of intraorganizational conflict. But with regard to the hypotheses, the three types of conflict tend to reflect similar relationships between type of structure and level of intraorganizational conflict. So the relationships between structure and conflict appear to be fairly robust and unvarying across different types of task-related conflict.

5.4 Discussion

5.4.1 Overall Findings

It is important to remember that the primary issue addressed by the study is largely absent from the existing literature. This issue is the impact of different types of matrix structure on intraorganizational conflict. It is

5 Understanding the Causes of Conflict in Matrix Structure Firms

probably impossible to identify or evaluate this from clinical research and case studies. To make such a comparison, one needs to quantify the measurement of conflict and vary the type of matrix structure across a sufficiently large sample of firms. The previous absence of such research explains the absence of this issue from the existing literature. As a result, the literature suggests that all matrix structures—regardless of type—lead to increased levels of intraorganizational conflict. This general hypothesis (Hypothesis 5.1 in our study) and its logical extensions (Hypotheses 5.2a, 5.2b, 5.2c, and 5.3) are largely rejected by the empirical results of our study.

These empirical results highlight a primary issue for further discussion and potential new theory development. They reveal that all of the hypotheses are only supported for the product division—geographical region relationship. As hypothesized, conflict between product division and geographical region managers is significantly higher in the product division × geographical region and the product division × geographical region × functional division matrix structures than in the product division and geographical region elementary structures. This is the relationship most frequently associated with MNC matrix structures (Stopford and Wells 1972; Davis and Lawrence 1977; Galbraith 2009). But our sample shows that for German MNCs, the functional division × product division and functional division × geographical region forms of matrix structure are also widely used. And for these types of matrix structure, conflict between the matrixed dimensions tends to be similar to the levels of conflict found in the elementary functional division and product division structures (the elementary geographical region structure could not be adequately tested). This contradicts both the hypotheses and the commonly held assumptions about conflict in matrix structure MNCs.

As previously discussed, the existing conceptualization of conflict in matrix structure MNCs is quite simple and not explicitly related to the type of matrix structure. Consequently, it provides no explanation for the mixed findings of the study. Clearly, some new, more specified logic is required to explain the mixed findings. In this case we believe the pattern of the findings that emerged can be used to help derive such new logic. An important difference between the product division–geographical region relationship and the other relationships (functional division–product division and functional division–geographical region) is that both the product division dimension and the geographical region dimension tend to organize their subunits as profit centers. The HQ of a worldwide product division attempts to optimize worldwide profits for the product area, while the geographical region HQ for Europe attempts to optimize profits within the region. It is easy to imagine how conflict between the two HQs might increase as they both attempt to manage foreign subsidiaries in Europe to realize their respective goals. This increase is clearly reflected in the empirical findings.

But if one of the dimensions in the MNC matrix is a series of worldwide functional division HQs (a worldwide R&D division HQ, a worldwide manufacturing division HQ, a worldwide marketing division HQ), it is unlikely that any of these will be profit centers, attempting to optimize the profits of some segment or activity. Functional subunits are typically cost centers rather than profit centers, since none can independently provide a product or generate outside revenue. So conflict between the functional division dimension and either the product division or geographical region dimension will not be over profits, but some other issues. Whatever these non-profit issues are, they seem to cause similar levels of conflict between functional division managers and product division or geographical region managers when (1) the interface occurs horizontally in a matrix structure, and (2) the interface occurs vertically in an elementary structure. In contrast, when the interface between product division and geographical region managers occurs vertically in an elementary structure, where one dimension is subordinate to the other, there is significantly less conflict than when the interface occurs horizontally at the same level in a matrix. Our tentative conclusion and suggestion is that profit issues are probably easy to reconcile vertically in a hierarchical manner (low conflict), but difficult to reconcile horizontally in a non-hierarchical manner (high conflict). Non-profit issues, in contrast, are more equally difficult to reconcile under a horizontal or a vertical relationship (similar levels of conflict). This line of reasoning is consistent with the empirical findings.

To facilitate further research on this issue it is useful to develop the following two propositions:

5 Understanding the Causes of Conflict in Matrix Structure Firms

Proposition 5.1 When the interface between interdependent product division and geographical region subunits occurs horizontally in a matrix structure, there will be higher levels of intraorganizational conflict than when the interface occurs vertically in an elementary structure.

Proposition 5.2 When the interface between interdependent functional division and product division subunits (or functional division and geographical region subunits) occurs horizontally in a matrix structure, there will be similar levels of intraorganizational conflict as when the interface occurs vertically in an elementary structure.

These propositions propose a meaningful extension to the existing theory about intraorganizational conflict in matrix MNCs. Since they are derived from our existing database, they need to be further tested and investigated with new data.

5.4.2 Limitations of the Study

The research design of the study involves two primary limitations. The first is an inadequate number of MNCs with an elementary geographical region structure, and the second is relatively weak measurement or operationalization of some of the constructs. While the single MNC with an elementary geographical region structure tends to satisfy Hypotheses 5.2a, 5.2b, 5.2c, and 5.3, this is not a meaningful test of this aspect of the hypotheses. Generally firms in consumer goods and service industries are more likely to use this structure, and such industries tend to be weakly represented among large German MNCs. Testing the hypotheses and propositions of the present study with a different national sample would hopefully overcome this problem and also extend the generalizability of the findings.

The second limitation refers to the use of a single respondent in each firm and single measures of the various types of conflict. Using multiple respondents in a firm and multiple measures of a concept like "frequency of conflict," that is largely judgmental, improves the reliability of its measurement. Such measurement will require a narrower and more focused study than the present one. The logic and propositions developed by the present study should facilitate moving subsequent research in this direction.

While the above limitations might make the present study unsuitable for testing and refining a well-developed theory about conflict in matrix MNCs, this was not the context of the study. We believe this is the first study to hypothesize and empirically test the above relationships in a meaningful sample of matrix and elementary structure MNCs.

5.5 Implications for Future Research and Practitioners

The implications of the present study for future research on conflict in matrix structure MNCs have already been alluded to in the previous subsection. The two propositions and their accompanying logic suggest a new conceptual framework for understanding and predicting when confrontation between the dimensions of a matrix structure will lead to more conflict and when it will not. The proposed framework modifies and extends the existing view or theory that all types of matrix structure tend to be associated with greater conflict than their alternative elementary structures. Since the framework was derived from the relationships in the present study's database, it in turn needs to be tested and evaluated with new independent databases and studies of the phenomenon.

At the end of the Literature Review in Sect. 5.1, we also stated that conflict in formal matrix structure MNCs may need to be viewed more broadly as a specific example of conflict in MNCs with a multidimensional organization design, which includes those with various forms of network structure. If two interdependent subunits of an MNC are both profit centers (e.g., a product subunit and a geographical region subunit), conflict will be higher than if one is a profit center (product subunit or geographical region subunit) and the other a cost center (functional subunit). While this argument is empirically supported for matrix structures, there is no obvious reason why it should not be equally applicable to more non-hierarchical network designs. The process for reconciling differences

5 Understanding the Causes of Conflict in Matrix Structure Firms 127

between the subunits appears to be largely non-hierarchical in both the matrix structure and the network design. If this is true, it would be important to study and compare intraorganizational conflict in a matrix structure environment with similar conflict in a network design environment. It may be possible to understand both with a more common theory about intraorganizational conflict in multidimensional organizations.

Finally, we want to consider the implications of the present study for practitioners in MNCs. The study suggests that practitioners may need to adopt a more differentiated view of matrix structure conflict. Matrix conflict seems to vary with the structural design of a matrix structure. To the extent this is true, managers may be able to better anticipate the level of conflict associated with adopting a given matrix structure and more intelligently plan for the conflict resolution capabilities that are required to manage it. Galbraith (2009) describes how participative problem solving by both dimensions of a matrix can lead to constructive conflict resolution. This generally requires some training, experience, and a compatible company culture. We will not discuss this issue further, since our study did not address it and there is already a large literature on conflict resolution in organizations.

The other way to resolve conflict in a matrix structure is to escalate the issue or decision up both of the hierarchies in the matrix. While this will normally be frowned upon by senior management, there are situations where this would appear to be the preferred course of action from the perspective of the firm. If an issue or decision is likely to set a precedent or impact higher-level strategy, it is preferable that the issue or decision be escalated to the level where such precedent or strategy is typically approved. This ensures that the appropriate perspective and type of information-processing capacity have been used to make the decision. This issue will be further discussed in the following chapter.

A second issue for practitioners suggested by the study is whether it is wise for MNCs to operate with so many overlapping profit centers. Since overlapping profit centers appear to be associated with higher levels of intraorganizational conflict, a firm needs to consciously understand why it is choosing to use such a design. MNCs may want to treat national subsidiaries and geographical regions as profit centers, because they facilitate local motivation and control. But, when there is high global interdependency, attempts by geographic subunits to maximize profits at the national and regional levels can contradict the attempts of global product or functional divisions to optimize profits at the firm level. This is an issue that needs to be carefully evaluated by MNCs with significant global interdependencies across the geographical regions.

As international strategies grow in complexity, more MNCs will be forced to consider some form of matrix structure. Better understanding the impact of type of matrix structure on intraorganizational conflict should contribute to the rationality that can be brought to bear on this important consideration.

Bibliography

Aguilar, F. J., & Yoshino, M. Y. (1987). The Philips Group: 1987. *Harvard Business School Case* 9-388-050.
Ambos, T. C., & Birkinshaw, J. (2010). Headquarters' attention and its effect on subsidiary performance. *Management International Review, 50*(4), 449–469.
Andersson, U., Forsgren, M., & Holm, U. (2001). Subsidiary embeddedness and competence development in MNCs: A multi-level analysis. *Organization Studies, 22*(6), 1013–1034.
Barker, J., Tjosvold, D., & Andrews, I. R. (1988). Conflict approaches of effective and ineffective project managers: A field study in matrix organization. *Journal of Management Studies, 25*(2), 167–178.
Bartlett, C. A., & Ghoshal, S. (1989). *Managing across borders: The transnational solution.* Boston, MA: Harvard Business School Press.
Bernasco, W., de Weerd-Nederhof, P. C., Tillema, H., & Boer, H. (1999). Balanced matrix structure and new product development process at Texas Instruments Materials and Controls Division. *R&D Management, 29*(2), 121–131.
Birkinshaw, J. (2000). *Entrepreneurship in the global firm.* Thousand Oaks, CA: Sage.
Brings, K. (1976). Erfahrungen mit der Matrixorganisation. *Zeitschrift fuer Organisation, 45*(2), 72–80.
Buehner, R. (1993). *Strategie und Organisation: Analyse und Planung der Unternehmensdiversifikation mit Fallbeispielen* (2nd ed.). Wiesbaden: Gabler.

Burns, L. R., & Wholey, D. R. (1993). Adoption and abandonment of matrix management programs: Effects of organizational characteristics and interorganizational networks. *Academy of Management Journal, 36*(1), 106–138.

Carr, L. P. (2003). Serono. *Babson College Case* BAB043.

Chi, T., & Nystrom, P. (1998). An economic analysis of matrix structure, using multinational corporations as an illustration. *Managerial and Decision Economics, 19*(3), 141–156.

Ciabuschi, F., Martin Martin, O., & Stahl, B. (2010). Headquarters' influence on knowledge transfer performance. *Management International Review, 50*(4), 471–491.

Davis, S. M., & Lawrence, P. R. (1977). *Matrix*. Reading, MA: Addison-Wesley.

Dougherty, D. (1992). Interpretive barriers to successful product innovation in large firms. *Organization Science, 3*(2), 179–202.

Drumm, H. J. (1974). Zur Koordinations- und Allokationsproblematik bei Organisationen mit Matrix-Struktur. In J. Wild (Ed.), *Unternehmensfuehrung* (pp. 323–348). Berlin: Duncker & Humblot.

Ford, R. C., & Randolph, W. A. (1992). Cross-Functional structures: A review and integration of matrix organization and project management. *Journal of Management, 18*(2), 267–294.

Forsgren, M., Holm, U., & Johanson, J. (2005). *Managing the embedded multinational: A business network view*. Cheltenham, UK: Edward Elgar.

Galbraith, J. R. (2009). *Designing matrix organizations that actually work*. San Francisco, CA: Jossey-Bass.

Garvin, D.A. (2006). Executive decision making at General Motors. *Harvard Business School Case* 5-305-026 and 5-306-026.

Ghemawat, P., & Nueno, P. (2004). Revitalizing Philips (A). *Harvard Business School Case* 9-703-501.

Ghoshal, S., Korine, T., & Szulanski, B. (1994). Interunit communication in multinational corporations. *Management Science, 40*(1), 96–110.

Ghoshal, S., & Nohria, N. (1997). *The differentiated MNC: Organizing the multinational corporation for value creation*. San Francisco, CA: Jossey-Bass.

Goggin, W. C. (1974). How the multinational structure works at Dow Corning. *Harvard Business Review, 52*(1), 54–65.

Hedlund, G. (1986). The hypermodern MNC: A heterarchy. *Human Resource Management, 25*(1), 9–35.

Janger, A. R. (1983). *Matrix organization of complex businesses* (Conference Board Report No. 763). Amsterdam: Elsevier.

Joyce, W. F. (1986). Matrix organization: A social experiment. *Academy of Management Journal, 29*(3), 536–561.

Kuprenas, J. A. (2003). Implementation and performance of matrix organization structure. *International Journal of Project Management, 21*(1), 51–62.

Laslo, Z., & Goldberg, A. I. (2001). Matrix structures and performance: The search for optimal adjustment to organizational objectives. *IEEE Transactions on Engineering Management, 48*(2), 144–156.

Lawrence, P. R., & Lorsch, J. W. (1967). *Organization and environment.* Homewood, IL: Irwin.

Ojha, A. K. (2010). Bosch group in India: Transition to a transnational organization. *Indian Institute of Management Bangalore Case IMB, 301.*

Peters, T. J. (1979). Beyond the matrix organization. *Business Horizons, 22*(5), 15–27.

Piekkari, R., Nell, P. C., & Ghauri, P. N. (2010). Regional management as a system: A longitudinal case study. *Management International Review, 50*(4), 513–532.

Piskorski, M.J., & Spadini, A.L. (2007). Procter & Gamble: Organization 2005 (A) & (B). *Harvard Business School Cases* 9-707-519, 9-707-402, and 5-708-450.

Rahim, A., & Bonoma, T. V. (1979). Managing organizational conflict: A model for diagnosis and intervention. *Psychological Reports, 44*(3), 1323–1344.

Simons, R., & Bartlett, C. (1992). Asea Brown Boveri. *Harvard Business School Case* 9-192-139, 9-192-141, and 9-192-142.

Simons, T. L., & Peterson, R. S. (2000). Task conflict and relationship conflict in top management teams: The pivotal role of intragroup trust. *Journal of Applied Psychology, 83*(1), 102–111.

Stopford, J. M., & Wells Jr., L. T. (1972). *Managing the multinational enterprise.* New York: Basic Books.

Wagner, H. (1978). Mehrdimensionale Organisationsstrukturen. *Die Betriebswirtschaft, 38*(1), 103–115.

Wolf, J., & Egelhoff, W. G. (2013). An empirical evaluation of conflict in MNC matrix structure firms. *International Business Review, 22*(3), 591–601.

6

Decision-Making Within Matrix Structures

This chapter evaluates the way decision-making occurs within matrix structure MNCs. It reports on recent exploratory research conducted by the authors in 15 German MNCs with matrix structures. Details of the study are described in the below Footnote.[1] A key finding of the study was that the mode of decision-making within many of the firms appears to be changing from the joint or balanced mode of decision-making inherent in the classical balanced matrix structure (Davis and Lawrence 1977), toward what we describe as a "rule-based" mode of decision-making. Since this appears to be an important emerging or ongoing change in many of the firms, we want to better conceptualize and understand it.

---

[1] During 2011 and 2012, the authors conducted interviews in 15 German MNCs with matrix structures. The firms were selected in an opportunistic manner, using whatever connections we had to gain access to a high-level manager who would have a company-wide perspective of how the matrix structure functioned. Four of the interviewees were CEOs, two were other members of the board of management, three directly reported to the CEO or board level and were at the matrix manager level, four were the chief organizational planners for the firm (reporting directly to the CEO or a board member), and two were direct reports of the chief organizational planner. The interviews lasted from one to three hours and covered the strategy and organization design of the firm and how each had evolved over the past several years. In each case we tried to outline the formal matrix structure and understand how it functioned. There were several topics that we ensured were covered in each interview, but aside from these the interviewee largely steered the conversation. The firms were at different points in developing or changing their matrix structure, and had different levels of experience with it.

© The Author(s) 2017
W.G. Egelhoff, J. Wolf, *Understanding Matrix Structures and their Alternatives*, DOI 10.1057/978-1-137-57975-1_6

The next section of this chapter identifies and contrasts the two different modes of decision-making that can occur within a matrix structure. The classical balanced mode of decision-making involves joint decision-making by the two dimensions of a matrix. The new rule-based mode of decision-making, on the other hand, pre-assigns certain types of decisions to one dimension or the other for unitary decision-making. A following section reconceptualizes the design of matrix structures, which currently focuses primarily on the structural configuration of a matrix structure (i.e., what type of structural dimensions it contains). This section argues that along with structural configuration, the mode of decision-making within a matrix should be viewed as a new second dimension of matrix structure design. It uses the information-processing perspective of organization design (Galbraith 1973; Tushman and Nadler 1978; Egelhoff 1991) to develop and compare the information-processing capacity of a rule-based mode of decision-making against the information-processing capacity of a balanced mode of decision-making. Using the differences in their information-processing capacities, a subsequent section develops propositions specifying which types of situation can be better addressed by a rule-based mode of decision-making or a balanced mode of decision-making. A concluding section then describes how firms might attempt to utilize both modes of decision-making on a contingency basis to create a more flexible type of matrix structure—one which can simultaneously address a wider range of situations.

6.1 The Modes of Decision-Making in a Matrix Structure

As previously described, the earlier classical conceptualization of a matrix structure was a balanced matrix. That is, both dimensions of the matrix have relatively equal power and influence over most significant decisions. While the balance of power in a matrix often shifts from one dimension to the other, reflecting changes in strategies and environments, and the personalities of the relevant managers, the underlying assumption is that there is always a meaningful level of shared power and influence between the dimensions of a matrix. In contrast to this, many of the firms we interviewed were attempting to shift to more of a rule-based mode of

6 Decision-Making Within Matrix Structures

decision-making, where explicit or tacit rules pre-assign different types of decisions to a specific dimension of the matrix for unitary decision-making. We view this as a significant change from the earlier balanced mode of decision-making that was a key characteristic of the classical balanced matrix. The differences between the earlier classical balanced mode of decision-making and the new rule-based mode of decision-making described to us are summarized in Table 6.1.

Table 6.1 Characteristics of the Classical Balanced Mode and the New Rule-based Mode of Decision-Making

	Classical balanced mode	*New rule-based mode*
Influence of the two hierarchies on decisions	balanced	unbalanced
How decision-making operates	Reconciles divergent viewpoints of the two hierarchies through the exchange of information and, when necessary, escalation up the hierarchy	Rules and formally designed processes guide decision-making so there is less overlapping responsibility for specific decisions; escalation is available, but rarely required
Speed of decision-making	Slow	Fast
Nature of information processing	Rich, exhaustive, largely reciprocal information processing	Efficient, largely sequential information processing
Level of conflict	High, driven by shared responsibilities and different goals	Reduced, minimized by more narrowly-defined and non-overlapping responsibilities
Importance of shared values and culture	Very important. Without shared values and culture, reconciliation of divergent viewpoints is difficult and too many decisions have to be escalated too far up the hierarchy	Less important. Specified rules and processes make responsibilities clear and less overlapping, so shared values/culture is less important

The classical matrix was not always equally balanced in terms of the influence each dimension could exert over important decisions, but in theory it was supposed to be (Davis and Lawrence 1977). An earlier chairman of Dow Chemical, which at the time had a highly regarded and seemingly very successful matrix, once said a matrix structure is inherently unstable, always shifting power toward one dimension or the other. He said it was the job of top management to continually prop up the weaker dimension so it remained influential. Without such support the firm would lose the benefit of a matrix structure. We did not hear this kind of concern from the companies we visited. The matrix at present appears to be more stable and predictable, with the primary influence over a given decision frequently assigned to one dimension or the other in advance. Few decisions seem to be equally exposed to influence by both dimensions of a matrix, so in this sense, the current mode of decision-making is deliberately unbalanced. The functional dimension may have primary responsibility for a given set of decisions, while the geographical region dimension has primary responsibility for a different set of decisions. Some of the managers we interviewed referred to this design as a "rule-based matrix," and we adopted their terminology. Some firms have formally stated the rules, while in others they simply seem to be commonly understood. Virtually all firms indicated a desire to have such a rule-based mode of decision-making, as opposed to leaving the issue of influence over specific decisions undefined or equally shared by both dimensions of the matrix. In theory, such a mode of decision-making should lead to much more orderly and predictable behavior than was the case under the balanced mode of decision-making.

The new rule-based mode of decision-making also operates differently from the balanced mode of decision-making. The balanced mode seeks to reconcile the divergent viewpoints of the two hierarchies with overlapping responsibilities through the exchange of information, and when necessary escalation of the issue up the hierarchy. The first stage of the reconciliation process, however, is for the parties to exchange information and arguments in an *ad hoc*, non-hierarchical manner. This is shown in Fig. 2.1 with dashed lines between the two hierarchies. They seek a solution that best addresses the joint concerns of both hierarchies, and such a solution will frequently differ from what either hierarchy by itself would decide. In this sense, the joint solution is innovative, and not something either hierarchy acting alone could have produced. Ideally, it reflects the concerns and knowledge possessed by both dimensions of the matrix and is therefore a richer outcome, more likely to promote the overall interests of the firm, than the more limited outcome of a single hierarchy. Its cost is the additional length of time and number of man-hours required to reach reconciliation plus the risk that such non-hierarchical reconciliation may not emerge.

In contrast, the rule-based mode of decision-making relies on formal or informal rules and standard processes to guide most decisions to one hierarchy or the other for processing. As a result, there is significantly less overlapping responsibility for decision-making. Our interviews indicate that firms are increasingly formalizing these rules (putting them in writing). However, whether formal or informal, the important point is how consistently these rules are understood and followed within a firm. All firms stressed the need for an escalation process when decision-making lingers, although it appears this is seldom required by firms with rule-based decision-making.

The two modes of decision-making differ in the speed with which they can reach a decision, and also in the nature of their underlying information processing. A balanced mode of decision-making with overlapping responsibilities leads to reciprocal information processing between the two dimensions, as they seek to reconcile their differences and converge around a decision. This can be a lengthy, exhaustive process, involving numerous meetings and exchanges of information. Many concerns and inputs are typically considered before a decision is reached. The rule-based mode of decision-making seeks to make this process much faster and more efficient. While both dimensions of the matrix can still input information into the decision process, one dimension has been given primary responsibility for making the decision. This leads to less back-and-forth discussion, and a more sequential decision-making process. A decision is made more quickly, and fewer man-hours of managerial time are required to make it.

Another result of the more narrowly defined and non-overlapping responsibilities of the rule-based mode of decision-making is significantly reduced conflict between the two dimensions. While each dimension still has different goals, the priority of the goals for a given type of decision has already been prescribed by the rules. While the decision process should still attempt to accommodate the concerns and inputs of both dimensions, the designation of primary responsibility ensures a timely ending of the process with less opportunity for conflict. The balanced mode of decision-making, in contrast, combines shared responsibilities and different goals for the two dimensions. This involves a much greater potential for conflict, since neither dimension has priority over the other, and both feel responsible for the decision.

Shared values and a shared culture have generally been recommended for firms employing the balanced mode of decision-making (Davis and Lawrence 1977). The idea is that a sharing of more basic values will keep conflicts from becoming destructive and personal. The values and culture should appropriately guide individual behavior during times of stress and disagreement. Shared values and culture are less important under a rule-based mode of decision-making, where specified rules and processes make responsibilities clearer and less overlapping. While firms in general prefer a strong corporate culture, the firms we interviewed did not stress the criticality of culture to the functioning of matrix structures. Instead, they stressed the criticality of rules and specified processes.

Having defined the key characteristics of the new rule-based mode of decision-making relative to the characteristics of the balanced mode of decision-making, it is important to note how directly they address the problems and complaints involving matrix structures outlined back in Table 2.1. The characteristics of rule-based decision-making clarify responsibilities and improve accountability within a matrix. They reduce the causes of conflict and power struggles, and speed up decision-making. While not directly reducing overhead or personnel costs, the rule-based mode makes decision-making more efficient, freeing up time for other tasks. Indirectly, employee stress and anxiety are probably reduced by the reduction of uncertainty. Thus, it would appear that as MNCs are increasingly forced to use some form of matrix structure, they are actively seeking to minimize the problems listed in Table 2.1 that have been traditionally associated with matrix structures. The final problem in Table 2.1, suggested by the Peters and Waterman (1982) book, is interesting. It asserts that matrix structures can degenerate into anarchy and then become bureaucratic and non-creative. While none of the managers we interviewed spoke about "anarchy," their preferences for more defined rules and processes are undoubtedly making today's matrix structure a more bureaucratic structure (Weber 1947), as they seek to address the problems of earlier matrix structures.

The rule-based mode of decision-making described above is clearly the intended mode for most of the firms we interviewed. However, it is important to recognize that our exploratory study was not able to measure the extent to which a firm actually used rule-based decision-making as opposed to balanced decision-making. A different research methodology would be required to study this issue. In this chapter we are primarily concerned with defining the two different modes of decision-making and establishing that they can exist in firms with matrix structures. In reality, most firms with a matrix structure probably use both modes of decision-making, even if their intention is to primarily use one or the other. Rules usually won't cover every type of decision, and when such is the case the two dimensions of a matrix are likely to employ a balanced mode of decision-making. And even when a balanced mode of decision-making formally exists, some decisions will so obviously fit the knowledge possessed by one dimension of the matrix as opposed to the other, that the decision-making process will likely resemble that of a rule-based mode of decision-making. So, it is largely a matter of the extent to which the balanced or the rule-based mode of decision-making is used in a firm, and the types of decisions which are exposed to each mode of decision-making.

The reader needs to understand that at this point we are attempting to conceptualize two mutually exclusive ideal types of decision-making that can exist within a matrix structure—the balanced mode of decision-making and the rule-based mode of decision-making. Once the two ideal types are properly defined and their implications understood, the more complex reality of decision-making within a real matrix structure can be modeled and more easily understood as some combination of these two mutually exclusive and clearly defined modes of decision-making. By definition, ideal types tend to be more rigid and mutually exclusive than the fuzzy reality they seek to represent. This is necessary to simplify the task of developing theory. After the theory is developed and explained, we will discuss how one can relax the rigidity of the ideal types and still benefit from the knowledge inherent in the theory.

6.2 Further Conceptualizing the Design of Matrix Structures

In this section we want to reconceptualize the design of matrix structures, so that it better accommodates both the classical balanced mode of decision-making and the new rule-based mode of decision-making. An information-processing perspective will be used to better understand and further conceptualize the role of mode of decision-making within matrix structure theory. In order for matrix structure theory to better accommodate both the existing concept of a balanced mode of decision-making and the new concept of a rule-based mode of decision-making (as both are defined in Table 6.1), it is necessary to reconceptualize the design of a matrix structure to include the following two dimensions: (1) the structural configuration of a matrix structure, and (2) the mode of decision-making used within a matrix structure. The structural configuration of an organization specifies its principal subunits as well as the formal hierarchies of command and control that hierarchically order and link the subunits. In a matrix structure firm there must be at least two different command and control hierarchies operating at the level just below the firm's CEO (see Fig. 2.1). As already discussed, the mode of decision-making within a matrix structure can assume either of two values: a balanced or joint mode of decision-making and a rule-based or unitary mode of decision-making.

The structural configuration of subunits and hierarchies within an organization structure has long been the primary dimension of both elementary and matrix structure design. When one refers to a specific type of structure, one typically refers to its structural configuration (e.g., a product division structure, a product division × geographical region matrix structure). As discussed in Chap. 3, the information-processing capacity inherent in a structure varies with its structural configuration. The recent empirical research described in Chap. 4 has supported this theory for matrix structures by successfully fitting three different structural configurations of matrix structure to four different characteristics of a firm's strategy. Thus, current strategy–structure theory for matrix structures ends with varying the structural configuration of a matrix structure, just as it does for elementary structures. But, since matrix structures always possess at least two different hierarchies for information-processing and decision-making, they potentially have an additional degree of freedom that elementary structures lack when it comes to designing hierarchical coordination and information-processing at the firm level. They can send a decision to either of the two hierarchical dimensions of the matrix (rule-based decision-making), or they can simultaneously send it to both dimensions (balanced decision-making). It would appear that some firms are increasingly utilizing this additional degree of freedom—changing the mode of decision-making—to significantly change the information-processing capacity that a matrix structure provides to address a specific type of situation or set of decisions. If this is the case, it is time to consider mode of decision-making an important second dimension—along with structural configuration—of matrix structure design and theory.

While mode of decision-making is a potentially important dimension of design for matrix structures, it is either absent or conceptually underdeveloped in the existing literature. In most of the literature on matrix structures, the stated or implied assumption is that important decisions tend to be jointly made by both dimensions of a matrix. This is the balanced matrix assumption. When it is in effect, mode of decision-making essentially disappears as a dimension of matrix structure design, and the balanced mode of decision-making becomes more a permanent attribute of all matrix structures. This is the way matrix structures are represented in most of the existing matrix literature.

Interestingly, there are a few exceptions to the balanced matrix assumption in the literature. The earliest is "Corning Glass Works International," a Harvard Business School case written by Bartlett and Yoshino (1981). In the case, Corning establishes an international division and considers matrixing it with the product divisions in the company. The consulting firm McKinsey was retained to advise on the organization structure, and they recommended using a "decision grid" to clarify the roles that specific executives would play in making specific decisions that involved the interests of both the international division and the product division.

More recently, Galbraith (2009: 82) recommends a similar mechanism, which he calls "responsibility charts," to specify the decision-making authorities of managers from different subunits in a matrix structure.

Both of the above are applied examples of what we now refer to as a rule-based mode of decision-making in a matrix structure. They are the two instances of this phenomenon that we have encountered in the literature. Both reside at the applied end of the literature, where they have not been further conceptualized as part of a more general theory of matrix structure design. From an applied perspective, the advantages of such decision grids and responsibility charts are obvious. They reduce uncertainty, support quicker decision-making, and reduce conflict. What is largely missing from such specific recommendations by consultants is a deeper, more comprehensive understanding of what capabilities might be lost when there is a switch from a balanced mode of decision-making to more of a rule-based mode of decision-making. Addressing this subject requires more abstract conceptualization and theory building. It is interesting that the more conceptual or theory-building literature on matrix structures has not previously engaged this issue. It consistently holds to the balanced matrix assumption, which ignores mode of decision-making as a potential dimension of matrix design. We believe this has a lot to do with the age of most of this literature and the lack of recent research on matrix structures. The result is that there has been no apparent attempt to conceptualize or develop any theory that could help academics and practitioners to better understand the importance of the mode of decision-making used within a matrix structure. We regard this as an important gap in the current understanding of matrix structures that the present chapter can only begin to address.

At this point it is useful to clarify how decision-making varies between elementary structures and the two modes of decision-making that can occur within matrix structures. The salient points of this comparison are outlined in Table 6.2. An elementary structure provides unitary decision-making across all decisions. This means that the same subunits and individuals handle a wide variety of decisions. There is relatively low specialization. In a matrix structure there is shared decision-making between the two hierarchical dimensions, with two ways of sharing the decision-making. The first way is the rule-based mode of decision-making, where each dimension of the matrix provides unitary decision-making within a

6 Decision-Making Within Matrix Structures

Table 6.2 An Information-processing Perspective of Decision-Making within Elementary and Matrix Structures

	Elementary structure firms	Matrix structure firms
Structure	Elementary structure (e.g., a product division structure)	Matrix structure (e.g., a product division x geographical region matrix structure)
Mode of decision-making	Unitary decision-making across all decisions	Shared decision-making (two different ways of sharing decision-making):
		1. Rule-based mode of decision-making: 2. Balanced mode of decision-making:
		Each dimension of the matrix provides unitary decision-making within a pre-defined content area / Both dimensions of the matrix engage in joint decision-making for all important decisions
What decision-making looks like at the level of an individual decision	One-dimensional decision-making (where the dimension is constant across all decisions)	One-dimensional decision-making (where the dimensions change to better address the content of a decision) / Two-dimensional decision-making for all important decisions

pre-defined content area (e.g., the product division dimension will make all pricing decisions, and the geographical region dimension will make all tax and government-related decisions). Thus, decision-making here is similar to that in an elementary structure, but for a reduced or smaller set of decisions. There is more specialization (a stronger fit between the knowledge of the decision-maker and the decision), since a decision can now go to one of two different hierarchies. And there may even be quicker decision-making than in an elementary structure, if the decision-maker is more specialized and has fewer types of decisions to make. Thus, in terms of information-processing capacity, the rule-based mode of decision-making in a matrix structure provides some potential advantages over the unitary decision-making process in an elementary structure.

Under the balanced mode of decision-making, both dimensions of the matrix engage in joint decision-making for all important decisions. This provides two-dimensional decision-making, which is much richer than the unitary decision-making found in the two preceding designs. This difference will become much more elaborated as the next section focuses on contrasting and better understanding the information-processing capacities of the two modes of decision-making used within a matrix structure.

6.3 Defining the Information-Processing Capacities of the Two Modes of Decision-Making

In Chap. 3 we described how the information-processing capacities of the various types of structure or structural configuration (e.g., a product division structure) were defined, so that subsequently they could be used to fit structure to strategy and environment. In an analogous manner, we now want to develop a new conceptual framework that defines the information-processing capacities of the two modes of decision-making, so that subsequently they can be used to fit mode of decision-making to strategy and environment. These are the values of the new second dimension of matrix design called mode of decision-making within a matrix, just as the different types of structure that have previously been modeled are the values of the structural configuration dimension. Table 6.1

already summarizes the key characteristics of the two modes of decision-making which can exist in a matrix structure. From these characteristics we identified five dimensions or types of information-processing capacity that vary significantly between the two modes of decision-making. These five types of information-processing capacity are as follows:

1. Accountability during decision-making,
2. Speed of decision-making (in terms of elapsed time),
3. Economizing on human and monetary costs during decision-making,
4. Novelty and innovativeness of alternatives generated during decision-making, and
5. Thoroughness with which alternatives are evaluated during decision-making.

Table 6.3 shows the extent to which the balanced and the rule-based modes of decision-making can provide each type of information-processing capacity. Next, we want to discuss each type of information-processing capacity in more detail.

Table 6.3 Information-processing Capacities of the Two Modes of Decision-Making

Types of information-processing capacity	Balanced mode of decision-making	Rule-based mode of decision-making
Accountability during decision-making	low	high
Speed of decision-making (in terms of elapsed time)	low	high
Economizing on human and monetary costs during decision-making	low	high
Novelty and innovativeness of alternatives generated	high	low
Thoroughness with which alternatives are evaluated	high	low

Level of information-processing capacities provided by:

6.3.1 Accountability During Decision-Making

This refers to the extent to which an individual can be held accountable for his or her decisions when the individual is engaged in organizational decision-making. Since the rule-based mode of decision-making assigns responsibility for a decision to a single hierarchy, and there is clear accountability within a hierarchy, this mode of decision-making provides high accountability. Alternatively, the balanced mode of decision-making jointly assigns responsibility for a decision to both dimensions of a matrix. This frustrates assigning accountability to individuals.

6.3.2 Speed of Decision-Making

While the relationship between speed of decision-making and a rule-based mode of decision-making may appear obvious, it is useful to understand what is going on at a deeper level. Under a rule-based mode of decision-making, information is processed within a single hierarchy, where there is typically high familiarity among the actors and a high degree of goal congruence. As a result, only a limited amount of information has to be exchanged before a decision is produced. Under a balanced mode of decision-making, information is typically processed first within each of the two hierarchies of the matrix. The time required to do this should be similar to the above example, if both dimensions are simultaneously working on the problem. But now additional information-processing is required between the two hierarchies before a decision can be made. This information processing will be network information processing, not hierarchical information processing. Consequently, there will be less familiarity among the actors and less goal congruence. To reach a common decision, more information will probably have to be exchanged here than was previously exchanged within each of the two hierarchies. If the goals of the two hierarchies are difficult to reconcile within the common decision, several cycles of what has already been described may be required before a common decision is produced. Thus, it is the information processing that occurs between the hierarchies that typically adds so much additional (and often unpredictable) time to the total elapsed time required by the balanced mode of decision-making.

6.3.3 Economizing on Human and Monetary Costs During Decision-Making

This refers to a decision mode's capacity to avoid conflict and minimize the man-hours required to make a decision. Both of these can be significant costs in a matrix structure. The capacity to avoid conflict varies significantly between the two modes of decision-making. Since the rule-based mode of decision-making processes information within a hierarchy where there tends to be high familiarity and high goal congruence, conflict is minimized and differences are more easily reconciled. The balanced mode of decision-making, in contrast, involves information processing between hierarchies where there is less familiarity and less goal congruence. Here, conflict is much more likely and much more difficult to reconcile. There are both psychological and monetary costs associated with managing conflict in an organization.

The costs related to the man-hours of managerial time required to reach a decision are once again significantly lower under a rule-based mode of decision-making than under a balanced mode of decision-making. With the rule-based mode there is little or no need to process information between the two hierarchies to reconcile differences. In addition, there is no need for both dimensions to independently do the information processing required to make a responsible decision. Only one of the dimensions needs to do this. The monetary costs associated with committing more man-hours of managerial time to decision-making are difficult to estimate. When there is insufficient managerial slack in an organization, they can become extremely high, since they are the opportunity cost of managerial time at that moment.

6.3.4 Novelty and Innovativeness of Alternatives Generated During Decision-Making

The novelty and innovativeness of the alternatives generated during information processing depend a lot on the different kinds of knowledge and capabilities that can be brought together and recombined in a new way (Kogut and Zander 1992). The rule-based mode of decision-making brings together the knowledge and capabilities that reside within a single hierarchy that possesses a congruent set of goals. This lack of differentiated inputs constrains the novelty and innovativeness of the alternatives that such information processing is likely to generate. Alternatively, the balanced mode of decision-making combines the knowledge inputs of two hierarchies that are typically much more differentiated from each other in terms of knowledge, capabilities, and goals. These inputs will largely be specified by the configuration dimension of a matrix structure's design. The knowledge, capabilities, and goals that reside within a product division hierarchy, a geographical region hierarchy, and a functional division hierarchy are usually quite different from each other, even within the same company. This difference provides the potential for generating more novel and innovative alternatives when it is constructively brought together in joint decision-making.

6.3.5 Thoroughness with Which Alternatives Are Evaluated During Decision-Making

The logic supporting this kind of information-processing capacity is similar to the logic supporting the previous information-processing capacity, even though the two capacities are conceptually different. The previous type of information-processing capacity concerned the ability of an organization to internally develop innovative alternatives for addressing a problem or situation. But many times alternatives are generated by the external environment, and then the information-processing task facing the organization becomes one of recognizing, evaluating, and selecting from among the available alternatives. As in the previous discussion, the limited differentiation inherent in a single hierarchical dimension limits the thoroughness that the rule-based mode of decision-making can bring to such an evaluation. The balanced mode of decision-making, in contrast, brings multiple perspectives and a much more differentiated set of knowledge, capabilities, and goals to the evaluation process. The latter is more likely to represent the broader or total interests of a firm.

The above are the information-processing capacities inherent in the two different modes of decision-making that can be used in a matrix structure. These capacities largely describe key characteristics of the decision-making process (its accountability, speed, cost, richness, thoroughness).

The structural configuration dimension, on the other hand, largely describes the kinds of knowledge that can enter the decision-making process. Together, they provide a more complete picture of the information-processing capacity associated with a specific matrix structure.

6.4 Identifying the Situations Best Addressed by the Two Different Modes of Decision-Making

Since the information-processing capacities of the two modes of decision-making are so different, one would expect each mode to fit different types of situations. While some of the situations arose during our interviews with managers, all of them can be logically deduced from the information-processing capabilities of the two modes of decision-making.

6.4.1 Situations that Fit a Rule-Based Mode of Decision-Making

Situations where accountability and compliance are important tend to require a single chain of command and responsibility. There are reported cases of firms with matrix structures having trouble with the illegal payment of bribes in foreign markets. When such payments came to light, it was unclear who had authorized them, since responsibility was shared by the two dimensions of the matrix (often a geographical region dimension and a product dimension). To address such situations, government regulators and corporate compliance officers are increasingly requiring a unitary chain of command over certain critical decisions and activities. Since the balanced mode of decision-making involves shared responsibility and shared decision-making between the two hierarchies of the matrix, it fails to fit this requirement. The rule-based mode of decision-making, in contrast, can meet these requirements by specifying which hierarchy is responsible for making a potentially sensitive set of decisions where clear accountability is required. For example, a global engineering hierarchy (a functional division hierarchy) may be responsible for reviewing and approving the safety of all new manufacturing facilities and processes within a firm, to ensure that the firm's global safety standards are not compromised by varying local standards and practices. At the same time, a regional hierarchy of country managers and their subordinates and superiors (a geographical region hierarchy) may be responsible for effectively and appropriately dealing with local, national, and regional government officials. They will be responsible for reconciling the global ethical standards of the firm with the need for local cultural sensitivity. In this example, a functional division × geographical region matrix structure is using rules to assign two different responsibilities and sets of decisions to two different hierarchies within the matrix. This focuses the right kind of information-processing capacity on each situation and provides for clear accountability. A balanced mode of decision-making would not provide this focus or this accountability.

Proposition 6.1 Situations requiring strict accountability and compliance with legal and social norms will be best addressed with a rule-based mode of decision-making within a matrix structure.

The most frequent reason provided to us by managers for employing the rule-based mode of decision-making was the need to speed up decision-making in an MNC. The conceptual logic for this fit is straightforward. As already developed in the previous section, the elapsed time required to reach a decision is minimized with the rule-based mode of decision-making because information processing occurs within a single hierarchy where there is relatively high familiarity and high goal congruence. Alternatively, the balanced mode of decision-making requires additional information processing between the two hierarchical dimensions of a matrix to reconcile differences and reach a common decision. Since there is low familiarity and low goal congruence between the two dimensions, this kind of information processing can require a substantial amount of time.

Proposition 6.2 Situations requiring quick decision-making will be best addressed by a rule-based mode of decision-making within a matrix structure.

6 Decision-Making Within Matrix Structures 149

The two situations just discussed arose during our interviews with high-level managers in MNCs with matrix structures. The remaining two situations that seem to fit a rule-based matrix come from our own deductive reasoning, and not from the comments of managers. The third situation that fits the rule-based mode of decision-making is where efficiency and low cost are required because of the high volume and low criticality of such decisions. When decisions that occur with some frequency are shared between the dimensions of a matrix, they will slow down and impair the efficiency of decision-making much more than when decisions are infrequent. It is especially important to identify such decisions and attempt to address them with rule-based decision-making as opposed to balanced decision-making. The former economizes on human and monetary costs to a much greater extent than the latter. In hindsight, it would appear that the failure to do this was a common problem back in the 1970s, when many US MNCs abandoned their matrix structures. For example, Texas Instruments reported having too many decisions moving between the dimensions of its matrix. This led to delays in product launches and ultimately to the resignation of its CEO. When the CEO resigned, he blamed the matrix, which at the time was operating with a balanced mode of decision-making. Since rule-based decision-making can process decisions with more efficiency than balanced decision-making, it can allow a firm to retain a matrix structure even as the volume of decision-making increases.

Proposition 6.3a Situations where efficiency and low cost are required because of the high volume and low criticality of such decisions will be best addressed by a rule-based mode of decision-making within a matrix structure.

The fourth situation that best fits the information-processing capacity of rule-based decision-making is when there is a low probability that combining the perspectives of the two dimensions will produce new insight. Under these conditions, economizing on the human and monetary costs is required, since the anticipated benefit to be derived from joint decision-making is extremely low. The classical balanced matrix perspective was that all potentially significant decisions in a firm should be considered from the two macro perspectives that are inherent in a matrix structure (e.g., a product perspective and a geographic perspective). The underlying assumption was that often enough this dual-perspective information processing would yield some new insight that would justify the added cost. Early proponents of matrix structures used to delight in providing surprising examples of such insights—insights that were invisible to decision-makers who had previously approached the situation from just one perspective. Since it was not possible to anticipate when such insight would occur, the general feeling was that it was necessary to expose most significant decisions to both dimensions of the matrix—the two different sets of goals and the two different types of knowledge that these dimensions represented. This perspective may appear unrealistic and overly idealistic today, but it was held by many managers in the 1970s. To illustrate this point, we want to briefly describe an incident from our own research during this period.

In 1977 one of the authors of this book was conducting research on strategy and organizational design in a number of the largest US and European MNCs. Part of the research in each company was a one-hour structured interview with a high ranking corporate manager. The incident I will relate took place in a large European-headquartered chemical company, where the interviewee was a member of the board of management. At some point during the interview he informed me that after we were through with the structured interview instrument, there was an issue he wanted to discuss with me. When the interview was nearly over, another gentleman appeared to fetch the interviewee for their next meeting. He was introduced to me as the CEO of the company. The interviewee told the CEO that he still needed to discuss something with me and that he would join the CEO in the meeting after he did this. I remember being somewhat surprised at what was happening. A short time after the interview I read in a newspaper that my interviewee had just become the new CEO of the company. The subject he was so intent on discussing with me was this. He believed that he had discovered a major flaw with the company's matrix structure. Like most board members, he was responsible for overseeing several of the firm's businesses (e.g., coatings) and several of its geographies (e.g., South America). As head of coatings and of South America, his problem was how should he be dealing with decisions regarding the coatings business in Brazil. I distinctly remember him asking me: "Am I supposed to be arguing with myself?"

I don't remember the specifics of our subsequent discussion, but I remember it going on for some time and my feeling increasingly uneasy over his absence from the other meeting. He obviously felt that what he was attempting to discuss with me was more important than what was going on in the other meeting. The take-away from this incident is that many managers in the 1970s, like the interviewee, felt that a matrix structure should provide for the constructive confrontation of two different macro-level perspectives (in this case a product perspective and a geographic perspective). This confrontation and its outcome or reconciliation were widely regarded as the great contribution of matrix structures to decision-making and the management of the firm. It was supposed to produce innovation and originality that would otherwise be lacking with more uni-dimensional decision-making.

The above view of a matrix structure, which was prevalent in the 1970s, is quite different from the present view of a matrix structure. The latter generally emphasizes a rule-based mode of decision-making, which seeks to economize on the human and monetary costs associated with decision-making. It is useful to consider why this change of view might have occurred. The strategies and competitive environments of most MNCs in the 1970s were undoubtedly simpler and less dynamic than they are today. Since complexity and change increase information-processing requirements, most firms today will have to make more decisions and process more information than they did in the 1970s. But the information-processing capacities of a balanced matrix structure and the managers within it probably haven't increased as much as the information-processing requirements have increased, and this is especially true if one is talking about strategic decisions. In order to keep information-processing requirements in line with information-processing capacities, most MNCs today will have to keep reducing the percentage of decisions made with balanced decision-making. One would expect them to do this by moving decisions least likely to benefit from joint decision-making to rule-based decision-making.

Proposition 6.3b Situations where there is a relatively low probability that combining the perspectives of the two dimensions of a matrix will produce new insight will be best addressed by a rule-based mode of decision-making within a matrix structure.

6.4.2 Situations that Fit a Balanced Mode of Decision-Making

The balanced mode of decision-making especially fits situations where the goals of both dimensions of a matrix are meaningfully involved and need to be reconciled. A decision to support a standardized technology platform may fit the long-run goals of a global engineering division, but it could frustrate the sales and market share goals of national subsidiaries and geographical regions. Such decisions are especially common under transnational strategies, which generally attempt to realize conflicting goals. To resolve such problems a firm requires decision-making that is capable of either (1) generating novel or innovative alternatives, or (2) thoroughly evaluating and selecting from a range of available alternatives the one that optimizes a company's goals. Which situation exists will depend on whether alternatives need to be developed or whether they are already clearly defined. In any case, the balanced mode of decision-making possesses both kinds of information-processing capacity. This kind of global versus local debate and trade-off occurs in many firms, and it typically requires reciprocal (back-and-forth) information processing between a global functional or product dimension arguing for global goals and a geographical region dimension arguing for local goals. The balanced mode of decision-making facilitates this debate occurring at multiple levels of the organization. Looking at Fig. 2.1, this debate between the two dimensions can occur at all of the levels lying between the two-boss manager and the CEO. In many MNCs this could involve three or four levels of management. As both dimensions of managers exchange information and seek to reach agreement, the global engineering division managers will become much more familiar with the differences between local markets and environments. Similarly, the geographical region managers will become more familiar with the economic benefits that might accrue from the further standardization of products and processes. If such sharing of information and decision-making can be accomplished in a constructive manner, the result should be a more creative and optimal decision from the perspective of the firm.

If this same problem were addressed with a rule-based matrix structure, the information processing that would occur and the resultant decision are likely to be different. If the global functional or product dimension has priority when it comes to selecting technology platforms, there will probably be less attempt to accommodate local differences and a more globally standardized technology platform than in the preceding case. Similarly, giving priority to the geographical region dimension would likely lead to more accommodation of local differences and less global standardization. This kind of unitary information processing and decision-making is more likely to maximize the goals of one dimension at the expense of the other. It is less likely to optimize the combined goals of both dimensions. Thus, when the overall goals of a firm require that high attention be given to the goals of both dimensions, the balanced mode of decision-making should lead to a superior firm-level decision.

Proposition 6.4 Situations where the goals of both dimensions are clearly involved and need to be reconciled within the decision will be best addressed by a balanced mode of decision-making within a matrix structure.

The second situation that fits a balanced mode of decision-making is when uncertainty is especially high, and it is not clear which dimension possesses the most relevant knowledge or information-processing capability to address the situation. As an example, imagine the case where some global political or financial shock has led to a sudden and precipitous decline in the demand for a firm's products. Normally, the firm has a global supply plan administered by global product divisions. National subsidiaries and geographical regions do their implementation planning within the parameters of the global supply plan. In reaction to the shock, the global product divisions may attempt to shut down or idle the most expensive sources of supply, in order to contain the buildup of inventories. While this may be an optimal decision based on information available within the product division dimension, it may not be optimal if additional information from the geographical region dimension could be made available. Some subsidiary managements may be aware of additional sources of demand that were previously ignored because the margins were too low (government contracts, private label contracts). Others may know of opportunities to do subcontract work for sectors less affected by the external shock. These may be more optimal solutions than shutting down production capacity. In such an unprecedented or uncertain situation, it is not clear where the information required to produce the optimal solution might lie. While this situation may require rapid decision-making, it is also clear that a balanced mode of decision-making will bring together a wider range of information and potentially a more optimal solution or response.

Proposition 6.5 Situations where uncertainty is especially high and it is not clear which dimension possesses the most relevant knowledge or information-processing capability to address the situation will be best addressed by a balanced mode of decision-making within a matrix.

The third situation that fits a balanced mode of decision-making is when a firm is seeking a radically new response to a problem, which will benefit from bringing together a wider array of knowledge inputs and perspectives. As an example, imagine a global automobile company with a functional division × geographical region matrix structure. Product development tends to be done on a global basis by a global engineering division. Information about customer demands and preferences largely enters the design process through information exchanges between the global marketing hierarchy and the global engineering hierarchy. Information about customers largely enters the marketing hierarchy at the bottom, from local market research and direct inputs from the national sales organizations. Now assume the company wants to more radically differentiate its cars from the cars of its competitors, so customers will see more difference between the models and features of the cars. One way to attempt this would be to have the geographical region hierarchy interact directly with the engineering hierarchy and perhaps even share some of the decision-making at critical points during the design process. The geographical region hierarchy is directly responsible for selling and providing after-sales service for the cars. It possesses information and a perspective that are not presently entering the design process.

In our example the national sales forces occupy the two-boss manager position and send information up both the geographical region hierarchy and the global marketing division hierarchy. These two hierarchies or dimensions process the same basic information quite differently, since they have different goals and concerns. The geographical region dimension is very interested in the current sales and market shares of specific products in national and regional markets and the current servicing and quality problems they are encountering. These issues will tend to vary between geographies. The global marketing division is less concerned with local sales and servicing problems and more concerned with the strategic positioning of the models and car lines relative to those of competitors. As a result, the way information is filtered and combined as it moves along the geographical region dimension differs substantially from the way this occurs along the global marketing dimension. The resultant perspectives and concerns of the two dimensions should be significantly different. Since the design process has primarily been exposed to the influence of the global marketing dimension, further exposing it to direct inputs from the geographical region dimension could potentially lead to new insights about the customer–product relationship. The global marketing dimension will necessarily aggregate and generalize its understanding of customer requirements and preferences across geographies as information moves up the hierarchy. This is needed by any global design process. The geographical region dimension, in contrast, will leave customer information and understanding disaggregated and differentiated by geography. This kind of information may reveal that the way a car line is divided into models fits certain geographies better than it fits other geographies. Or that certain subsystems or features of a car could benefit from more regional adaptation.

Proposition 6.6 Situations where the firm is seeking a radically new response to a problem, which will benefit from bringing together a wider array of inputs, will be best addressed by a balanced mode of decision-making within a matrix.

The above is only a hypothetical example. But it serves to illustrate how the two dimensions of a matrix represent different perspectives and kinds of knowledge and how a balanced mode of decision-making can facilitate combining the two different sets of inputs to produce a greater variety of new and potentially useful strategic options for a firm to consider. It may appear that using a balanced mode of decision-making to address (1) situations characterized by high uncertainty and (2) situations where the firm is seeking a radically new response to a problem are not altogether different situations. What they have in common is "uncertainty," but the cause of the uncertainty in the two situations is quite different. In the first situation, where there is high uncertainty, this uncertainty is caused by the external environment, and the firm uses the balanced mode of decision-making to better deal with it. In the second situation, where the firm seeks a radically new response to a familiar problem, the firm itself deliberately causes the increase in uncertainty. It does this by using a balanced mode of decision-making instead of rule-based decision-making along a single dimension of the matrix to address the problem at hand. This increases uncertainty about the outcome of such information processing and widens the range of potential responses to the problem, thereby increasing the chance that a new viable solution might emerge.

Our theory does not provide a final or definitive answer for when to use rule-based decision-making and when to use balanced decision-making within a matrix structure. Many real situations will be characterized by two or more of the situations specified in the theory. For example, a situation (new product design) may require information processing that (1) develops innovative alternatives (so products are differentiated), and (2) economizes on the human and monetary costs that go into such information processing (because the firm already has too many other high-priority situations that require balanced decision-making). The theory can't directly address the contradiction inherent in this situation, but it isolates and clarifies the trade-off in a way that helps one to focus on solutions that might best accommodate and reconcile the contradiction. In this case, one might use rule-based decision-making to economize on the cost accompanied by advice from the second dimension of the matrix. This would broaden the information inputs while avoiding the costs associated with reconciling conflict and divergent goals.

6.5 Designing a More Flexible Matrix Structure

Given the very different information-processing capacities of the two modes of decision-making, it would appear that matrix firms should attempt to employ both, using the contingency logic inherent in the above propositions. They should use rule-based decision-making to address certain situations and balanced decision-making to address other situations. This integration should result in a higher quality of decision-making than would occur with the exclusive use of either mode—there will be a better fit between the information-processing capacities of the mode of decision-making employed and the information-processing requirements of the situation addressed.

To the extent that a firm can employ both modes of decision-making on a contingency basis, it can create a more flexible form of matrix structure—one that can potentially fit a greater variety of information-processing requirements than any other type of hierarchical structure. Such a structure can provide quick decision-making with high accountability and low cost to address certain situations, while at the same time providing decision-making that develops novel and innovative alternatives as it addresses other situations. This new, more optimized form of matrix structure differs from the classical balanced matrix structure described in the literature, and it probably differs from the more rule-based kind of matrix structure that seems to be emerging in many matrix firms today. Our sense is that the current move toward more rule-based decision-making is largely being driven by the immediate need for quicker decision-making, often with little regard for the capacities that are lost when a firm moves away from more balanced decision-making.

This chapter has sought to develop the more comprehensive theory that is required to more optimally fit both rule-based and balanced decision-making to their most appropriate situations. Without such a theory we doubt that firms can tap the flexibility described above. It is important to observe that the information-processing capacities provided by rule-based decision-making (accountability, speed, lower costs) tend to be immediately apparent and are easy to evaluate and appreciate.

On the other hand, the information-processing capacities provided by balanced decision-making (more innovative and thoroughly evaluated alternatives) take longer to become apparent and are more difficult to evaluate and appreciate. Thus, without a theory to facilitate an unbiased evaluation, there is likely to be a natural bias favoring the selection of rule-based over balanced decision-making in firms with matrix structures.

The insight, that the difference between a rule-based matrix and a balanced matrix structure depends on a difference in the mode of decision-making, is an important observation. Because the mode of decision-making in a matrix structure is more changeable than its structural configuration, it provides additional potential for flexibility. An organization's structural configuration consists of certain types of sub-units, staffed with certain types of people, and one or more hierarchies that link them together. These are relatively permanent characteristics of an organization's design that cannot be easily or frequently changed. Since the mode of decision-making can be incrementally changed more frequently without disturbing the configuration of a matrix structure, it provides a way to more frequently and flexibly alter the information-processing capacities of a matrix structure so that they can better adjust to changes in the firm's strategy and environment.

The following analogy might be helpful. The structural configuration of a matrix structure can be seen as analogous to the hardware of an information-processing system, while the mode of decision-making used within a matrix structure is analogous to the software that guides information flows within the hardware. There usually are many more ways to change and modify the software that operates inside an information-processing system than there are ways to change its hardware. Consistent with this analogy, the mode of decision-making within a matrix structure can potentially assume more values than the two ideal types assigned to it in this chapter. For example, top management in a matrix firm could say something like the following: "Previously the product design decisions for this business have been assigned to the product division management. But given the recent technology breakthroughs that have occurred and the resultant market turmoil, we now want the product design decisions to be made by balanced decision-making, involving both the product division and geographical region managements. When the technology and markets stabilize, we will reconsider going back to a rule-based mode of decision-making, with just the product division management making these decisions."

Still another way to adjust the information-processing capacity inherent in a mode of decision-making would be to make subtle adjustments to the ways that different subunits can participate in the decision-making process. For example, the product design decisions may remain the responsibility of the product division management, but with "advice" from the geographical region managements. Under this mode of decision-making, product division management would have to keep geographical region management informed of their deliberations and solicit input from the geographical region managements. But in the end, product division management would make the decisions. The information-processing capacity of this design would lie somewhere between the capacities associated with the rule-based mode and the balanced mode of decision-making. This design distinguishes between line and staff roles in decision-making, a system which has its origin in military organizations. It preserves unity of command while bringing knowledge not possessed by the ultimate decision-makers into the decision-making process. But these are only examples of how the mode of decision-making within a matrix structure can be modified and tweaked to provide a more tailored kind of information-processing capacity.

We would argue that a matrix structure with a flexible mode of decision-making, as described above, should be considered a new form of organizing. Unlike any other form of hierarchical structure, it would dynamically allocate tasks—their associated problems and decisions—to the most relevant type of hierarchical information processing. As described above, the flexible matrix structure appears to have a particularly interesting fit with the requirements for a more ambidextrous organization (O'Reilly and Tushman 2011). The following chapter will develop this idea more fully.

Bibliography

Bartlett, C. A., & Yoshino, M. Y. (1981). Corning Glass Works, *Harvard Business School Cases* 9-381-160 thru 164 (A, B-1, B-2, C-1, C-2).

Davis, S. M., & Lawrence, P. R. (1977). *Matrix*. Reading, MA: Addison-Wesley.

Egelhoff, W. G. (1991). Information-processing theory and the multinational enterprise. *Journal of International Business Studies, 22*(3), 341–358.

Galbraith, J. R. (1973). *Designing complex organizations.* Reading, MA: Addison-Wesley.

Galbraith, J. R. (2009). *Designing matrix organizations that actually work.* San Francisco, CA: Jossey-Bass.

Kogut, B., & Zander, U. (1992). Knowledge of the firm, combinative capabilities and the replication of technology. *Organization Science, 3*(3), 383–397.

O'Reilly, C. A., & Tushman, M. L. (2011). Organizational ambidexterity in action: How managers explore and exploit. *California Management Review, 53*(4), 5–22.

Peters, T. J., & Waterman, R. U., Jr. (1982). *In search of excellence: Lessons from America's best-run companies.* New York: Warner.

Tushman, M. L., & Nadler, D. A. (1978). Information processing as an integrating concept in organizational design. *Academy of Management Review, 3*(3), 613–624.

Weber, M. (1947). *Essays in sociology.* London: Paul, Trench, Trubner & Co.

7

How a Flexible Matrix Structure Supports a More Ambidextrous Organization

7.1 The Need for Ambidexterity in Organizations

March (1991) argues that the exploitation and refinement of existing knowledge and the exploration of new possibilities outside of the existing knowledge are two fundamentally different learning activities within organizations. In order to survive, organizations must succeed in doing both. Those that engage in exploration to the exclusion of exploitation will have "too many undeveloped new ideas and too little distinctive competence." Those "that engage in exploitation to the exclusion of exploration are likely to find themselves trapped in suboptimal stable equilibria." (March 1991: 71). While exploitation and exploration are both essential for survival, they compete for the same scarce resources within an organization. As a result, organizations make explicit and implicit choices between the two. The purpose of this chapter is to better understand how this choice is made—to see if the available options can be better clarified, so that the choice can be made in a more explicit way from an expanded range of options.

The concept of ambidexterity has frequently been linked to the above conceptual framework. Ambidexterity can be defined as "an organization's ability to be aligned and efficient in its management of today's business demands while simultaneously being adaptive to changes in the environment" (Raisch and Birkinshaw 2008: 375). In other words, ambidexterity means winning in both the short run and the long run—in the short run through efficiency and in the long run through adaptation to a changing competitive environment. Ambidexterity would be unimportant if competitive environments were stable and never changed. But competitive environments tend to be extremely dynamic, and most firms that were initially successful go out of business within two decades of their founding. As a result, ambidexterity is increasingly being viewed as a capability that firms need to possess in order to survive over time. It is firms' ability to regenerate and remake themselves, their strategies and organization designs, to fit a changing competitive environment that count in the long run. But the long run is a moot question if a firm cannot first succeed in the short run.

7.2 How Ambidexterity Is Currently Implemented in Organizations

In this section of the chapter we describe how the present literature seeks to understand and implement ambidexterity in organizations. Ambidexterity is still very much in the process of developing into a new research paradigm in organization theory. As a result, research on ambidexterity is diverse, and difficult to summarize. More research has focused on identifying the elements of ambidexterity and the benefits of ambidexterity than on how to implement or achieve ambidexterity (Raisch and Birkinshaw 2008). The approaches to creating ambidexterity vary. They include structural approaches, leadership-based approaches, and contextual approaches. The latter involves creating a context where exploitative and exploratory behaviors can co-exist in the same organizational unit. Lubatkin et al. (2006) argue that leadership-based approaches are most appropriate for small firms, while structural approaches are more appropriate for larger firms. Gibson and Birkinshaw (2004) conclude that contextual ambidexterity is most appropriate for small firms and the business-unit level of larger firms. Most of the empirical research on ambidexterity appears to be at the level of a single-business unit or lower. We found no conceptual or empirical research that specifically addresses how to create ambidexterity at the corporate or firm level of a large, complex organization such as an MNC, which embraces both product and geographic diversity.

While it is difficult to generalize across the existing literature, exploration is generally associated with organic structures, loosely coupled systems, path breaking, improvisation, autonomy, and chaos, while exploitation tends to be associated with mechanistic structures, tightly coupled systems, path-dependence, routinization, control, and bureaucracy (He and Wong 2004). One of the most common ways of achieving ambidexterity at the business unit level or lower is by having two separate but interdependent subunits (one engaged in exploratory behavior and the other in exploitative behavior) interacting with each other around some common purpose (such as transferring technology from one subunit to the other). The physical and organizational separation of the two subunits protects and maintains their differentiated goals, subcultures, and behaviors. The targeted integration that occurs between these subunits varies from situation to situation and appears to be largely arranged in an *ad hoc* manner by senior management at the business unit level. Such targeted integration may involve informal networking by managers or the establishment of task forces or committees which include representatives from both subunits, to facilitate the transfer of real-world information to the exploratory subunit or the transfer of new technology to the exploitative subunit. While much of the literature emphasizes the role of informal relations, Jansen et al. (2009) found that ambidextrous organizations often used formal organizational integration devices as opposed to relying so heavily on informal social relations for integration between exploitative and exploratory subunits.

O'Reilly and Tushman (2011) provide one of the most complete discussions of how to create ambidexterity at the business unit level. They state that ambidexterity requires senior managers to accomplish two critical tasks:

1. They must be able to accurately sense changes in their competitive environment, including potential shifts in technology, competition, customers, and regulation.
2. They must be able to act on these opportunities and threats and to be able to seize them by reconfiguring both tangible and intangible assets to meet new challenges.

Since the rest of this chapter will be concerned with addressing the second task, we would like to digress at this point and briefly discuss the first task. It calls for senior managers to have good insight into a firm's environment. It is important to realize that a firm with a matrix structure will be monitoring more of the firm's competitive environment than a firm without a matrix structure. This is not just a function of the flexible matrix structure, but of all matrix structures. Since a matrix structure has two different hierarchies (e.g., a product division hierarchy and a geographical region hierarchy) stretching from the two-boss manager at the bottom to the second hierarchical level just below the CEO (see Fig. 2.1), it will absorb environmental information at multiple levels of each hierarchy and process it up to the product or business strategy level and the geographical region strategy level. Since much of the information flow along each hierarchy is different, senior management in a matrix structure firm should have significantly more information available concerning environmental opportunities and threats than they would in a firm that possesses only one of the two hierarchies. As a result, senior managers at the level of the CEO and the top of the product division and geographical region HQs should have good multidimensional insight into the firm's environment. We refer to the above as firm-level management, since the heads of these hierarchical divisions tend to sit on the board of management along with the CEO in most European companies, while in US firms they are often part of a senior management committee.

The second task is the primary subject of the O'Reilly and Tushman article, and it identifies five conditions or requirements for ambidexterity in an organization. These are tested with data from 15 case studies, and empirical support is found for four of the requirements:

1. An articulation of a common vision and values that provide for a common identity across the exploitative and exploratory units.
2. A senior team that explicitly owns the unit's strategy of exploration and exploitation, there is a common-fate reward system, and the strategy is communicated relentlessly.
3. Separate but aligned organizational architectures (business models, structure, incentives, metrics, and cultures) for the exploratory and exploitative units and targeted integration at both senior and tactical levels to properly leverage organizational assets.
4. The ability of the senior leadership to tolerate and resolve the tensions arising from separate alignments.

This is a relatively complete description of how ambidexterity can be created at the business unit level, and it has some empirical support. Our objective in this chapter is to develop an analogous description of how ambidexterity can be created at the firm level of large, complex organizations like MNCs. Before attempting to do this, we want to discuss a hypothetical example of a flexible matrix structure contributing to ambidexterity at the firm level.

7.3 A Hypothetical Example of a Flexible Matrix Structure Contributing to Ambidexterity

Since a flexible matrix structure can readily alter the kind of information processing that surrounds an activity, such as product technology development, it has the potential to make a firm more ambidextrous. Ambidexterity at the macro level is keeping a firm's strategy and organization design aligned with the overall evolution of the firm's environment. The contingency theory developed in Chap. 6 describes when to use rule-based decision-making and when to use balanced decision-making. Consistent with this contingency theory, it is apparent that the information-processing capacities inherent in rule-based decision-making (accountability, speed, economy) strongly fit the information-processing requirements associated with exploitation or incremental innovation, while the information-processing capacities of balanced decision-making (the innovativeness of alternatives generated and the thoroughness with which alternatives are reviewed) strongly fit the information-processing requirements associated with exploration or discontinuous innovation. Since a flexible matrix structure can rationally fit each of these information-processing capacities to the different information-processing requirements associated with the need for exploitative or exploratory behavior, it should be a viable structural approach to creating a more ambidextrous organization at the macro level. As such, it differs from existing approaches for achieving ambidexterity at lower levels of an organization. The latter are frequently leadership-based and generally emphasize the use of non-hierarchical information-processing mechanisms.

If a firm has a product division × geographical region matrix structure, firm-level management can specify whether the decision-making surrounding new product technology development will be guided by rule-based decision-making or by balanced decision-making. The implications of this decision are sufficiently predictable that management can use the decision to steer the technology development process—to make it more exploitative or more exploratory.

If rule-based decision-making is specified and the product division dimension is given primary responsibility for new product technology decisions, technology development will largely be guided by the goals and knowledge available within the worldwide product division. The goals and knowledge about the product that reside within the geographical region dimension of the matrix structure may enter the decision-making process to a limited extent at the two-boss manager level, but they will be more weakly represented than the goals and knowledge of the product division dimension. If there already exists a dominant technology for the product, the product division's strategy could seek to create its differential advantages by staying at the forefront of this existing technology curve. If firm-level management believes this is a sustainable strategy for long-run success, it will want to support the product division in exploiting and maintaining its current leadership position within the technology. It does this by specifying rule-based decision-making, with the product division having primary responsibility for product technology development decisions. This makes such decision-making fast and efficient, which should support an orderly, consistent, and rapid development of new product technology.

If, in contrast, firm-level management views the product category in danger of becoming more commodity-like (as all the major competitors attempt to race down the same technology curve), it may want to encourage a more exploratory approach to new product technology development. It can do this by specifying balanced decision-making, where both the product division and geographical region dimensions will have joint responsibility for making new product technology decisions. Relative to the above example, it would probably lead to a more disorderly, heterogeneous, and slower development of new product technology. By introducing more radically different goals and knowledge to the same technology development process, one could argue that the reconciliation process here is going to be more exploratory and less predictable than the above search for new technology. Introducing the geographical region dimension increases the chances for a different outcome, since previously its goals and knowledge have had little impact on technology development.

The managers in the geographical region hierarchy (the national product managers, the country managers, and managers in the geographical region HQs) may have observed that the current product technology bypasses a number of extremely attractive niche markets for the product in a number of countries. These niche markets are much less competitive and support higher profit margins. Under a mode of balanced decision-making, one would expect the geographical region managers to pressure the product division management to develop a new technology that can address this new opportunity to improve market share and profits. The goals and thoughtworld of the global product division might emphasize maintaining a uniform technology so that the company can stay at its forefront and also realize global economies of scale in manufacturing. The efforts to reconcile these divergent goals and views may push technology development out of its current trajectory of incremental improvement and into a more exploratory trajectory. For example, technology development might seek to move more of a product's functioning and control away from the hardware and into the software. This might allow the product to be more easily altered to address some of the attractive niche markets while still maintaining the uniform technology and economies of scale underlying the present technology strategy.

Whether it succeeds or not, the above shift to pursue a more exploratory technology development strategy stems directly from the change in the mode of decision-making to be used within the matrix structure. It illustrates how the existing information-processing capacities of the two hierarchies in a matrix can be constructively deployed to develop new knowledge, simply by changing the mode of decision-making. Without such a matrix structure and firm-level management's call for balanced decision-making, it is doubtful the knowledge possessed by the geographical region managers would have so meaningfully influenced, or even been brought into the technology development process.

As an alternative to the above, it is useful to consider what might have happened without the context of the matrix structure. Assuming senior management wanted to include both the product and geographic perspectives, the firm would probably have created a task force consisting of product division and geographical region managers to study the problem. Since the geographical region managers would be under global product division managers in a non-matrix worldwide product division structure, it is less likely they could study the problem and organize their arguments as effectively as when there are geographical region HQs at the same hierarchical level as the product division HQs. The goals and thought-worlds of geographical region managers within a worldwide product division structure will be closer to those of the product managers, and they will also have less influence over decision-making. It is important to observe that the balanced mode of decision-making ensures that one dimension of a matrix cannot move to end discussion without concurrence from the other dimension. In a properly functioning matrix, this leads to exchanging information and trying to work things out. The latter necessarily involves exploration and increases the chances for innovation. It is important to realize that it is the presence of two hierarchical structures, with more or less equal influence, operating at the same level on the same problem that creates this unique condition favoring exploration and innovation.

As developed in Chap. 6, the costs associated with balanced decision-making in a matrix are high, and few issues can continually favor exploration over exploitation. But, when firm-level management believes there is a meaningful opportunity for exploration and innovation, the flexible matrix structure would appear to provide an effective organizing mechanism for responding to such an opportunity. Equally important, the flexible matrix can readily change the information processing addressing an issue from exploration to exploitation. After the above shift to embedding more of a product's design in software and less in hardware has taken hold and shown signs of succeeding, firm-level management might return technology development to rule-based decision-making by specifying that the product division dimension will have primary responsibility for such decisions. This reduces the cost of such decision-making both in terms of reduced conflict and reduced man-hours. It frees up information-processing capacity along both dimensions of the matrix so that it can be reallocated to other issues. Thus, a flexible matrix structure seems like a more specified and a more reliable way to implement the dynamic capability of ambidexterity in large, complex organizations like MNCs, than the alternative non-hierarchical organizational designs.

7.4 How Ambidexterity at the Macro Level Compares to Ambidexterity at Lower Levels

The above example illustrates both the concept of ambidexterity at the macro level and the concept of "evolutionary engineering" (March 1991). The latter occurs when prior knowledge and understanding are used to guide change and evolution instead of leaving it to random forces. The ability of senior management to flexibly alter the emphasis to be placed on exploration and exploitation for significant subunits of the company helps to operationalize the concept of evolutionary engineering at the macro level of large, complex organizations. It respects the bounded rationality of firm-level managers and keeps them from having to intervene in more detailed decision-making that they can't adequately understand.

It is apparent that at the macro level of large, complex organizations, ambidexterity needs to be conceptualized in a way that differs from the way it is currently conceptualized for the business unit level of analysis or lower. At the macro level it cannot be based on selectively integrating the behaviors or information-processing capacities of separate exploratory and exploitative subunits, but rather on integrating the information-processing capacities of two different hierarchical dimensions. Like the two subunits, these two hierarchies represent different groupings of goals, capabilities, and knowledge, and different types of information-processing capacity. When these two types of information-processing capacity are combined to address a problem, they have a high probability of creating new knowledge that is useful. The reason this is so is because the two subunits and the two hierarchical dimensions are not random groupings of knowledge. They are groupings that are deliberately designed to be most relevant to the strategy of the firm. In the case of a product division × geographical region matrix structure, they are relevant from a product and technology perspective and from a geographical or local environment perspective. When these two different perspectives are focused on the same problem, it is highly probable that new insights will result—insights that could not have been developed by either of the two perspectives alone. These new insights are the necessary raw material for reformulating strategy and redeploying the tangible and intangible assets of the firm. A different but analogous logic applies to the targeted integration that occurs between the two subunits at the business unit level.

Our approach to implementing ambidexterity at the macro level represents a structural approach, in that it alters the mode (or structure) of decision-making addressing a problem. It changes the structure of decision-making from one that favors exploitation (rule-based decision-making) to one that favors exploration (balanced decision-making), and *vice versa*. Thus, decision-making for a given task or issue can embrace both exploitation and exploration, but not at the same time. For a given task and its associated subunits, time differentiates between the two inconsistent behaviors (exploration and exploitation). At the macro level, a firm will be more concerned with reconciling and integrating across periods of time—periods of exploration and change and periods of exploitation and relative stability. The same managers and HQ will address both situations at the strategic level. Most successful general managers are capable of doing this. The above picture is consistent with the punctuated equilibrium theory of change (Romanelli and Tushman 1994). It is our understanding of how the process of ambidexterity can work at the macro level of large, complex organizations. The flexible matrix structure is the organizational structure that facilitates implementing the above ambidexterity process.

In contrast to the above, the ambidexterity process is typically conceptualized in a different way at lower levels of an organization. Here exploration and exploitation activities are not separated by periods of time, but by physical location within an organization (they tend to be done in different subunits of the organization on a permanent basis). Thus, the same managers and subunits do not have to embrace both kinds of activities. This respects their particular kinds of bounded rationality and specialization. Some individuals and subunits specialize in exploration, while others specialize in exploitation. At this more micro level, the problem now becomes one of reconciling and integrating between differentiated subunits, not time periods, as at the macro level. Like the above problem of integrating between periods of change and stability, the problem of integrating between differentiated subunits is one that individuals and organizations are already familiar with. So the critical thing to recognize is that the problem of organizing to implement the process of ambidexterity at the macro level of large, complex organizations is fundamentally different from the problem of organizing to implement the process of ambidexterity at more micro levels of the organization. The flexible matrix structure creates a context where exploitative and exploratory behaviors can co-exist at the highest levels of large, complex organizations and be deployed in a rational manner. Consciously creating ambidexterity at this macro level is a new phenomenon, at least for organization theory. It can supplement—not replace—the creation of ambidexterity at lower levels of organizations (where current theory about ambidexterity is concentrated).

Next, we want to discuss how a flexible matrix structure and ambidexterity at the macro level relate to the four requirements for ambidexterity identified by O'Reilly and Tushman (2011). The first requirement calls for a common vision and set of values that provide for a common identity across the exploitative and exploratory subunits. A matrix structure provides for a convergence of vision and values as an issue moves up both hierarchies of the matrix. While there is total convergence and a single firm-level identity at the CEO level, successful matrix firms also require a high level of convergence and common identity at the second hierarchical level, which is where the matrix structure begins. Managers at this level should have the capacity to think like the CEO and fully identify with firm-level goals. As one moves down both hierarchies of the matrix, divergence increases.

The second requirement is a senior management team that explicitly owns the joint strategy of exploration and exploitation and that shares a common-fate reward system. A matrix structure says little about this issue beyond what has already been stated above, under the first requirement. But, this is a potentially important issue. Rewards based on firm-level performance (both short run and long run) are clearly appropriate for CEO-level managers, but when a manager's responsibilities involve the performance of a specific hierarchy (as occurs at the second hierarchical level), it becomes problematic how much to reward on the performance of a product division, a geographical region, or a functional division, and how much to reward on the shared overall performance of the firm. Unfortunately, we are not aware of any current literature on this subject in matrix structure companies. But, if the goal is to implement ambidexterity at the macro level, managers at the second hierarchical level need to identify more with optimizing total firm performance than the individual performance of the hierarchy they head. In most cases these two performances should not conflict, but when they do, firm-level performance needs to dominate. In other words, ambidexterity at the macro level requires the same kind of uniformity and consensus across the senior management team as is required by ambidexterity at the business unit level.

The third requirement calls for separate but aligned organizational architectures (business models, structure, incentives, metrics, and cultures) for the exploratory and exploitative units and targeted integration at both senior and tactical levels to properly leverage organizational assets. At the macro level a flexible matrix structure responds strongly to this general requirement for differentiation and integration. It provides a relatively stable differentiation of subunits (based on structural configuration) and a more dynamic way of aligning or integrating their goals and behaviors (based on the specified mode of decision-making). While some lower-level subunits in a matrix structure may be associated with largely exploitative goals and behaviors (e.g., a national sales subsidiary or manufacturing operation at the country level), most levels of HQs above the country level are more likely to be associated with both exploitative and exploratory goals and behaviors. Naturally, specific individuals within a HQ may have one orientation or the other, but the HQ itself should increasingly share both orientations as one moves up a hierarchy. So the flexible matrix structure provides a generic or pre-specified mechanism for beginning to align the differentiated orientations (goals and behaviors) associated with exploitation and exploration below the level of firm-level management. This should reduce the burden which would otherwise be placed on firm-level management.

The current design for creating ambidexterity at the business unit level or below relies on targeted or customized integration that seems to be largely arranged on a case-by-case basis by senior management. This approach to achieving integration would overwhelm firm-level management if it were applied to the macro-level problem. Instead, the flexible matrix uses integration mechanisms that are pre-specified and known by the participants (information processing up and down a hierarchy, balanced decision-making between hierarchies). These pre-specified and familiar mechanisms won't handle all of the information-processing requirements needed for integration, but they should be able to handle a high percentage of them and relieve the burden that would otherwise be placed on firm-level management.

The fourth requirement associated with a more ambidextrous organization calls for the ability of the senior leadership to tolerate and resolve the tensions arising from separate alignments. This capability already exists and is a standard characteristic of any properly functioning matrix structure. The cost to develop this capability can be great, but once it is developed, a formal matrix structure perpetuates such capability in the norms, values, processes, and routines that managers joining the organization are required to learn. Once established, this capability can be leveraged for multiple purposes, including the implementation of more ambidexterity. Thus, the flexible matrix structure satisfies this requirement for a more ambidextrous organization. In summary, there are similarities and differences in the way ambidexterity is achieved at the business unit level and lower, and the way we suggest it could be achieved at the more macro level of large, complex organizations. Ambidexterity at both levels relies on being able to develop and integrate differentiated inputs. The way both are accomplished varies between the two levels of analysis.

7.5 How a Flexible Matrix Structure Supports Ambidexterity at the Macro Level of Large, Complex Organizations

After describing how ambidexterity at the macro level can be created and contrasting its characteristics against those of ambidexterity at lower levels of an organization, we would now like to conceptualize macro-level ambidexterity as succinctly and insightfully as we can and discuss how it can be used to renew and prolong the life of large, complex organizations. We begin with the following definition:

> Ambidexterity at the macro level of large, complex organizations like MNCs is the capability to occasionally and selectively deploy multi-dimensional, hierarchical decision making to a limited number of problems that involve the long-run position of the firm and its principal businesses in their competitive environments.

Let us first consider the meaning of "occasionally and selectively." Balanced decision-making within a matrix structure, which is the way one accomplishes multidimensional, hierarchical decision-making, is a scarce resource. This is especially true when the decision-making concerns firm-level and business-level strategies and involves the higher levels of both hierarchies. As a scarce resource, balanced decision-making must be used selectively (the result of a rational deployment) to drive innovation and discontinuous change at this level of the organization.

Change at this higher level will be less frequent than change at lower levels, where there are more narrowly defined product lines, technologies, and competitive markets. Some elements of this lower level can even undergo continuous change (Brown and Eisenhardt 1997). But significant changes at higher levels of large firms will tend to be less frequent and can best be described by the punctuated equilibrium model of change. This model assumes that long periods of small, incremental change are interrupted by brief periods of discontinuous, radical change (Tushman and Anderson 1986; Romanelli and Tushman 1994; Utterback 1994). The occasional deployment of balanced decision-making is consistent with the punctuated equilibrium model of change.

Chapter 6 identified three situations where balanced decision-making is required to attain the optimal result: (1) situations where the goals of both dimensions of a matrix are clearly involved and need to be reconciled, (2) situations where uncertainty is especially high and it is not clear which dimension possesses the most relevant knowledge or information-processing capacity to address the situation, and (3) situations where the firm is seeking a radically new response to a problem, which will benefit from bringing together a wider array of inputs. The first type of situation is especially important to MNCs trying to implement transnational strategies, since they typically involve reconciling conflicting goals that are held by different dimensions of the matrix. When this kind of interdependency exists between the two dimensions, any significant changes to firm and business-level strategy should be reached through balanced decision-making between the two dimensions. This will ensure that both sets of goals are jointly optimized, instead of one set being optimized at the expense of the other.

The second type of situation, which involves high levels of uncertainty, typically arises when there is some kind of external shock. If both dimensions of the matrix are involved, the number of alternatives generated for addressing the uncertainty should increase, and thus increase the chances of finding a more optimal solution. Times of high uncertainty frequently involve great risk and great opportunity. Better insight into the situation is extremely valuable, and joint information processing and decision-making between the two dimensions increase the chances that such insight can be developed. When high uncertainty is also associated with the need for quick decision-making, this requirement, which implies the need for rule-based decision-making, needs to be weighed against the need for deeper insight.

The third type of situation that requires balanced decision-making is where the existing strategy of the firm or business has gradually lost fit with its competitive environment. Often this occurs due to small but continual change in that environment, that the firm only responds to when the misfit becomes too large to ignore. Reformulating the strategy and redeploying the firm's assets generally require the joint information-processing capacities of the two dimensions of a matrix for the same reasons as those provided above. The joint information processing and decision-making are more likely to optimize the common goals of the firm instead of the individual goals of each hierarchy. This is especially important when a firm's strategy is no longer working well. It could imply that the goals of the two hierarchies no longer fit or adequately implement the overall goals of the firm. Subtle but continuous changes in the environments of the individual businesses, the geographical regions, and the overall firm can easily erode the advantages that were once inherent in a strategy. Gaining sufficient insight into this situation and reformulating so that the competitive advantages are restored will be aided by the multidimensional information processing provided by balanced decision-making.

The first two types of situation generally depend on some internal or external event (e.g., the development of a new technology, the loss of a major customer, some financial or political crisis). This naturally leads to a kind of periodic reconsideration of strategy, which is consistent with the punctuated equilibrium model of change. The third situation is different. The gradual but continual evolution of many competitive environments is difficult to detect and properly interpret. While some firms argue that they continually monitor such change and evolve their own strategies and behaviors to keep up with it, we are skeptical of most firms' ability to do this. Collecting data on a continuous basis is relatively easy, but interpreting it in a way that meaningfully and comprehensively evaluates strategy requires the broader, multidimensional perspective discussed above. Our view is that firm-level management in a company with a flexible matrix structure can, on occasion, specify balanced decision-making for an important issue that requires this kind of consideration, so that it can be brought back into fit with changes in the competitive environment and the firm's goals. This is a structural approach to achieving more ambidexterity at the macro level of large, complex organizations. It is important to observe that a flexible matrix structure primarily provides more ambidexterity to strategic decision-making. It has little direct effect on the large amount of tactical decision-making and its associated behavior that go on at the lower levels of such organizations.

In conjunction with the above, there is the need for a concerted effort to increase the use of rule-based decision-making in large, complex organizations with matrix structures. This will free up management time so that it is available for the occasional use of balanced decision-making. We believe much of the earlier failure with matrix structures can be attributed to using balanced decision-making for both exploration and exploitation decisions. This tends to convert decisions of exploitation (which should have short time horizons) into decisions which invite the exploration of alternatives (which have longer time horizons). This tendency both overloaded the information-processing capacity of the firm and led to serious delays in decision-making. Two revealing examples of this are reported in case studies. Texas Instruments (Vancil 1984) insisted on using its three-dimensional matrix structure to make decisions regarding specific products and specific markets. As the firm rapidly increased in size, this mode of decision-making proved unsustainable. Product launches were delayed, deadlines were missed, and firm performance suffered. Ultimately, the CEO had to resign, and the firm abandoned its matrix structure.

A second case involved California Bank (Goossen 1978), which was actually Bank of America before it became a national bank. Its Personal Finance Group, which focused on providing a range of financial products (e.g., banking, investments, trusts, financial counseling) to five different groups of wealthy clients (e.g., inherited wealth, emerging wealth), was organized with a product × customer matrix structure. The person actually supplying the financial product to the customer (e.g., a trust officer) reported to both the trust department and the customer's account manager (who oversaw all of the financial products delivered to the customer). When balanced decision-making was employed, this design resulted in slow decision-making, poor customer service, and high costs. In both cases the firms failed to distinguish the very different information-processing requirements associated with exploration and exploitation. Balanced decision-making, which both firms were employing, is very appropriate to the development and creation of new products, but it is inappropriate when one is trying to deliver the new products to customers. The latter task should have employed rule-based decision-making, which would have given decision-making responsibility to one dimension of the matrix or the other.

The balance between rule-based decision-making and balanced decision-making will vary with a firm's need for strategic change. While the search for more ambidexterity frequently emphasizes the advantages that can be gained from better exploration, significant improvements can also be realized from better exploitation. The latter can be significantly improved in a matrix structure firm using rule-based decision-making when compared to exploitation in an elementary structure firm. As was indicated in Table 6.2 and discussed at that point, the use of rule-based decision-making in a matrix structure allows each of the dimensions in a matrix to further specialize its information-processing capacities. This increases the speed and efficiency with which such information-processing capacity can be deployed relative to that of an elementary structure. The only way an elementary structure can respond is to add more non-hierarchical network information-processing capacity. As will be discussed in the next chapter, the network option may not be an equivalent alternative to the hierarchical information processing.

This chapter is more speculative, more a work in process than the other chapters in this book. It relies on firm-level management being able to rationally and flexibly change the mode of decision-making within a matrix structure. We have not witnessed this taking place in any firm, although we believe the seeds for being able to develop such a design—the flexible matrix structure—are germinating in many firms with matrix structures. The interest and attempts we have witnessed of firms seeking to specify rule-based decision-making in matrix structure firms are promising first steps. Retaining or redeveloping the capacity to engage in constructive balanced decision-making and learning how to intelligently specify the occasional use of balanced decision-making to make strategic decision-making more exploratory and innovative are still the missing or uncertain pieces of this design. We believe most firms already using matrix structures can probably develop these capabilities and begin to implement a more flexible matrix structure. This, in turn, would support becoming a more ambidextrous and long-lived organization. In this chapter we are frequently describing the potential for something, in place of fact or reality. But with the kind of engineered evolution we are advocating, the identification of potential always precedes the subsequent creation of reality.

Bibliography

Brown, S. L., & Eisenhardt, K. M. (1997). The art of continuous change: Linking complexity theory and time-paced evolution in relentlessly shifting organizations. *Administrative Science Quarterly, 42*(1), 1–34.

Gibson, C. B., & Birkinshaw, J. (2004). The antecedents, consequences, and mediating role of organizational ambidexterity. *Academy of Management Journal, 47*(2), 209–226.

Goossen, M. E. (1978). California Bank's Personal Finance Group. *Harvard Business School Case* 9-478-055.

He, Z. L., & Wong, P. K. (2004). Exploration vs. exploitation: An empirical test of the ambidexterity hypothesis. *Organization Science, 15*(4), 481–494.

Jansen, J. J. P., Tempelaar, M. P., Van den Bosch, F. A., & Volberda, H. W. (2009). Structural differentiation and ambidexterity: The mediating role of integration mechanisms. *Organization Science, 20*(4), 797–811.

Lubatkin, M. L., Simsek, Z., Ling, Y., & Veiga, J. F. (2006). Ambidexterity and performance in small- to medium-sized firms: The pivotal role of top management team behavioral integration. *Journal of Management, 32*(5), 646–672.

March, J. G. (1991). Exploration and exploitation in organizational learning. *Organization Science, 2*(1), 71–87.

O'Reilly, C. A., & Tushman, M. L. (2011). Organizational ambidexterity in action: How managers explore and exploit. *California Management Review, 53*(4), 5–22.

Raisch, S., & Birkinshaw, J. (2008). Organizational ambidexterity: Antecedents, outcomes, and moderators. *Journal of Management, 34*(3), 375–409.

Romanelli, E., & Tushman, M. L. (1994). Organizational transformation as punctuated equilibrium: An empirical test. *Academy of Management Journal, 37*(1), 1141–1166.

Tushman, M. L., & Anderson, P. (1986). Technological discontinuities and organizational environments. *Administrative Science Quarterly, 31*(3), 439–465.

Utterback, J. M. (1994). *Mastering the dynamics of innovation: How companies can seize opportunities in the face of technological change.* Boston, MA: Harvard Business School Press.

Vancil, R. F. (1984). Texas instruments, incorporated: 1983. *Harvard Business School Case* 9-184-109.

8

The Joint Use of Matrix Structures and Network Designs to Implement Multidimensional Strategies

8.1 Introduction

As already stated, the growth in large, complex organizations like MNCs is driven by the growth in complex, multidimensional strategies. The latter are largely driven by the growing interconnectedness of the world and its economic activity. Firm strategies first became national, then regional, and now global. The complex, multidimensional strategies pursued by most large MNCs seek to implement certain differential advantages at the global level, other differential advantages at the regional level (and these vary between regions), and still other advantages at the national or local level (and these also vary between countries). Now multiply the above by the number of businesses a company engages in. This is the multidimensional strategy that a firm's organizational design is attempting to implement.

Multidimensional strategies create multidimensional interdependencies and information-processing requirements among the subunits of an

---

Major portions of this chapter are reprinted from "How the Parent Headquarters Adds Value to an MNC" by William G. Egelhoff, published in *Management International Review* Volume 50, Number 4 by permission of *Management International Review*. Copyright 2010 by Gabler Verlag.

© The Author(s) 2017
W.G. Egelhoff, J. Wolf, *Understanding Matrix Structures and their Alternatives*, DOI 10.1057/978-1-137-57975-1_8

MNC. Throughout this book we have discussed how these interdependencies or requirements must be satisfied by either hierarchical or non-hierarchical information processing for a firm to perform well. Since the subject of this book is matrix structures, which embraces a high level of hierarchical information processing, we have so far emphasized the fitting of hierarchical information processing to such information-processing requirements. When this fails to satisfy the requirement, we have stated that a firm needs to also use some form of non-hierarchical, network-like information processing (e.g., informal communication, task forces, committees, liaison roles). This ordering may have created the impression that we want to first satisfy as much of the information-processing requirement as possible with hierarchical information processing and then fill in the remainder with non-hierarchical information processing. But the situation is not this simple, and we are not recommending this approach. In most cases the information-processing capacities of hierarchical mechanisms (e.g., formal structure, hierarchical planning and control systems) differ significantly from the information-processing capacities of non-hierarchical mechanisms (e.g., informal network communication, committees, task forces). As a result, one is generally not a good substitute for the other, and a firm should strive to employ each against the information-processing requirement it best fits. In order to understand this issue more deeply, we want to briefly review the literature that describes hierarchical structures and network designs, and then attempt to conceptualize and contrast their different information-processing capacities. Following this, the chapter will develop some propositions specifying when hierarchical information processing should be superior to non-hierarchical network information processing, and *vice versa*. Finally, we consider a number of situations where both the information-processing capacities of networks and matrix structures are required (Wolf and Egelhoff 2012).

8.2 Literature Review

8.2.1 Hierarchical Structures

Classical management theorists such as Taylor (1911), Fayol (1949), and Weber (1947) tended to view hierarchy as a necessary kind of vertical specialization, where HQ specialized in strategic- and higher-level tactical thinking and decision-making, while lower levels of the organization specialized in executing these decisions. It was the obvious complement to horizontal task specialization within organizations. Chandler's (1962) research on strategy and structure subsequently revealed that a properly designed hierarchical structure was important to strategy implementation. The earlier chapters of this book have already described the substantial literature that relates strategy and structure in MNCs, and the research that uses an information-processing framework to fit different types of hierarchical structure to different elements of strategy has been presented in detail. In this chapter we want to develop an analogous information-processing framework that can fit either a hierarchical structure or a network design to different types of task situation.

Hierarchical referral or using the chain of command to process information and provide coordination is one of Galbraith's (1973) five types of information-processing mechanism. It is capable of providing non-routine information processing, but vulnerable to information-processing overload (Egelhoff 1988b). From an information-processing perspective, the most important attributes of organizational hierarchy are vertical specialization and centralization. Vertical specialization provides a difference in perspective (a strategic versus a tactical perspective) that is generally not available from a non-hierarchical form of organization. Centralization of decision-making facilitates the aggregating of diverse information (from different horizontal subunits and different vertical levels) for comprehensive decision-making. Again, this is a relatively unique capability of a hierarchy. Organizational hierarchies also tend to be associated with a hierarchical distribution of power and authority in an MNC. But, this is less a unique characteristic of a hierarchical structure, since the possession of critical knowledge and resources by lower-level subunits can create a countervailing power to challenge such hierarchical authority (Forsgren et al. 2005).

8.2.2 Network Designs

About 30 years ago, network organizations or network designs arose as an alternative organizational design to hierarchical structures for

MNCs (Hedlund 1986; Bartlett and Ghoshal 1989; Ghoshal and Nohria 1997; Birkinshaw and Hagstrom 2000). Since they appear to address the most severe limitations of hierarchical structures, many theorists view network designs as the most promising way to organize large contemporary organizations, like MNCs. It is important to distinguish between a network design, as reflected in the work of Hedlund (1986), Bartlett and Ghoshal (1989), Ghoshal and Nohria (1997), and a network perspective of organizations, as reflected in the work of Andersson et al. (2002) and Forsgren et al. (2005). Both are prominent in the MNC literature. The former views a network design as a type of organizational design that is usually argued to be superior to a hierarchical structure for addressing the situations facing today's MNCs. The latter network perspective, on the other hand, is a conceptual framework rooted in business/social network theory. It seeks to understand all organizational designs (hierarchical structures, network designs) in terms of their network characteristics. The present chapter views the choice between network designs and hierarchical structure as its dependent variable. It will attempt to develop a contingency model specifying when each type of organization design is most appropriate.

As defined above, the general concept of a network design embraces a variety of conceptualizations of non-hierarchical form in the MNC literature: heterarchy (Hedlund 1986), multifocal firm (Prahalad and Doz 1987), interorganizational network (Ghoshal and Bartlett 1990), horizontal organization (White and Poynter 1990), transnational firm (Bartlett and Ghoshal 1989), network-based structures (Malnight 1996), differentiated network (Ghoshal and Nohria 1997), and structured network (Goold and Campbell 2003). Although there may be subtle differences among these, most forms are not sufficiently specified to make these differences clear or meaningful. While there cannot be a definitive or universally agreed upon definition of a network design, characteristics that generally distinguish it from hierarchical forms of structure are summarized in Table 8.1.

In a network design, subsidiaries tend to directly process information with each other, as opposed to going through HQ under a more hierarchical hub and spoke design. Each subsidiary develops and

8 The Joint Use of Matrix Structures and Network Designs... 185

Table 8.1 Characteristics of Network Designs in the MNC Literature

- MNC is conceptualized as a differentiated network of HQ and subunits connected by relationships or linkages (Ghoshal and Nohria 1997; Forsgren, Holm and Johanson 2005).
- Core capability is flexibility. Flows of information and knowledge can readily be reconfigured to address a variety of problems (Hedlund 1986; Birkinshaw 2000).
- Roles of subunits in terms of knowledge, action, and position of authority will vary over time and circumstance (Hedlund 1993).
- Subunits interact on a quasi-market basis, where participation is voluntary and governed by norms of reciprocity rather than hierarchy (Birkinshaw 2000).
- Subunits are involved in cooperative as well as competitive relationships with each other. This has increased the scope for intrafirm coalition building and bargaining (Kotabe and Mudambi 2004; Forsgren, Holm and Johanson 2005).
- Subunits develop and are embedded in their own external networks of customers and suppliers. These networks provide knowledge, resources, and power to subunits, and can become important contributors to overall firm competence development (Birkinshaw and Hagstrom 2000; Andersson, Forsgren and Holm 2001, 2002; Forsgren, Holm and Johanson 2005).
- Subunits become centers of excellence within a firm, receiving mandates to take strategic responsibility for specific technologies and/or products (Holm and Pedersen 2000; Frost and Birkinshaw 2002).
- Network cohesion is primarily achieved by normative integration (shared objectives and knowledge, common organizational culture) (Ghoshal and Nohria 1997; Hedlund 1993).

becomes embedded in its own external network of suppliers and customers (Forsgren et al. 2005). This exposes most subunits to divergent pulls from inside and outside of the firm. The result is a more fluid and market-like shifting of power and resources across the subunits of a firm. The internal network becomes an arena for creation and experimentation rather than just for the exploitation of given knowledge and other resources (Hedlund 1993). Internal networks facilitate learning through problem solving among subsidiaries that are complementary and knowledge transfer between subsidiaries that are similar (Forsgren et al. 2005). Thus, as conceptualized in Table 8.1, the network design is a radically different organizational design from the traditional hierarchical structure.

8.3 The Information-Processing Characteristics of Hierarchies and Networks

Information processing in organizations has already been defined as including the gathering of data, the transformation of data into information, and the communication and storage of information in the organization (Galbraith 1973; Tushman and Nadler 1978). Here we want to contrast some important differences between hierarchical structures and network designs that can potentially influence their respective information-processing capacities. These differences are summarized in Table 8.2.

8.3.1 Goal Structure

Galbraith (1973) considered goal setting and planning, along with the resultant goals and plans, to be an important information-processing mechanism. Goals and plans help to inform and coordinate the actions of subunits within a firm. The goal structures associated with hierarchical structures and network designs are likely to be quite different. In an organizational hierarchy there tends to be a hierarchy of goals. HQ primarily identifies and works with strategic and other firm-level goals, while subunits largely identify and work with more local subunit goals. This implies a difference in HQ and subunit perspectives. A HQ will generally use its institutional power to ensure some reasonable level of goal congruence between the diverse subunit goals and the overall firm-level goals. This congruence will tend to exist along the organizing dimension of a structure, while there may well be incongruence along other dimensions not emphasized by the hierarchical structure.

In a network design without any hierarchical structure, it is unclear how firm-level goals will arise. Local subunits' goals will tend to evolve to fit the local situations. In the networks literature, the primary mechanism for achieving goal congruence across subunits or with some firm-level goal seems to be shared vision (Bartlett and Ghoshal 1989) or firm-level

Table 8.2 Important Differences between Hierarchical Structures and Network Designs that Influence Their Information-processing Capacities

Hierarchical structure	Network design
Goal structure	
• Strategic firm-level goals held by HQ; diverse subunit goals held by subunits. • Provides a reasonable level of goal congruence across levels and subunits, along the organizing dimension.	• Diverse subunit goals held by subunits; unclear how firm-level goals will arise without some hierarchy. • Primary mechanism for achieving congruence is shared vision and firm-level culture.
Information flows	
• Formal information flows along the hierarchy are directed by fiat; augmenting informal flows develop from high position familiarity & trust. • Hierarchies centralize information as it moves up and becomes more strategic and disperse it as it moves down and becomes more tactical.	• Information flows among subunits are voluntary, informal, and flexible; they are influenced more by personal familiarity & trust than by position familiarity. • Networks can take many shapes, so no single pattern to the shaping of information flows.
Motivation & behavior	
• Provides a system of incentives that supports extrinsic motivation and the processing of explicit (as opposed to tacit) information.	• Facilitates intrinsic motivation and the development and transfer of tacit knowledge.
Decision-making	
• Tends to push decisions up the hierarchy when there is interdependency across subunits. • Tends to standardize many decisions (often through centralization) to reduce complexity and achieve efficiency. • Facilitates centralized, comprehensive decision-making by a HQ (where firm-level goals & knowledge are more important than subunit goals & knowledge).	• Tends to keep decisions at the subunit level and exchange the necessary information to take interdependency into account. • Tends to tolerate diversity in decisions and decision-making. • Facilitates decentralized, incremental decision-making by the local subunits (where subunit goals & knowledge are more important than firm-level goals & knowledge).

culture (Edstrom and Galbraith 1977). But the emergence and existence of shared vision and firm-level culture is not specified in the networks literature; it is largely assumed. Thus, the network design perspective seems to be associated with a rather incomplete picture of how firm-level goals develop and evolve within MNCs.

8.3.2 Information Flows

The mechanisms influencing information flows in hierarchies and networks are also fundamentally different. The formal flows of information within a hierarchy are largely directed by fiat (Williamson 1975). This makes them reliable and predictable. The levels and subunits in a hierarchy tend to be mutually familiar with each other. They are familiar with who is responsible for something, who knows something, and who needs to know. Much of this kind of familiarity relates more to the positions in a hierarchy than to the actual persons filling the positions. Familiarity, frequent interaction, and goal congruence within a hierarchy leads to trust—trust that information will be conscientiously provided and properly attended to. Despite the maladies of hierarchies, both familiarity and trust are generally greater within a hierarchy than between individuals or subunits not linked by a hierarchy. When familiarity and trust are high within a hierarchy, there is generally a high level of informal information flow within the hierarchy, which parallels and enriches the formal information flows. The shape of a hierarchy naturally centralizes information as it moves up and becomes more strategic, and disperses information as it moves down and becomes more tactical.

In contrast to a hierarchy, there is little formally specified information flow in most network designs. Instead, information flow is largely informal and voluntary, driven by the need to coordinate interdependent tasks or address mutual problems (Hedlund 1986; Forsgren et al. 2005). Information flow in a network will depend heavily upon personal familiarity and trust between the nodes, since organizational positions and position familiarity have reduced meaning outside of a hierarchy. Unlike a hierarchy, a network design has no fixed shape, so it can potentially accommodate a wide variety of information flow patterns. Since all information networks depend on some kind of familiarity between the nodes, the variety and density of specific information flow networks within a network design will depend heavily upon the degree of familiarity among the subunit nodes.

8.3.3 Motivation and Behavior

Hierarchies are more strongly associated with providing extrinsic motivation than intrinsic motivation. With such incentives as pay and promotion deliberately linked to realizing the formal hierarchical goals of the firm, extrinsic motivation is very powerful in many firms. There is even some empirical evidence that strong extrinsic motivation can "crowd out" intrinsic motivation in organizations (Deci 1975; Lepper and Greene 1978), as it preempts the limited attention and focus of employees. Extrinsic motivation favors the development and transfer of explicit information over the development and transfer of tacit knowledge, since the former can be monitored and rewarded (Osterloh and Frey 2000). Thus, hierarchies are better designed to process explicit information than tacit knowledge.

Network designs, in contrast, are associated with supporting intrinsic motivation and the development and transfer of tacit knowledge (Osterloh and Frey 2000). When the network design is applied to an MNC, most of the extrinsic motivation resides at the subunit level. Above this level relationships tend to be more informal and voluntary, and there is more opportunity for intrinsic motivation to exert its influence. Thus, network designs should be superior to hierarchical structures in facilitating the development and transfer of tacit knowledge in MNCs.

8.3.4 Decision-Making

Decision-making is also quite different under a hierarchical structure and a network design. When there is interdependency across subunits so that information from various subunits has to be combined to make a decision, a hierarchy will tend to centralize the decision-making above the subunit level. Facing the same situation, a network design will attempt to exchange the necessary information among the subunits and either jointly arrive at a decision or allow each subunit to individually make its own decision, based on the same shared information. This centralized versus decentralized approach to handling interdependency has different consequences for different situations.

In a hierarchy there is also a tendency to standardize many decisions across the subunits. This reduces the complexity and information-processing requirements faced by a HQ, but it may result in insufficient sensitivity to local differences at the subunit level. A network design generally decentralizes most decisions to the subunit level and tolerates diversity in decisions and decision-making styles. This provides a lot of sensitivity to local differences, but leads to a more complex, heterogeneous, and less consistent decision-making environment within the firm. Consistent with this, a hierarchy facilitates centralized, comprehensive decision-making, where firm-level goals and contextual knowledge are more important to the decision than subunit goals and knowledge. Conversely, a network design facilitates more decentralized, incremental decision-making, where subunit-level goals and knowledge are of primary importance.

8.4 Situations Where Hierarchical Structures Should Outperform Network Designs

In this section we want to employ the conceptualization developed above to understand three important task situations where a hierarchy should outperform a network design, that is, where the information-processing capacities of a hierarchy better fit the information-processing requirements of the task than the information-processing capacities of a network design. Each of these tasks has been previously identified by Milgrom and Roberts (1992), using transaction cost economics analysis, as a situation where hierarchy should be superior to markets in providing the appropriate coordination. Since markets and network designs share certain properties (both involve relationships that are flexible, voluntary, and governed by norms of reciprocity instead of by hierarchy), our intention is to use the insight provided by Milgrom and Roberts (1992) to suggest where hierarchy may also provide superior coordination to network designs. We want to evaluate and understand each task using the information-processing perspective.

8.4.1 Tight Coupling

According to Milgrom and Roberts (1992), firms frequently have to address problems involving synchronization, where certain patterns or fits between interdependent behaviors are desirable and known. For example, the physical completion and startup of a new factory needs to be synchronized with the hiring and training of a work force and the delivery of equipment and raw materials. Since the information-processing requirements are known and relatively narrow (and hence suitable for addressing with centralization), Milgrom and Roberts (1992) conclude that firms (hierarchies) are superior to markets or pricing mechanisms for coordinating such problems of synchronization. The question we want to address is whether a hierarchy or a network should be used to coordinate this type of problem. We view the synchronization of events or behaviors as a specific example of the more general concept of tight coupling in organizations (Orton and Weick 1990), where there is high interdependency and no independency among the subunit behaviors. Our intention is to extend Milgrom and Roberts' specific example into a wider conceptual framework for distinguishing tightly coupled situations from more loosely coupled situations and relate these to the kinds of coordination provided by hierarchies and network designs. Applying the information-processing conceptualization developed above to two different practical problems of coordination leads to some useful insight and a preliminary proposition.

8.4.1.1 First Applied Example

Consider an MNC that supplies an important type of component to manufacturers of PCs and other electronic products. The component tends to be custom-designed and manufactured for each customer. The firm has three regional subsidiaries: North America, Europe, and Asia. Each subsidiary has its own value chain (sales, product design, manufacturing) and is responsible for conducting business in its region. Initially, the firm pursues a multidomestic strategy, where each subsidiary largely develops its own unique strategy. Europe, for example, tries to avoid competing on price. It focuses on providing superior customer service and quick cycle times for relatively short production runs of a product. Asia, in contrast, emphasizes low cost production for large volumes of a product. While the three subsidiaries use similar technical knowledge, they otherwise operate independent of each other. The general manager of each subsidiary reports to the firm's CEO.

At some point, the subsidiaries realize there is substantial duplication going on in the product design area (largely circuit design). They establish an "Engineering Council," which consists of the three product design heads, who begin to discuss how they can share and better leverage design knowledge. This leads first to some informal transfer of specific design information among the three subsidiaries and later evolves into a central electronic library of certain designs. A designer in any subsidiary can access these designs, select one that is similar to his needs, and modify or borrow ideas from the design to create a new design. The result of this coordination was a substantial reduction in design costs. It is apparent that the firm used a network design (the Engineering Council) and network information processing to achieve this coordination. The question we want to address is whether this coordination could have been better provided by a hierarchy or a network design.

From an information-processing perspective, the network is the preferred mode of coordination for this type of problem. It decentralizes all of the decision-making to the subsidiary level, where local knowledge of the customer's needs and priorities and the manufacturing plant's capabilities and costs are best understood. This level of independency among subsidiaries is important, since customer characteristics and manufacturing characteristics vary widely across the three regions. At the same time, designers can informally and voluntarily share with each other the technical knowledge that is accumulated in their past designs. They will be motivated to do this because they all expect to benefit from it (the norm of reciprocity applies). This level of interdependency among subsidiaries is also important, since it provides new, valuable information to the task of designing a new product. This information was previously lacking when decisions were decentralized and there was no network design to connect the designers in the three subsidiaries.

An alternative would be to address this task situation with a hierarchy. Here, all designs executed by the three subsidiaries would be sent to a central design office in the firm's HQ. This office would organize them into a central library and make them available to all designers. If the role of the central design office stopped here, the end result might be similar to what it was with the network design alternative (although the cost of maintaining the central design office would undoubtedly be greater). But with all of this centralized design information available, the central office will be tempted to play an additional role. It may attempt to evaluate the designs to determine preferred designs for given problems, and it may begin to press for more standardization in design approaches. We are not in a position to say whether this would be good or bad for the firm, but clearly it would be inconsistent with the current multidomestic strategy of the firm. It is important to realize that the projected difference in outcome arises from the different information-processing capabilities of the network design and the hierarchy. The network design facilitates information sharing and decentralized decision-making. It gives priority to subunit, not to firm-level goals. The hierarchy not only brings the interdependent information together, but also encourages making some kind of centralized evaluation of the situation (a hierarchy that failed to do this would be considered remiss). It also develops firm-level goals for its areas of responsibility. If the intended strategy of the firm is a multidomestic strategy, coordinating interdependency in the design area with a hierarchy is problematic.

8.4.1.2 Second Applied Example

As a result of increased competition, our MNC decides it must move to a more global strategy in the design and manufacturing areas of the value chain. The plan is to concentrate certain types of products in certain plants and also to better balance the production across the plants. As part of the transition to a global strategy, the firm wants to develop and install an integrated CAD/CAM (computer-aided design/computer-aided manufacturing) system across all plants and design centers. This will reduce the time and cost associated with transferring design work and manufacturing among the various sites. Sales remains a regional or local activity to fit the customers.

This task situation involves a much higher level of interdependency and tighter coupling of subunit behaviors than the previous example. Local subsidiary information about the range of product designs that must be accommodated and the manufacturing capabilities of each site need to be accumulated during the design phase and explicitly built into the firm-level CAD/CAM software system, or they will subsequently be ignored by the standardized decision process. This accumulated local knowledge needs to be combined with leading-edge knowledge about CAD/CAM systems so that comprehensive evaluation and decision-making regarding the design of the system can occur. In this case, the manufacturing central office at HQ understands better than any of the local sites what kinds of coordination the new CAD/CAM system should provide. This knowledge largely comes from outside of the firm. A similar perspective, one that can take all of this interdependency into account, is required when it comes to maintaining and improving the CAD/CAM system. On the basis of the information in Table 8.2, a hierarchy as opposed to a network design tends to provide the kind of centralized, comprehensive decision-making and firm-level perspective required by this task.

Following this logic, the firm should create central design and manufacturing offices at parent HQ, with the local subsidiary design centers and manufacturing plants reporting to the respective office. Sales activities remain decentralized and local, but instead of relating directly with the local design center and manufacturing plant, they must now turn their orders in to the central offices at HQ, since the order may now be designed and manufactured in a different region from the sales office.

Now we want to compare the two examples and propose a logic that captures their difference. Coordinating the designing of new products so that the process benefits from a common or firm-level experience curve while it remains responsive to local conditions requires both firm-wide technical design knowledge (the central library of designs) and local subsidiary knowledge about customers and manufacturing capabilities. Since the technical design knowledge is codified and easy to transfer and the local customer and manufacturing knowledge is difficult to transfer, it is best to keep decision-making at the local subsidiary level. Such coordination problems, which require both firm-level and subunit-level knowledge, where the latter is more difficult to transfer, are well suited to a network design. Such problems require independency among the subunits to respect the variation in local knowledge, and they require interdependency to construct and leverage a single experience curve for technical design knowledge. A network design fits this situation precisely because it is a loosely coupled system.

Coordinating the development and implementation of a firm-wide CAD/CAM system within the context of a global strategy requires combining externally imported information about CAD/CAM systems with aggregated product design and manufacturing information from the subunits. Since developing the system requires comprehensive decision-making at the firm level, a hierarchy is the preferred design to coordinate this task. In this case, subunits do not autonomously seek to improve their decisions, as in the previous example. Instead, they act in a cooperative manner that contributes to the overall quality of firm-level decisions. They provide information requested by HQ and follow directives provided by HQ, ensuring that the high degree of firm-level optimization built into the comprehensive decisions and directives of HQ is accurate and fully realized. The CAD/CAM problem requires high interdependency (actually standardization) across the design and manufacturing sites with little or no local independency. A hierarchical structure fits this situation precisely because it is a tightly coupled system.

Proposition 8.1 Developing and implementing tight coupling of subunit behaviors across a firm is best coordinated with a hierarchical structure, while the loose coupling of subunit behaviors is best coordinated with a network design.

The need for tight coupling among geographically dispersed subunits in MNCs is increasing. It is especially driven by (1) the need to deal with tightly coupled financial and commodity markets around the world, (2) the demands of customers pursuing global strategies for more global account management, and (3) the need to respond in a more integrated way to the threats of competitors pursuing global strategies.

8.4.2 Significant Economies of Scale and Scope

Milgrom and Roberts (1992) point out markets are not good at coordinating economic activity when significant economies of scale and scope are present. It is useful to understand the logic underlying this conclusion. Market coordination depends on each actor possessing two pieces of information: (1) the market price of the product or service, and (2) local actor-specific knowledge about the product or service. The latter varies from actor to actor and allows each actor to personally assess the marginal value of the product or service (i.e., each buyer knows how much he/she values the product, each producer know his/her cost to produce the product). With these two pieces of information, markets efficiently exchange goods and services and coordinate economic activity. But since no actor has an overall picture of the market (e.g., what total demand at any given price might be), there is no way this model can identify and define the economies of scale and scope that might be present. To do this one needs to bring the dispersed local information together and evaluate it as a whole, not incrementally as the market does.

It is obvious that a hierarchy can pull together the dispersed information from all of the markets its subsidiaries participate in and centrally evaluate the opportunities to realize economies of scale, and even economies of scope across the various product markets. The question is whether a network design can also do this? The answer depends on how one sees a network processing information. In the previous example, we viewed networks as facilitating decentralized decision-making by all of the nodes. This would lead to a lot of incomplete information processing, incremental decision-making, and autonomous adjustment by the individual subunits. A subsidiary might typically receive information from a few other nodes before making a decision, but it is unlikely to bring together all of the relevant information in the network before making a decision. And, typically, a network would tend to make many subsidiary-level decisions about a subject, while a hierarchy would tend to make a much smaller number of comprehensive firm-level decisions about the subject. The latter approach, involving a hierarchy, is more appropriate for addressing issues like economies of scale and scope.

If a network organization were to evaluate a comprehensive issue like economies of scale and scope, it would require aggregating information from the various subunits. For example, assume one of the subsidiaries of our electronic components MNC develops a product that it thinks might have the potential to become a standard product, suitable for multiple customers' applications. The economies of scale or cost to produce the product at different volume levels will be easy to determine, since the required information processing lies within the producing subsidiary. The difficulty will be to estimate the potential sales volume at different price points. This information would have to come from the sales areas of the three subsidiaries and be aggregated. While the Engineering Council provided a network linking the three design subunits, there is no comparable network linking the sales subunits. As the number of subsidiaries in a firm increases, so will the difficulty aggregating the necessary sales information. In general, it would appear that network designs suffer from the same deficiencies as markets when it comes to bringing all relevant information to a central point and making a comprehensive evaluation.

Proposition 8.2 Hierarchical structures are superior to network designs in identifying and defining economies of scale and scope.

One of the most significant advantages of MNCs is their ability to exploit economies of scale and scope to a greater extent than purely domestic firms. Primary examples of this occur with the optimal configuring and sizing of subunits and facilities to address global demands, the purchasing of raw materials, and the outsourcing of information systems, human resource management, and public relations services. Identifying and implementing such global advantages require the information-processing capacity associated with hierarchical structures.

8.4.3 Significant Innovation

Another shortcoming of markets is the way they coordinate and manage situations involving significant innovation. Milgrom and Roberts (1992) state that problems involving significant newness or innovation frequently require information that is not available at the operating level of firms. To the extent that this is true, the decentralized decision-making associated with network organizations, as well as markets, would not appear to fit situations involving significant innovation.

From an information-processing perspective, we see two reasons why a hierarchical structure should be superior to a network design for addressing problems involving high levels of newness or innovation. First, it can readily pull together at a central point the relevant internal and external information (much as it previously did for problems involving economies of scale). It will be more difficult for a network to accomplish this, and there may also be a tendency for subunits in a network to incrementally make decisions before a comprehensive evaluation has occurred. The second reason for preferring a hierarchical structure is that it adds increased vertical specialization to the decision process. It will be easier for HQ managers in a hierarchy to assume a longer time horizon and view new innovation as discontinuous from the present, since they do not have to directly manage current operations. Subunit managers in a network organization, on the other hand, will have primary responsibility for current operations and performance. It would be natural for them to see the future as continuous with the present. In a mature industry with little prospect of significant change this may be fine, but it will be inappropriate if a firm faces significant new innovations. The advantage a hierarchical structure has over a network design is that it can simultaneously support more radically different views of the present and future organization.

Proposition 8.3 Hierarchical structures are superior to network designs in identifying and incorporating significant new innovation into firm strategies.

This issue is especially important for MNCs, where newness in both markets and technologies often originates in different locations around the world. Making strategic sense out of such dispersed information, which potentially involves opportunities and threats, requires bringing it together at a point where there is a comprehensive and deep understanding of the firm's strategy. This is facilitated by a hierarchical structure.

The view expressed in Proposition 8.3 may appear to contradict some of the virtues currently attributed to network designs in MNCs. Many scholars believe that a lot of innovation either enters or could potentially enter an MNC through its network of foreign subsidiaries (Birkinshaw 2000; Forsgren et al. 2005; Dellestrand 2011). A critical part of this view is the embeddedness of subsidiaries in their local environments, whereby they pick up new innovative knowledge, which can be distributed and further developed through a network design. Birkinshaw (2000), for example, explicitly argues that a good deal of new firm-level strategy should emerge from such subsidiary initiatives. Our view is that while subsidiary-level initiatives which seek to alter corporate-level strategy might initially be generated by a network design, they should be further developed and adopted through a hierarchical structure rather than through a horizontal network design. This exposes the new initiatives or innovations to a more comprehensive evaluation and a different perspective, as discussed in the logic supporting Proposition 8.3.

There is support for this argument elsewhere in the literature. In their analysis of the "metanational" firm, Doz et al. (2001) found vertical HQ–subunit links were more important for sensing and exploring, while lateral links between subunits were more important for mobilizing knowledge. Schulz (2001) found a similar pattern and believed the reason for such a pattern of flows was the uncertain relevance of new knowledge generated by a subsidiary for other subunits. He concluded it was more efficient to verify the relevance of such new knowledge by sending it up the hierarchy to HQ than to send it laterally to other subsidiaries. Using a somewhat different logic, Andersson et al. (2002) also found that the HQ has an important role to play in further developing external relationships that were initiated by subsidiaries (converting subsidiary-level relationships and opportunities into broader firm-level relationships and opportunities). Thus, a varied literature supports the need for a hierarchical structure and HQ when significant new innovation is to be incorporated into a firm's strategy.

In order to reconcile these seemingly opposing views—that networks and hierarchies both contribute to the level of new innovation in an MNC—it is necessary to further conceptualize the specific contributions of each. New innovations originating at the subsidiary level are often associated with a good deal of tacit knowledge (about customers, supply chains, production processes, and product technologies). To further develop such knowledge to the point where it can be identified and evaluated as a new innovation, different kinds of network information processing are usually required. Cross-functional networks within subsidiaries allow an idea that might have originated within a single function to be tested from different functional perspectives (R&D, manufacturing, marketing). Functional networks between subsidiaries (an R&D network, manufacturing network, marketing network, each across subsidiaries) allow a higher level of functional specialization and experience effects to modify and enrich the original idea. External networks with customers, suppliers, and competitors surround each subsidiary and also inform new innovations at the subsidiary level. This kind of flexible network information processing exposes new ideas to a potentially wide variety of inputs, increasing the chance that some valuable recombination of knowledge will occur. Since all transfers of knowledge encourage making it more explicit, the amount of time innovations spend in subsidiary-level networks also helps to codify innovative knowledge so that it can be vertically transmitted by a hierarchy. This line of reasoning leads to the following proposition.

Proposition 8.4 The level of new innovations generated at the subsidiary level of an MNC will be positively influenced by (1) the density of cross-functional (and cross-product) networks within subsidiaries, (2) the density of between subsidiary networks within functions (or within products), and (3) the embeddedness of subsidiaries within local environments (external networks between subsidiaries and local environments).

The above discussion describes the creation or generation phase of bottom-up innovations in MNCs. For such innovations to be incorporated into firm-level strategy, the information-processing perspective would require that they subsequently undergo an evaluation and selection phase that involves hierarchical information processing. As already discussed, this subjects new ideas to a review that involves a firm-level strategic perspective, which tends to differ from the perspectives that were present during the generation phase. For example, imagine a new product innovation that has been generated by one or more subsidiaries of an MNC. As this innovation requires more resources (to develop, produce, market), it will typically be transmitted up some kind of hierarchy within the MNC. This hierarchical information processing will evaluate and probably modify the innovation before it is included in the MNC's firm-level strategy. If the innovation moves up the hierarchy of a worldwide product division structure, there will be a tendency to globally standardize the product, design the product for a few major markets, and realize global economies of scale in sourcing and production. These are the goals and perspectives that a product division hierarchy typically brings to the task. Subsidiary-level innovations that are not valued by this perspective are likely to be rejected and discouraged by such a hierarchy. In contrast, if the same innovation moves up a geographical region hierarchy, there will be a tendency to: regionally standardize the product (with tolerance for local variations varying by region), design the product for a wider range of markets, and forego global economies of scale.

As illustrated above, changing the hierarchical structure changes the way information is aggregated and the kind of vertical specialization (in terms of goals, perspectives, and knowledge) that managers bring to the task of evaluating and incorporating subsidiary-level innovations into higher levels of strategy. Subsidiary-level innovations that are rejected by one type of hierarchical structure may be embraced by another type, and the way different types of hierarchical structure further develop and incorporate such innovations into firm-level strategy differ significantly. Since one of these outcomes is likely to be superior to the other in terms of the firm-level advantages it provides, it is important for an MNC to have the most appropriate or suitable hierarchical structure in place. This line of reasoning leads to the following proposition:

Proposition 8.5 The level of subsidiary-generated new innovations selected for inclusion in an MNC's firm-level strategy will be positively influenced by (1) the level of new innovations generated and codified as explicit knowledge, and (2) the existence of a suitable hierarchy (functional, product, geographic) for transmitting and evaluating new innovations above the subsidiary level.

Thus, the proposed reconciling argument is that network designs facilitate the generation of subsidiary-level innovations, while suitable hierarchical structures are critical to the selection and incorporation of such innovations into MNC strategy.

8.5 Two Alternative Conceptualizations of the Matrix Idea

Now that we have described the information-processing capacities of hierarchical structures and network designs and identified a number of task situations where one is preferable to the other, we want to discuss two alternative conceptualizations of the matrix idea: (1) the concept of a "structured network" as proposed by Goold and Campbell (2003), and (2) the concept of a matrix in the mind of a manager, as proposed by Bartlett and Ghoshal (1990).

8.5.1 The Concept of a "Structured Network"

Goold and Campbell (2003) describe the concept of a "structured network" and provide a good description of how its largely non-hierarchical network coordination can be used to address multidimensional strategies in place of more traditional matrix structures. A structured network stresses clarity about the responsibilities of subunits, mutual learning, and cooperation, along with shared responsibility among the subunits. Upper-level management provides the subunits a lot of slack and only intervenes when necessary. There is a good deal of self-management and local initiative at the subunit level. Goold and Campbell believe this kind of network design can achieve the benefits of a matrix structure without most of the matrix structure's problems (see Table 2.1). Under certain conditions we believe this kind of network design could work.

Vertical specialization is not as well represented in the structured network model as in our hierarchical model of a matrix structure. The structured network model assumes lower-level managers will share the goals and perspectives of higher-level managers, at least for the task at hand. When this condition is true, the design can probably substitute for a matrix structure. But when higher-level knowledge and a higher-level perspective that are not shared by the subunit managers are required, this kind of design will not provide the same kind of information-processing capacity that a matrix structure will provide. Since the nodes of a non-hierarchical network tend to exist at a similar hierarchical level in an organization, they usually can't provide the vertical differentiation and specialization that are frequently required for dealing with strategic matters in a large, complex organization.

8.5.2 The Concept of a Matrix in the Mind of the Manager

Back in 1990, Bartlett and Ghoshal (1990) proposed yet another alternative to formal matrix structures. In a well-read article entitled "Matrix Management: Not a Structure, a Frame of Mind," they argue for "focusing less on the quest for an ideal structure and more on developing the abilities, behavior, and performance of individual managers." The idea was to create a matrix of the possibilities in the minds of individual managers and let them "make the judgments and negotiate the trade-offs that drive the organization toward a shared strategic objective" (Bartlett and Ghoshal 1990: 145). Our criticism of this approach is that it fails to adequately respect the bounded rationality of managers. It assumes that a single mind can contain all of the knowledge required to make a proper judgment. It provides an insightful contrast to the way decision-making occurs in a matrix structure with balanced decision-making. The latter deliberately brings together and integrates the viewpoints of multiple managers who possess different kinds of knowledge (horizontal differentiation) and different perspectives (vertical differentiation).

8.6 Expanding Information-Processing Capacity Through Matrix Structures and Network Designs

In this section we want to discuss two of the most common organizational design problems faced by MNCs: (1) simultaneously managing local adaptation and global integration, and (2) managing significant innovation. Our view is that a deeper understanding of hierarchical structures and network designs can allow firms to more rationally address both of these problems.

8.6.1 The Problem of Simultaneously Managing Local Adaptation and Global Integration in a Firm

At some point most large, complex firms possessed a single product line and a functional division structure. Then they typically increased product diversity, just as DuPont did in Chap. 2. Following the DuPont example, most firms will then change to a product division structure, so that they can employ hierarchical information processing to coordinate the significant interfunctional interdependencies that exist around each product line. These significant interdependencies are now contained within separate product divisions, each with its own hierarchical structure. If the interdependency between product divisions is small, it will be either ignored or coordinated by network information processing (e.g., sales people may exchange information about common customers). If these interdependencies are significant, the firm may decide to create a functional division × product division matrix structure, so that the critical interdependencies within functions can be hierarchically coordinated across the product divisions.

When the firm expands geographically into foreign markets, the need to process geographically differentiated information usually enters the picture. For US MNCs, the typical response has been to leave the domestic product division structure intact and to add a separate international division structure to manage the foreign operations. This is what Corning did in the mid-1960s (Bartlett and Yoshino 1981). The problem Corning encountered was that the substantial product knowledge it possessed resided in the domestic product divisions, and it was extremely difficult transferring this knowledge to the geographically and organizationally distant foreign subsidiaries. At first it attempted to establish various types of network information processing between the two, including committees that contained both members of the international division and the product divisions. This was not very successful. It did not transfer enough knowledge or adequately integrate the foreign and domestic operations. At this point, Corning adopted an international division × product division matrix structure. This made the product divisions responsible for the foreign operations and created hierarchical information processing between the centers of product knowledge and the foreign subsidiaries.

The above example is representative of what occurred in many US MNCs. When foreign sales grow to more than 35 % of total company sales, most firms will abandon the international division structure. At this point the product divisions will no longer be domestic product divisions; they will contain internationally experienced personnel and have a global understanding and perspective of the product line or business. If the product divisions all pursue global strategies (with little or no multidomestic or locally oriented strategy), the firm will probably stay with an elementary worldwide product division structure. The relatively weak interdependencies between product divisions will largely be coordinated with network information processing (e.g., local committees to coordinate the sharing of a site, an environmental protection council at the national or regional level to provide a unified company approach to dealing with national or regional government agencies).

The real complexity arises when the above product or business strategies are not strictly global, but also embrace significant national and regional variation. This leads to a transnational strategy, which requires a firm to simultaneously manage local adaptation and global integration. The view of many scholars currently is that this situation can be adequately coordinated by a single elementary structure and high levels of network information processing in a firm. In contrast, our view is that this situation can be better coordinated by a product division × geographical region matrix structure. This structure provides two independent dimensions of hierarchical information-processing capacity. Each dimension overlays an important set of differences and interdependencies which need to be coordinated.

For example, a plastics product division distinguishes between different types of plastic that are used to make different end products. But all of these types share a lot of common technology and facility that the plastics division will attempt to synergistically leverage as it further develops and manufactures these products. Optimizing the plastics product line or business within the firm requires a lot of tightly coupled decision-making and behavior within the plastics division. As previously discussed, hierarchical information processing is the preferred way to implement high levels of tight coupling. Since significant economies of scale and scope are involved in developing and producing the various types of plastic, a lot of information will have to be brought together and optimized at the firm level. This requires both the centralizing capability and the firm-level perspective that are associated with a product division hierarchy.

The second hierarchical dimension in the matrix structure is the geographical region dimension. It consists of national product managers, national country managers, and various levels of hierarchy within a geographical region HQ. Here, the European Region also overlays an important set of differences and interdependencies, analogous to those just discussed for the plastics division. Consistent with the above example, assume our firm is a diversified chemical company, headquartered in the US, which develops, manufactures, and sells a range of chemical products around the world. Within this context, the European Region dimension, for example, distinguishes between the French and German markets, largely in terms of their economic, institutional, and cultural differences. While it focuses on such differences as it decides where to develop and produce products and which market segments to emphasize, it also seeks to integrate (tightly couple) operations as much as possible within Europe to realize European-level economies of scale and economies of scope across the firm's product lines. The latter could involve the production of multiple product lines at the same site or the marketing of multiple product lines by the same sales organization in some countries. While these kinds of decisions also require some product knowledge, they are largely distinguished by the high levels of national and European-level economic, institutional, and cultural knowledge that informs them. This is knowledge that the product division dimension of the matrix generally lacks.

The example presented above involves high levels of tight coupling at both the global and regional levels. It seeks some global economies of scale as well as some regional economies of scale and scope. This requires hierarchical information processing along both dimensions and justifies the product division × geographical region matrix structure. Beneath this higher-level structure, there are many requirements for network information processing within the firm. At the national level, the multiple products and sales forces could use network information processing to coordinate around a common customer. At the geographical region level, there could be many different network designs coordinating a wide variety of issues across the national subsidiaries. Typical examples include the launch of a new product in multiple countries, the servicing of a common customer in multiple countries, how to best address the new environmental standards, and the transfer of best practices among the manufacturing plants. Networks are the preferred way of coordinating tasks when the information being transferred needs to be combined with local knowledge that isn't available at higher levels. It leaves discretion with the local subunits, so that behavior can be adjusted to fit the immediate environment. The quality of network information processing depends heavily on the familiarity and trust that exist among the nodes of a network. This is likely to be higher within a geographical region such as Europe than on a global basis, where physical and cultural distances are much greater.

Before leaving this discussion of local adaptation and global integration, we want to discuss an example of where network information processing was employed at a high level of the organization in place of hierarchical information processing. The company was a diversified chemical company with a product division × geographical region matrix structure, similar to the one described above. At some point it dropped the worldwide product division dimension and operated with an elementary geographical region structure. Our understanding of this change is that most of the economies of scale and scope that were available to the company were already being realized within the geographical regions. Most of the product and process technologies had also become relatively mature. These characteristics reduced the need for tight coupling at the global level. There was still a need to transfer some product knowledge between the geographical regions. This was addressed by creating a small staff of product coordinators at the corporate level, one for each of the former worldwide product divisions. They were experienced managers who reported directly to the CEO, but had no decision-making authority. They traveled continually between the geographical regions and became the global experts on the respective product lines. They frequently facilitated direct contacts between individuals in different geographical regions. The company saw this as a lower cost alternative to the previous matrix structure. We would view this as a type of network design replacing a matrix structure when the need to realize tight coupling and economies of scale along one of the dimensions largely disappeared.

8.6.2 The Problem of Managing Significant Innovation in a Firm

Network information processing is important if a firm wants to learn from many different local environments. The more embedded subsidiaries are in their local environments, the more potentially valuable information they can receive from the environments (Andersson et al. 2001). This transfer necessarily involves network information processing and depends on the familiarity and trust that exist between a subsidiary and its customers, suppliers, regulators, and competitors. If the information gathered in this manner stays within the subsidiary, it adds value at this level. But if the information can be accumulated and combined at a higher level, it can potentially create value at the regional and even the firm level. Some external information may be hierarchically aggregated by the formal data collection systems of a company. But other, less explicit information will often be shared among subsidiaries, especially those that are in the same region and face similar problems and opportunities. Some of this information is likely to be tacit and not amenable to upward transmission. Yet, individuals in different subsidiaries who face similar situations can intelligently discuss such information and begin to interpret it. The more tacit information is exchanged and aggregated, the more insightful and valuable it can become. In the process, it also tends to become more codified, so that ultimately it can be transmitted upward and become a source for innovation at higher levels of the organization. The ability of a firm to leverage such diffuse and tacit information for purposes of innovation depends heavily on the strength of the external networks of the subsidiaries and the strength of the networks among the subsidiaries.

While networks are the originators of such bottom-up innovation, the selection of which innovations to support and further develop at the region and firm levels requires hierarchical information processing. This exposes the potential innovation to a more strategic perspective, which can further adjust it to optimize results at the region and firm levels. Thus, a well-designed combination of network and hierarchical information processing can be important for significant innovation in many MNCs. When the firm has a matrix structure (e.g., a product division × geographical region matrix), the hierarchical review and selection process can occur along either of the two dimensions, depending on which dimension has primary responsibility for such innovation. For very significant innovations, the review and selection process would probably occur along both dimensions and be subjected to balanced decision-making.

8.7 Conclusion

While the overall role of hierarchies in MNCs may have changed in recent years as more coordination and problem solving takes place outside of the formal hierarchical structure, there are still important tasks that require some hierarchical structure and an active corporate HQ in most MNCs. This chapter has identified three broad types of task that cannot be as effectively or efficiently performed by a network design, and there may be other types as well. Tasks involving: the development and implementation of tight coupling, the identification and definition of economies of scale and scope, and the identification and incorporation of significant innovation into firm strategy, all require hierarchical information processing and significant HQ involvement. Our argument is that network designs provide inadequate information-processing capacity to successfully accomplish the above tasks in large organizations. As a result, MNCs are likely to remain a mixture of hierarchy and networks, and the challenge is to understand the relative strengths and weaknesses of each well enough to properly design the mixture.

This chapter uses an information-processing perspective to evaluate the coordination properties of hierarchical structures and network designs. The first great advantage of a hierarchy is its ability to gather and centralize at a single point, information from disparate parts of an organization, so that it can be comprehensively evaluated and understood. The growing number of tightly coupled task situations in modern MNCs requires this type of capability. A second, related but somewhat different, advantage is a hierarchy's ability to move decision-making away from the point where the information originates to a higher point in the organization, where a different perspective resides. The growing complexity of global and transnational strategies creates more situations in modern MNCs that require a global or firm-level strategic perspective. From an information-processing perspective, both of these advantages are uniquely provided by a hierarchical structure with various levels of HQs.

In this book we have argued that formal organizational structure and its relationship to strategy are important to the organizational functioning and performance of firms. Critics of this view have generally argued that formal structure is too blunt a mechanism for designing coordination; that the strategy–structure model leads to an overly mechanical view of how organizations function. And this may be true, if one employs the simple view of formal structure that is typically presented in strategy–structure research articles. But the strategy–structure relationship is more than some consistent associations between a structure and various elements of strategy. In large, complex organizations like MNCs, formal structure has significant implications for coordination and motivation. It shapes and influences large amounts of organizational behavior. This neither contradicts nor is contradicted by recent views of network behavior in organizations. In fact, at the level of organization behavior the two views can be combined and reconciled.

8 The Joint Use of Matrix Structures and Network Designs... 211

The strategy–structure perspective doesn't (or shouldn't) say that coordination only occurs through formal structure or hierarchy. As the costs of informal communication go down in organizations (including MNCs), this kind of coordination is likely to increase. Along with this there may be a reduction in formal communiqués and formal meetings. One may tend to see the former as evidence of a network organization developing and the latter as evidence of a decline in the use of formal organization. But one needs to be careful in how one conceptualizes this growing network of informal communication.

Proponents of a network view of organizations are generally vague in specifying what causes or shapes networks. Most often they assume that networks are "all channel networks," where every subunit or person is directly connected to every other subunit or person in the network or organization. This kind of network clearly cuts across any divisions created by formal structure, and structure becomes irrelevant to communication and coordination. In contrast to the above assumption, we suggest that informal networks in MNCs are strongly influenced by formal structure and that they are likely to be partial or incomplete networks rather than all channel networks. By specifying organizational, cognitive, and physical distances between subunits of individuals, formal structure influences the type of informal communication networks that arise in an organization. Network models of the MNC are very incomplete if they ignore the influence of formal structure on organizational networks. Thus, the influence of formal structure goes well beyond its direct influence on formal communication. The need to fit strategy and structure is still important, even when network coordination and informal communication increase.

Matrix structures are the primary way of adding additional hierarchical information-processing capacity to a firm's organization design. They increase the potential to evaluate more information at a higher level with a different perspective. This chapter argues for reconsidering and better understanding the complementary roles of networks and hierarchy in MNCs. Currently, the dominant view is that network designs fit most environmental conditions better than hierarchies and matrix structures. This chapter proposes a more complex contingency model that better explains the complementary coordination capabilities of matrix structures and networks. Both are needed to implement the present-day's multidimensional strategies.

Bibliography

Andersson, U., Forsgren, M., & Holm, U. (2001). Subsidiary embeddedness and competence development in MNCs: A multi-level analysis. *Organization Studies, 22*(6), 1013–1034.
Andersson, U., Forsgren, M., & Holm, U. (2002). The strategic impact of external networks: Subsidiary performance and competence development in the multinational corporation. *Strategic Management Journal, 23*(11), 979–996.
Bartlett, C. A., & Ghoshal, S. (1989). *Managing across borders: The transnational solution.* Boston, MA: Harvard Business School Press.
Bartlett, C. A., & Ghoshal, S. (1990). Matrix management: Not a structure, a frame of mind. *Harvard Business Review, 68*(4), 138–145.
Bartlett, C. A., & Yoshino, M. Y. (1981). Corning glass works. *Harvard Business School Cases* 9-381-160 thru 164 (A, B-1, B-2, C-1, C-2).
Birkinshaw, J. (2000). *Entrepreneurship in the global firm.* Thousand Oaks, CA: Sage.
Birkinshaw, J., & Hagstrom, P. (2000). *The flexible firm: Capability management in network organizations.* Oxford: Oxford University Press.
Chandler Jr., A. D. (1962). *Strategy and structure: Chapters in the history of industrial enterprise.* Cambridge, MA: M.I.T. Press.
Deci, E. L. (1975). *Intrinsic motivation.* New York: Plenum Press.
Dellestrand, H. (2011). Subsidiary embeddedness as a determinant of divisional headquarters involvement in innovation transfer processes. *Journal of International Management, 17*(3), 229–242.
Doz, Y. L., Santos, P. J., & Williamson, P. J. (2001). *From global to metanational: How companies win in the knowledge economy.* Boston, MA: Harvard Business School Press.
Edström, A., & Galbraith, J. R. (1977). Transfer of managers as a coordination and control strategy in multinational organizations. *Administrative Science Quarterly, 22*(2), 248–263.
Egelhoff, W. G. (1988b). *Organizing the multinational enterprise: An information-processing perspective.* Cambridge, MA: Ballinger.
Fayol, H. (1949). *General and industrial management.* London: Pitman.
Forsgren, M., Holm, U., & Johanson, J. (2005). *Managing the embedded multinational: A business network view.* Cheltenham, UK: Edward Elgar.

Frost, T. S., & Birkinshaw, J. M. (2002). Centers of excellence in multinational corporations. *Strategic Management Journal, 23*(11), 997–1018.

Galbraith, J. R. (1973). *Designing complex organizations.* Reading, MA: Addison-Wesley.

Ghoshal, S., & Bartlett, C. A. (1990). The multinational corporation as an interorganizational network. *Academy of Management Review, 15*(4), 603–625.

Ghoshal, S., & Nohria, N. (1997). *The differentiated MNC: Organizing the multinational corporation for value creation.* San Francisco, CA: Jossey-Bass.

Goold, M., & Campbell, A. (2003). Structured networks: Towards the well-designed matrix. *Long Range Planning, 36*(5), 427–439.

Hedlund, G. (1986). The hypermodern MNC: A heterarchy. *Human Resource Management, 25*(1), 9–35.

Hedlund, G. (1993). Assumptions of hierarchy and heterarchy: With applications to the management of the multinational corporation. In S. Ghoshal & E. Westney (Eds.), *Organization theory and the multinational corporation* (pp. 95–113). New York: St. Martin's Press.

Holm, U., & Pedersen, T. (Eds.). (2000). *The emergence and impact of MNC centres of excellence.* London: Macmillan Press.

Kotabe, M., & Mudambi, R. (2004). From markets to partnerships and hierarchies to coalitions: Perspectives on the modern multinational corporation. *Journal of International Management, 10*(2), 147–150.

Lepper, M. R., & Greene, D. (1978). *The hidden costs of reward: New perspectives on the psychology of human motivation.* Hillsdale, NY: Erlbaum.

Malnight, T. W. (1996). The transition from decentralized to network-based MNC structures: An evolutionary perspective. *Journal of International Business Studies, 27*(1), 43–65.

Milgrom, P., & Roberts, J. (1992). *Economics, organization and management.* Englewood Cliffs: Prentice Hall.

Orton, J. D., & Weick, K. E. (1990). Loosely coupled systems: A reconceptualization. *Academy of Management Review, 15*(2), 203–223.

Osterloh, M., & Frey, B. S. (2000). Motivation, knowledge transfer, and organizational forms. *Organization Science, 11*(5), 538–550.

Prahalad, C. K., & Doz, Y. L. (1987). *The multinational mission: Balancing global integration with local responsiveness.* New York: Free Press.

Schulz, M. (2001). The uncertain relevance of newness: Organizational learning and knowledge flows. *Academy of Management Journal, 44*(4), 661–681.

Taylor, F. W. (1911). *The principles of scientific management.* New York: Harper.

Tushman, M. L., & Nadler, D. A. (1978). Information processing as an integrating concept in organizational design. *Academy of Management Review, 3*(3), 613–624.

Weber, M. (1947). *Essays in sociology.* London: Paul, Trench, Trubner & Co.

White, R. E., & Poynter, T. A. (1990). Organizing for world-wide advantage. In C. A. Bartlett, Y. L. Doz, & G. Hedlund (Eds.), *Managing the global firm* (pp. 95–113). New York: Routledge.

Williamson, O. E. (1975). *Markets and hierarchies: Analysis and antitrust implications: A study in the economics of internal organization.* New York: Free Press.

Wolf, J., & Egelhoff, W. G. (2012). Network or matrix? how information-processing theory can help MNCs answer this question. In A. Bøllingtoft, L. Donaldson, G. P. Huber, D. Døjbak Håkonsson, & C. C. Snow (Eds.), *Collaborative communities of firms: Purpose, process, and design* (pp. 35–57). New York: Springer.

9

Conclusion

9.1 The Future of Matrix Structures

At present, most large, complex organizations such as MNCs use some form of multidivisional structure (e.g., a worldwide product division structure, a geographical region structure). The multidivisional structure concentrates interdependency within a number of relatively autonomous divisions, where it can be effectively and efficiently coordinated. It minimizes interdependency between divisions, where it is difficult and costly to coordinate. This elegantly simple concept has served business organizations well for nearly a hundred years. But over the past 20 years, business strategies have become increasingly complex and multidimensional. They increasingly call for interdependencies across what were previously relatively autonomous divisions (or businesses). This increasingly violates the core principle of the multidivisional structure. It diffuses interdependencies across the firm in a way that a single dimension of hierarchical organizing can no longer coordinate it. To address this problem, a few firms have added a second hierarchical dimension and adopted a matrix structure. The majority, however, have added a significant amount of network design (e.g., task forces, committees, and informal networks of people who share information with each other) to coordinate the new interdependencies that do not lie along the principal dimension of organizing. In many firms, we believe this kind of organization design is already operating near full capacity. If this is true, it will not be possible to meaningfully expand the information processing provided by this kind of organization design. Yet, one can expect that competition will continue to increase the complexity of the multidimensional strategies these firms are required to implement. As a result, we expect that the use of matrix structures by such firms will grow.

Matrix structures increase the number of managers available at a given hierarchical level and specify how they should share decision-making and relate to each other. At the macro level of large organizations, there is a substantial amount of evidence that less structured network information processing usually cannot substitute for the information-processing capacity provided by a hierarchical dimension. This was apparent earlier in this book in Chandler's (1962) study of DuPont, where cross-functional committees could not substitute for a product division structure. And, the same was apparent later in the Corning Glass case, where boards including members of the international division and the product divisions could not substitute for an international division × product division matrix structure. The rare counterexample of this trend was reported in Chap. 8, when a diversified chemical company abandoned the product division dimension of its matrix structure and substituted a small staff of product coordinators. But, this only occurred after most product line interdependency was no longer global and was largely located within the geographical regions.

The other reason matrix structures should increase is because they are becoming more amenable to practitioners. As firms embrace the rule-based mode of decision-making within their matrix structures, many of the former problems and complaints associated with matrix structures are greatly reduced. Our fear, as organization theorists, is that firms may go too far in this direction and largely drive out balanced decision-making and the longer run benefits it can provide. Even if this were to happen, we would regard it as an improvement over an elementary structure, since it significantly increases the amount of hierarchical information-processing capacity available at the upper levels of the organization. The potential ability of senior management to flexibly alter the mode of decision-making within a matrix structure, as described in Chap. 7, should also make it more attractive to practitioners who feel the need for a more responsive and ambidextrous organization at the macro level. This is where the problem of defining and implementing multidimensional strategies is greatest.

9.2 The Need for Better Theory about the Functioning of Matrix Structures

Picking up on a theme we introduced at the beginning of this book, individuals are extremely bounded in what they by themselves can accomplish. Individuals working together have far greater possibilities to accomplish more. In most cases, we believe there is more to be gained from improving collective behavior in large organizations than from improving individual behavior. Unfortunately, collective behavior involves interdependencies. The more benefit we seek from collective behavior, the more complex the interdependencies become. How to better manage and coordinate across these interdependencies has been the broad subject of this book. At the leading edge of this subject lie matrix structures and network designs. This book has especially sought to better understand matrix structures, since they have been so ignored by the current literature and, in most cases, tend to be poorly understood by the business community that could benefit from them.

If matrix structures and network designs are supposed to address more complex interdependencies, they need to be conceptualized in a way that supports this kind of understanding. Our approach to dealing with complex interdependencies has been a series of contingency models. Under certain conditions, hierarchical information processing is preferable to network information processing (Chap. 8). Under other conditions, a given structural configuration (e.g., a product division × geographical region matrix structure) is preferable to other structural configurations (e.g., a product division × functional division matrix structure) (Chap. 4).

And under still other conditions, a balanced mode of decision-making within a matrix structure is preferable to a rule-based mode of decision-making (Chap. 6). This contingency theory approach breaks down a complex problem into a series of less complex problems, which can then be addressed by some existing theory.

All three of the contingency theories mentioned above are in need of empirical testing and further refinement. The theory surrounding the matrix structure configurations in Chap. 4 has only been empirically tested in the reported study, and important aspects of this theory (such as the missing contingency variable that will hopefully define the strategic domain of the three-dimensional tensor structure) still need to be developed. The other two contingency theories described in Chaps. 6 and 8 were logically deduced and presented as a series of propositions. While it is unlikely these propositions can be directly tested, other forms of empirical research can be designed that could further inform and develop these theories.

Underlying all of the individual contingency theories is the same conceptual framework: an information-processing approach to organizational design. This creates a kind of common physics for relating various elements of organization design to a variety of different contingency conditions, all of which create some kind of information-processing requirement. As described in Chap. 2, the roots for an information-processing approach to organization design go back to the early days of organization theory. This history is consistent with our philosophy of science. In general, we believe one must attempt to understand the present-day problems within the context of past problems that one has been successful in addressing. We did this when we attempted to extend the knowledge used to understand elementary structures and their relationship to strategy to matrix structures. We believe that most valuable and sustainable new knowledge usually doesn't arrive as an isolated flash of inspiration. Rather, it accumulates on top of and extends existing knowledge.

Although the information-processing perspective of strategy and organizational design was previously discussed at some length in Chap. 2, it seems appropriate to reconsider the subject now that the reader has observed how this conceptual framework has been used to develop a number of more specific contingency theories. It is important to realize that information-processing models are implicitly process models. Their logic and relationships are based on a rather detailed description of how information is actually processed inside a specific type of organization. All of this understanding is implicitly a part of the information-processing framework and model, even if the explicit variables used by the model (and measured in a study) tend to be structural. Other approaches to modeling macro design tend to be more structural and lack a link to the functioning of the organization. For example, knowledge-based studies of the firm generally don't describe or analyze the underlying processes that actually develop and transfer knowledge in organizations (Kogut and Zander 1992). As a result, information-processing models provide a deeper understanding of how an organization functions and how this functioning varies when some contingency variable varies. And, since information processing tends to be important at all levels of an organization, it can support theory building across an organization.

9.3 The Need for More Academic Research

In closing, we want to argue that it is time for academic research to reengage the subject of matrix structures. While academics have largely ignored matrix structures, concerned practitioners have not been idle. Managers and consultants have clearly been trying to address the problems associated with the classical balanced matrix structure. It would appear that a rule-based mode of decision-making has been incrementally evolving in many matrix structure MNCs, as a direct response to the problems firms encountered with the balanced mode of decision-making. A more academic understanding of this phenomenon is still largely lacking, and, to date, there has been little academic contribution to the current understanding of how matrix structures are being used in today's MNCs. More specifically, academic research needs to study, evaluate, and attempt to understand in a more conceptual way the incremental changes that practitioners have been making to matrix structures in MNCs. The exploratory research which underlies significant parts of this book is an early attempt to do this. The theory developed from this research is tentative and suggestive. It will hopefully motivate more systematic research to test, revise, and extend it.

The need for a more manageable and flexible matrix structure to better implement the complex multidimensional strategies of MNCs is great. But the complexity of both the strategies and the matrix structure means that their relationship needs to be understood with some reliable and insightful theory, not a number of unrelated rules of thumb. Developing such a theory is going to require more than incremental experimentation and learning by practitioners. It will require the more comprehensive inquiry and conceptual theorizing that academics are supposed to provide to practitioners.

Bibliography

Chandler Jr., A. D. (1962). *Strategy and structure: Chapters in the history of industrial enterprise.* Cambridge, MA: M.I.T. Press.

Kogut, B., & Zander, U. (1992). Knowledge of the firm, combinative capabilities and the replication of technology. *Organization Science, 3*(3), 383–397.

Bibliography

Aguilar, F. J., & Yoshino, M. Y. 1987. The Philips Group: 1987. *Harvard Business School Case* 9-388-050.

Aldrich, H. E., & Pfeffer, J. 1976. Environments of organizations. *Annual review of sociology 82*, 929–964.

Ambos, B., & Schlegelmilch, B. B. (2007). Innovation and control in the multinational firm: A comparison of political and contingency approaches. *Strategic Management Journal, 28*(5), 473–486.

Ambos, T. C., & Birkinshaw, J. (2010). Headquarters' attention and its effect on subsidiary performance. *Management International Review, 50*(4), 449–469.

Anand, J. (2011). Permeability to inter- and intrafirm knowledge flows: The role of coordination and hierarchy in MNEs. *Global Strategy Journal, 1*(3–4), 283–300.

Andersson, U., Forsgren, M., & Holm, U. (2001). Subsidiary embeddedness and competence development in MNCs: A multi-level analysis. *Organization Studies, 22*(6), 1013–1034.

Andersson, U., Forsgren, M., & Holm, U. (2002). The strategic impact of external networks: Subsidiary performance and competence development in the multinational corporation. *Strategic Management Journal, 23*(11), 979–996.

Barker, J., Tjosvold, D., & Andrews, I. R. (1988). Conflict approaches of effective and ineffective project managers: A field study in matrix organization. *Journal of Management Studies, 25*(2), 167–178.

Barnard, C. I. (1938). *The functions of the executive*. Cambridge, MA: Harvard University Press.

Bartlett, C. A. (1979). *Multinational structural evolution: The changing decision environment in international divisions*. Unpublished doctoral dissertation, Harvard Business School, Boston, MA.

Bartlett, C. A., & Ghoshal, S. (1989). *Managing across borders: The transnational solution*. Boston, MA: Harvard Business School Press.

Bartlett, C. A., & Yoshino, M. Y. (1981). Corning glass works. *Harvard Business School Cases* 9-381-160 thru 164 (A, B-1, B-2, C-1, C-2).

Bernasco, W., de Weerd-Nederhof, P. C., Tillema, H., & Boer, H. (1999). Balanced matrix structure and new product development process at Texas Instruments Materials and Controls Division. *R&D Management, 29*(2), 121–131.

Birkinshaw, J. (2000). *Entrepreneurship in the global firm*. Thousand Oaks, CA: Sage.

Birkinshaw, J., & Hagstrom, P. (2000). *The flexible firm: Capability management in network organizations*. Oxford: Oxford University Press.

Brings, K. (1976). Erfahrungen mit der Matrixorganisation. *Zeitschrift fuer Organisation, 45*(2), 72–80.

Brown, S. L., & Eisenhardt, K. M. (1997). The art of continuous change: Linking complexity theory and time-paced evolution in relentlessly shifting organizations. *Administrative Science Quarterly, 42*(1), 1–34.

Buehner, R. (1993). *Strategie und Organisation: Analyse und Planung der Unternehmensdiversifikation mit Fallbeispielen* (2nd ed.). Wiesbaden: Gabler.

Burns, T., & Stalker, G. M. (1961). *The management of innovation*. London: Tavistock.

Burns, L. R., & Wholey, D. R. (1993). Adoption and abandonment of matrix management programs: Effects of organizational characteristics and interorganizational networks. *Academy of Management Journal, 36*(1), 106–138.

Burton, R. M., Obel, B., & Hakonsson, D. D. (2015). How to get the matrix organization to work. *Journal of Organizational Design, 4*(3), 37–45.

Carr, L. P. (2003). Serono. *Babson College Case* BAB043.

Chandler Jr., A. D. (1962). *Strategy and structure: Chapters in the history of industrial enterprise*. Cambridge, MA: M.I.T. Press.

Channon, D. F. (1973). *The strategy and structure of British enterprise*. Boston, MA: Division of Research, Harvard University Press.

Chi, T., & Nystrom, P. (1998). An economic analysis of matrix structure, using multinational corporations as an illustration. *Managerial and Decision Economics, 19*(3), 141–156.

Chi, T., Nystrom, P. C., & Kircher, P. (2004). Knowledge-based resources as determinants of MNC structure: Tests of an integrative model. *Journal of International Management, 10*(2), 219–238.

Ciabuschi, F., Martin Martin, O., & Stahl, B. (2010). Headquarters' influence on knowledge transfer performance. *Management International Review, 50*(4), 471–491.

Cyert, R. M., & March, J. G. (1963). *A behavioral theory of the firm*. Englewood Cliffs, NJ: Prentice Hall.

Daniels, J. D., Pitts, R. A., & Tretter, M. J. (1984). Strategy and structure of U.S. multinationals: An exploratory study. *Academy of Management Journal, 27*(2), 292–307.

Daniels, J. D., Pitts, R. A., & Tretter, M. J. (1985). Organizing for dual strategies of product diversity and international expansion. *Strategic Management Journal, 6*(3), 223–237.

Davidson, W. H., & Haspeslagh, P. (1982). Shaping a global product organization. *Harvard Business Review, 60*(4), 125–132.

Davis, S. M., & Lawrence, P. R. (1977). *Matrix*. Reading, MA: Addison-Wesley.

Deci, E. L. (1975). *Intrinsic motivation*. New York: Plenum Press.

Dellestrand, H. (2011). Subsidiary embeddedness as a determinant of divisional headquarters involvement in innovation transfer processes. *Journal of International Management, 17*(3), 229–242.

Donaldson, L. (2009). In search of the matrix advantage: A re-examination of the fit of matrix structures to transnational strategy. In J. Cheng, E. Maitland, & S. Nicholas (Eds.), *Managing subsidiary dynamics: Headquarters role, capability development, and China strategy, advances in international management series* (pp. 3–26). Bingley, UK: Emerald Publishing.

Dougherty, D. (1992). Interpretive barriers to successful product innovation in large firms. *Organization Science, 3*(2), 179–202.

Doz, Y. L., Santos, P. J., & Williamson, P. J. (2001). *From global to metanational: How companies win in the knowledge economy*. Boston, MA: Harvard Business School Press.

Drumm, H. J. (1974). Zur Koordinations- und Allokationsproblematik bei Organisationen mit Matrix-Struktur. In J. Wild (Ed.), *Unternehmensfuehrung* (pp. 323–348). Berlin: Duncker & Humblot.

Duncan, R. B. (1972). Characteristics of organizational environments and perceived environmental uncertainty. *Administrative Science Quarterly, 17*(3), 313–327.

Duncan, R. B. (1973). Multiple decision-making structures in adapting to environmental uncertainty: The impact of organizational effectiveness. *Human Relations, 26*(3), 273–291.

Dyas, G. P., & Thanheiser, H. T. (1976). *The emerging European enterprise: Strategy and structure in French and German industry*. London: Macmillan.

Edström, A., & Galbraith, J. R. (1977). Transfer of managers as a coordination and control strategy in multinational organizations. *Administrative Science Quarterly, 22*(2), 248–263.

Egelhoff, W. G. (1982). Strategy and structure in multinational corporations: An information-processing approach. *Administrative Science Quarterly, 27*(3), 435–458.

Egelhoff, W. G. (1988a). Strategy and structure in multinational corporations: A revision of the Stopford and Wells model. *Strategic Management Journal, 9*(1), 1–14.

Egelhoff, W. G. (1988b). *Organizing the multinational enterprise: An information-processing perspective*. Cambridge, MA: Ballinger.

Egelhoff, W. G. (1991). Information-processing theory and the multinational enterprise. *Journal of International Business Studies, 22*(3), 341–358.

Egelhoff, W. G., Wolf, J., & Adzic, M. (2013). Designing matrix structures to fit MNC strategy. *Global Strategy Journal, 3*(3), 205–226.

Emery, F. E., & Trist, E. L. (1965). The causal texture of organizational environments. *Human Relations, 18*(1), 21–31.

Fayol, H. (1949). *General and industrial management*. London: Pitman.

Ford, R. C., & Randolph, W. A. (1992). Cross-functional structures: A review and integration of matrix organization and project management. *Journal of Management, 18*(2), 267–294.

Forsgren, M., Holm, U., & Johanson, J. (2005). *Managing the embedded multinational: A business network view*. Cheltenham, UK: Edward Elgar.

Franko, L. G. (1976). *The European multinationals: A renewed challenge to American and British big business*. Stamford, CT: Greylock.

Frost, T. S., & Birkinshaw, J. M. (2002). Centers of excellence in multinational corporations. *Strategic Management Journal, 23*(11), 997–1018.

Bibliography 225

Galbraith, J. R. (1969). *Organization design: An information processing view.* Working Paper #425-69, M.I.T., Sloan School of Management.
Galbraith, J. R. (1970). Environmental and technological determinants of organizational design. In J. W. Lorsch & P. R. Lawrence (Eds.), *Studies in organization design* (pp. 113–139). Homewood, IL: Irwin.
Galbraith, J. R. (1971). Matrix organization design. *Business Horizons, 14*(1), 29–40.
Galbraith, J. R. (1973). *Designing complex organizations.* Reading, MA: Addison-Wesley.
Galbraith, J. R. (1977). *Organization design.* Reading, MA: Addison-Wesley.
Galbraith, J. R. (2000). *Designing the global corporation.* San Francisco, CA: Jossey-Bass.
Galbraith, J. R. (2009). *Designing matrix organizations that actually work.* San Francisco, CA: Jossey-Bass.
Garvin, D. A. (2006). Executive decision making at General Motors. *Harvard Business School Case* 5-305-026 and 5-306-026.
Ghemawat, P., & Nueno, P. (2004). Revitalizing Philips (A). *Harvard Business School Case* 9-703-501.
Ghoshal, S., & Bartlett, C. A. (1990). The multinational corporation as an interorganizational network. *Academy of Management Review, 15*(4), 603–625.
Ghoshal, S., Korine, T., & Szulanski, B. (1994). Interunit communication in multinational corporations. *Management Science, 40*(1), 96–110.
Ghoshal, S., & Nohria, N. (1997). *The differentiated MNC: Organizing the multinational corporation for value creation.* San Francisco, CA: Jossey-Bass.
Gibson, C. B., & Birkinshaw, J. (2004). The antecedents, consequences, and mediating role of organizational ambidexterity. *Academy of Management Journal, 47*(2), 209–226.
Goggin, W. C. (1974). How the multinational structure works at Dow Corning. *Harvard Business Review, 52*(1), 54–65.
Goold, M., & Campbell, A. (2003). Structured networks: Towards the well-designed matrix. *Long Range Planning, 36*(5), 427–439.
Goossen, M. E. (1978). California Bank's Personal Finance Group. *Harvard Business School Case* 9-478-055.
Habib, M., & Victor, B. (1991). Strategy, structure, and performance of U.S. manufacturing and service MNCs. *Strategic Management Journal, 12*(8), 589–606.

Hannan, M. T., & Freeman, J. (1977). The population ecology of organizations. *American Journal of Sociology, 82*(5), 929–964.

Harvey, E. (1968). Technology and the structure of organizations. *American Sociological Review, 33*(2), 247–259.

He, Z. L., & Wong, P. K. (2004). Exploration vs. exploitation: An empirical test of the ambidexterity hypothesis. *Organization Science, 15*(4), 481–494.

Hedlund, G. (1986). The hypermodern MNC: A heterarchy. *Human Resource Management, 25*(1), 9–35.

Hedlund, G. (1993). Assumptions of hierarchy and heterarchy: With applications to the management of the multinational corporation. In S. Ghoshal & E. Westney (Eds.), *Organization theory and the multinational corporation* (pp. 95–113). New York: St. Martin's Press.

Holm, U., & Pedersen, T. (Eds.). (2000). *The emergence and impact of MNC centres of excellence*. London: Macmillan Press.

Janger, A. R. (1983). *Matrix organization of complex businesses* (Conference Board Report No. 763). Amsterdam: Elsevier.

Jansen, J. J. P., Tempelaar, M. P., Van den Bosch, F. A., & Volberda, H. W. (2009). Structural differentiation and ambidexterity: The mediating role of integration mechanisms. *Organization Science, 20*(4), 797–811.

Jensen, R., & Szulanski, G. (2004). Stickiness and the adaptation of organizational practices in cross-border knowledge transfers. *Journal of International Business Studies, 35*(6), 508–523.

Joyce, W. F. (1986). Matrix organization: A social experiment. *Academy of Management Journal, 29*(3), 536–561.

Katz, D., & Kahn, R. L. (1966). *The social psychology of organizations*. New York: Wiley.

Kmetz, J. L. (1984). An information-processing study of a complex workflow in aircraft electronics repair. *Administrative Science Quarterly, 29*(2), 255–280.

Kogut, B., & Zander, U. (1992). Knowledge of the firm, combinative capabilities and the replication of technology. *Organization Science, 3*(3), 383–397.

Kotabe, M., & Mudambi, R. (2004). From markets to partnerships and hierarchies to coalitions: Perspectives on the modern multinational corporation. *Journal of International Management, 10*(2), 147–150.

Kuprenas, J. A. (2003). Implementation and performance of matrix organization structure. *International Journal of Project Management, 21*(1), 51–62.

Larson, E. W., & Gobeli, D. H. (1987). Matrix management: Contradictions and insights. *California Management Review, 29*(4), 126–138.

Laslo, Z., & Goldberg, A. I. (2001). Matrix structures and performance: The search for optimal adjustment to organizational objectives. *IEEE Transactions on Engineering Management, 48*(2), 144–156.

Lawrence, P. R., & Lorsch, J. W. (1967). *Organization and environment.* Homewood, IL: Irwin.

Lepper, M. R., & Greene, D. (1978). *The hidden costs of reward: New perspectives on the psychology of human motivation.* Hillsdale, NY: Erlbaum.

Lubatkin, M. L., Simsek, Z., Ling, Y., & Veiga, J. F. (2006). Ambidexterity and performance in Small- to medium-sized firms: The pivotal role of top management team behavioral integration. *Journal of Management, 32*(5), 646–672.

Malnight, T. W. (1996). The transition from decentralized to network-based MNC structures: An evolutionary perspective. *Journal of International Business Studies, 27*(1), 43–65.

March, J. G. (1991). Exploration and exploitation in organizational learning. *Organization Science, 2*(1), 71–87.

Miles, R. E., & Snow, C. C. (1984). Fit, failure, and the hall of fame. *California Management Review, 26*(3), 10–28.

Milgrom, P., & Roberts, J. (1992). *Economics, organization and management.* Englewood Cliffs: Prentice Hall.

Mudambi, R. (2011). Hierarchy, coordination, and innovation in the multinational enterprise. *Global Strategy Journal, 1*(3–4), 317–323.

Nell, P. C., Ambos, B., & Schlegelmilch, B. B. (2011). The benefits of hierarchy: Exploring the effects of regional headquarters in multinational corporations. *Advances in International Management, 24*, 85–106.

Ojha, A. K. (2010). Bosch group in India: Transition to a transnational organization. *Indian Institute of Management Bangalore Case IMB, 301.*

O'Reilly, C. A., & Tushman, M. L. (2011). Organizational ambidexterity in action: How managers explore and exploit. *California Management Review, 53*(4), 5–22.

Orton, J. D., & Weick, K. E. (1990). Loosely coupled systems: A reconceptualization. *Academy of Management Review, 15*(2), 203–223.

Osterloh, M., & Frey, B. S. (2000). Motivation, knowledge transfer, and organizational forms. *Organization Science, 11*(5), 538–550.

Paven, R. D. J. (1972). *The strategy and structure of Italian enterprise.* Unpublished doctoral dissertation, Harvard Business School, Boston, MA.

Perlmutter, H. V. (1969). The tortuous evolution of the multinational corporation. *Columbia Journal of World Business, 4*(1), 9–18.

Perrow, C. (1967). A framework for the comparative analysis of organizations. *American Sociological Review, 32*(3), 194–208.

Peters, T. J. (1979). Beyond the matrix organization. *Business Horizons, 22*(5), 15–27.

Peters, T. J., & Waterman Jr., R. U. (1982). *In search of excellence: Lessons from America's best-run companies.* New York: Warner.

Piekkari, R., Nell, P. C., & Ghauri, P. N. (2010). Regional management as a system: A longitudinal case study. *Management International Review, 50*(4), 513–532.

Piskorski, M. J., & Spadini, A. L. (2007). Procter & Gamble: Organization 2005 (A) & (B). *Harvard Business School Cases* 9-707-519, 9-707-402, and 5-708-450.

Pitts, R. A. (1977). Strategies and structures for diversification. *Academy of Management Journal, 20*(2), 197–208.

Pitts, R. A., & Daniels, J. D. (1984). Aftermath of the matrix mania. *Columbia Journal of World Business, 19*(2), 48–54.

Porter, M. E. (1986). *Competition in global industries.* Boston, MA: Harvard Business School Press.

Prahalad, C. K., & Doz, Y. L. (1987). *The multinational mission: Balancing global integration with local responsiveness.* New York: Free Press.

Qui, J. X., & Donaldson, L. (2010). The cubic contingency model: Towards a more comprehensive international strategy-structure model. *Journal of General Management, 36*(1), 81–100.

Rahim, A., & Bonoma, T. V. (1979). Managing organizational conflict: A model for diagnosis and intervention. *Psychological Reports, 44*(3), 1323–1344.

Raisch, S., & Birkinshaw, J. (2008). Organizational ambidexterity: Antecedents, outcomes, and moderators. *Journal of Management, 34*(3), 375–409.

Romanelli, E., & Tushman, M. L. (1994). Organizational transformation as punctuated equilibrium: An empirical test. *Academy of Management Journal, 37*(1), 1141–1166.

Rugman, A. M., & Verbeke, A. (2005). Towards a theory of regional multinationals: A transaction cost economics approach. *Management International Review, 45*(1), 5–17.

Rumelt, R. P. (1974). *Strategy, structure, and economic performance.* Boston, MA: Harvard University.

Sayles, L. R. (1976). Matrix management: The structure with a future. *Organization Dynamics, 5*(2), 2–17.

Schulz, M. (2001). The uncertain relevance of newness: Organizational learning and knowledge flows. *Academy of Management Journal, 44*(4), 661–681.
Simon, H. A. (1957). *Administrative behavior: A study of decision-making processes in administrative organization.* New York: Free Press.
Simons, R., & Bartlett, C. (1992). Asea Brown Boveri. *Harvard Business School Case* 9-192-139, 9-192-141, and 9-192-142.
Simons, T. L., & Peterson, R. S. (2000). Task conflict and relationship conflict in top management teams: The pivotal role of intragroup trust. *Journal of Applied Psychology, 83*(1), 102–111.
Stopford, J. M., & Wells Jr., L. T. (1972). *Managing the multinational enterprise.* New York: Basic Books.
Strikwerda, J., & Stoelhorst, J. W. (2009). The emergence and evolution of the multidimensional organization. *California Management Review, 51*(4), 11–31.
Sy, T., & D'Annunzio, L. S. (2005). Challenges and strategies of matrix organizations: Top-level and mid-level managers' perspectives. *Human Resource Planning, 28*(1), 39–48.
Taylor, F. W. (1911). *The principles of scientific management.* New York: Harper.
Thompson, J. D. (1967). *Organizations in action.* New York: McGraw-Hill.
Tushman, M. L. (1978). Technical communication in research and development laboratories: Impact of project work characteristics. *Academy of Management Journal, 21*(4), 624–645.
Tushman, M. L., & Anderson, P. (1986). Technological discontinuities and organizational environments. *Administrative Science Quarterly, 31*(3), 439–465.
Tushman, M. L., & Nadler, D. A. (1978). Information processing as an integrating concept in organizational design. *Academy of Management Review, 3*(3), 613–624.
Utterback, J. M. (1994). *Mastering the dynamics of innovation: How companies can seize opportunities in the face of technological change.* Boston, MA: Harvard Business School Press.
Van de Ven, A. H., Delbecq, A. L., & Koenig Jr., R. (1976). Determinants of coordination modes within organizations. *American Sociological Review, 41*(2), 322–338.
Vancil, R. F. (1984). Texas instruments, incorporated: 1983. *Harvard Business School Case* 9-184-109.
Wagner, H. (1978). Mehrdimensionale Organisationsstrukturen. *Die Betriebswirtschaft, 38*(1), 103–115.

Weber, M. (1947). *Essays in sociology*. London: Paul, Trench, Trubner & Co.
Weick, K. E. (1979). *The social psychology of organizing*. Reading, MA: Addison-Wesley.
White, R. E., & Poynter, T. A. (1990). Organizing for world-wide advantage. In C. A. Bartlett, Y. L. Doz, & G. Hedlund (Eds.), *Managing the global firm* (pp. 95–113). New York: Routledge.
Williamson, O. E. (1975). *Markets and hierarchies: Analysis and antitrust implications: A study in the economics of internal organization*. New York: Free Press.
Wolf, J., & Egelhoff, W. G. (2002). A reexamination and extension of international strategy-structure theory. *Strategic Management Journal, 23*(2), 181–189.
Wolf, J., & Egelhoff, W. G. (2013). An empirical evaluation of conflict in MNC matrix structure firms. *International Business Review, 22*(3), 591–601.
Woodward, J. (1965). *Industrial organization: Theory and practice*. London: Oxford University Press.
Yuchtman, E., & Seashore, S. E. (1967). A system resource approach to organizational effectiveness. *American Sociological Review, 32*(6), 891–903.

Author Index

A
Adzic, M., 75
Aguilar, F.J., 111
Aldrich, H.E., 98
Ambos, B., 39
Ambos, T.C., 113
Anand, J., 81
Anderson, P., 175
Andersson, U., 81, 113, 184–5, 199, 208
Andrews, I.R., 112

B
Barker, J., 112
Barnard, C.I., 32
Bartlett, C.A., 11, 32, 39, 45, 48, 57, 89, 111, 113, 139, 184, 186, 202–3, 205

Birkinshaw, J., 10, 32, 39, 81, 113, 162, 184, 185, 199
Bonoma, T.V., 112
Brings, K., 114
Brown, S.L., 175
Buehner, R., 114
Burns, L.R., 27, 113
Burns, T., 35, 56
Burton, R.M., 2

C
Campbell, A., 11, 184, 202
Carr, L.P., 111
Chandler, A.D., Jr., 6, 16, 18, 44, 54, 183, 216
Channon, D.F., 44
Chi, T., 28, 76, 77, 109, 112, 114
Ciabuschi, F., 113
Cyert, R.M., 33

Author Index

D

Daniels, J.D., 28, 44–5, 54, 75, 82
D'Annunzio, L.S., 28
Davidson, W.H., 45
Davis, S.M., 24–7, 76, 98, 109, 111–12, 114–15, 117, 123, 131, 134, 136
Deci, E.L., 189
Dellestrand, H., 199
Donaldson, L., 79
Dougherty, D., 53, 117
Doz, Y.L., 184, 199
Drumm, H.J., 117
Duncan, R.B., 33, 35, 37
Dyas, G.P., 44

E

Edström, A., 187
Egelhoff, W.G., 27, 38, 43–4, 46–7, 75–6, 78–9, 82–4, 86, 88, 96–7, 100–1, 104, 109, 110, 132, 181–3
Eisenhardt, K.M., 175
Emery, F.E., 56

F

Fayol, H., 28, 182
Ford, R.C., 27, 112
Forsgren, M., 32, 39, 113, 183–5, 188, 199
Franko, L.G., 27, 44, 54, 77, 82
Freeman, J., 98
Frey, B.S., 189

G

Galbraith, J.R., 26–7, 34–5, 46, 54, 77, 98, 109, 112, 114–15, 117, 123, 127, 132, 140, 183, 186–7
Garvin, D.A., 111
Ghemawat, P., 111
Ghoshal, S., 11, 32, 39, 81, 89, 113, 184–6, 202, 203
Gibson, C.B., 162
Gobeli, D.H., 28
Goggin, W.C., 27, 111
Goldberg, A.I., 113
Goold, M., 11, 184, 202
Goossen, M.E., 177
Greene, D., 189

H

Habib, M., 46, 77, 82, 97
Hagstrom, P., 32, 81, 184
Hannan, M.T., 98
Harvey, E., 55
Haspeslagh, P., 45
He, Z.L., 163
Hedlund, G., 32, 39, 81, 113, 184–5, 188
Holm, U., 185

J

Janger, A.R., 109, 115, 117
Jansen, J.J.P., 163
Jensen, R., 40
Johanson, J., 185
Joyce, W.F., 113

K

Kahn, R.L., 33
Katz, D., 33
Kmetz, J.L., 35
Kogut, B., 40, 145, 219
Kuprenas, J.A., 27, 113

L

Larson, E.W., 28
Laslo, Z., 113
Lawrence, P.R., 24–7, 33, 35, 54, 56, 66, 76, 98, 109, 112, 114, 115, 117, 123, 131, 134, 136
Lepper, M.R., 189
Lorsch, J.W., 33, 35, 54, 56, 66, 117
Lubatkin, M.L., 162

M

Malnight, T.W., 184
March, J.G., 33, 161, 169
Miles, R.E., 46
Milgrom, P., 190–1, 196–7

N

Nadler, D.A., 34, 132, 186
Nell, P.C., 70
Nohria, N., 81, 113, 184–5
Nueno, P., 111
Nystrom, P., 28, 76, 109, 112, 114

O

Ojha, A.K., 111
O'Reilly, C.A., 159, 163–4, 171

Orton, J.D., 191
Osterloh, M., 189

P

Pavan, R.D.J., 44
Perlmutter, H.V., 89–90
Perrow, C., 55
Peters, T.J., 28–9, 75, 109, 117, 136
Peterson, R.S., 117
Pfeffer, J., 98
Piekkari, R., 113
Piskorski, M.J., 111
Pitts, R.A., 45, 54, 75
Porter, M.E., 89
Poynter, T.A., 184
Prahalad, C.K., 184

Q

Qui, J.X., 79

R

Rahim, A., 112
Raisch, S., 10, 162
Randolph, W.A., 27, 112
Roberts, J., 190–1, 196–7
Romanelli, E., 171, 175
Rugman, A.M., 89
Rumelt, R.P., 44

S

Sayles, L.R., 27
Schlegelmilch, B.B., 39
Schulz, M., 199
Seashore, S.E., 98
Simon, H.A., 15, 33

Simons, R., 111
Simons, T.L., 117
Snow, C.C., 46
Spadini, A.L., 111
Stahl, B., 113
Stalker, G.M., 35, 56
Stoelhorst, J.W., 28
Stopford, J.M., 27, 44–6, 48, 54, 57, 58, 77–8, 82, 96–7, 105, 123
Strikwerda, J., 28
Sy, T., 28
Szulanski, G., 40

T
Taylor, F.W., 16, 182
Thanheiser, H.T., 44
Thompson, J.D., 14, 33–4, 60
Trist, E.L., 56
Tushman, M.L., 34–5, 37, 132, 159, 163–4, 171, 175, 186

U
Utterback, J.M., 175

V
Van de Ven, A.H., 35, 37

Vancil, R.F., 177
Verbeke, A., 89
Victor, B., 46, 77, 82, 97

W
Wagner, H., 114
Waterman, R.U., Jr., 28–9, 75, 136
Weber, M., 15–16, 137, 182
Weick, K.E., 30, 191
Wells, L.T, Jr., 27, 44–6, 48, 54, 57–8, 77–8, 82, 96, 97, 105, 123
White, R.E., 184
Wholey, D.R., 27, 113
Williamson, O.E., 188
Wolf, J., 27, 46, 75, 76, 78, 79, 82, 84, 88, 100, 110, 182
Wong, P.K., 163
Woodward, J., 55

Y
Yoshino, M.Y., 111, 139, 205
Yuchtman, E., 98

Z
Zander, U., 40, 145, 219

Subject Index

A

aerospace industry, 5, 27–8, 113
ambidexterity of organizations, 10, 161–79
  definition of, 10, 162, 174
army/military organizations, 5, 159

B

balanced matrix structure, 10–11, 26, 114, 131–59, 165–70, 174–9
  definition of, 131–6
  situations where it fits, 152–6
bounded rationality, 4, 15, 21, 23, 169–71, 203, 217

C

California Bank, 177
centralization/decentralization, 17, 19, 20, 23, 30, 35, 51–7, 59–60, 67, 83, 90, 103, 183, 187–94, 196, 198, 206, 210
committee, 19–21, 71–2, 163–4, 182, 205, 215–16
complexity of strategy, 1–2, 16, 20, 23, 27, 54–5, 67, 79, 114, 128, 181, 203–5, 210, 215–17
conflict. *See* matrix structures, conflict in
Corning Glass, 139, 204–5, 216
culture and shared vision, 110–11, 113, 133, 136, 165, 172

D

decision-making
balanced mode of, 9–11, 26, 114, 131–59, 166–78, 203, 209
in matrix structures, 9–11, 131–59
rule-based mode of, 9–10, 131–59, 165–7, 169–70, 176–8
distribution of power and authority, 28, 32, 34, 115–21, 183, 185
Dow Chemical, 134
DuPont, 16–21, 23, 72, 204, 216

E

economies of scale (and scope), 11, 16, 55, 57–8, 60, 70–1, 84–9, 91, 103–4, 167–8, 196–8, 201, 206–9
elementary structure, 3, 6–9, 43–54, 115–25, 140–2
environment, 6, 10, 17–20, 23, 26, 29–31, 33, 36, 39, 162
escalation of issues/decisions, 111, 127, 133–5
evolutionary engineering, 169
exploitation of knowledge, 161–79
extent of acquisitions, 54, 60–2, 68
extent of outside ownership, 38, 59 63, 68

F

fit *vs.* causation, 37–8
flexible matrix structure, 10–11, 157–9, 161–79

functional division structure, 6–9, 16–21, 23–4, 49–55, 57–71

G

geographical region structure, 6–7, 16, 22–4, 44, 49–53, 56–60, 62, 64–5, 67–71
global *vs.* local, 204–8
goal structure, 186–7

H

healthcare industry, 103
heterarchy, 113, 184
hierarchical coordination. *See* information processing, hierarchical information processing
hierarchical structures, 49–53, 79–82, 181–202
situations where they fit, 190–202

I

information processing
as an abstract intervening concept, 36–9
approach to organization design, 5–6, 32–40, 43–8, 217–20
capacities of balanced and rule-based modes of decision-making, 142–7
capacities of elementary structures or dimensions, 49–61
capacities of matrix structures, 79–91

Subject Index 237

dimensions of, 38–40
hierarchical information processing, 25, 81, 83, 182, 190–211
information overload, 34–5, 55, 83, 87, 93, 95, 100–2, 183
information-processing capacity of balanced matrix, 143–6
information-processing capacity of rule-based matrix, 143–6
network information processing, 25, 81–2, 182–90, 192–212
requirements of strategy, 53–61
strategic *vs.* tactical, 38–9, 49, 51–60, 69–72, 82–3, 85, 88
subject (content), 39, 49–53, 56–60, 69, 70, 82–3, 85, 87
innovation, significant, 197–2, 208–9
interdependency, 4, 14–21, 35, 54–60, 69, 72, 89–90, 103, 112–13, 125–8, 163, 175, 181–2, 187–95, 204–6, 215, 217
international division structure, 7, 24, 44–6, 48–53, 56–60, 62, 64–5, 68–70, 84–6, 139, 204–5, 216
intervening concept, 29, 33, 36–9
intraorganizational communication, 32, 34–5

L

lateral coordination. *See* information processing, network information processing

M

matrix in the mind, 11, 202–3
matrix managers, 25, 111, 114, 118
matrix structures
accountability during decision-making, 28, 111, 136, 143–4, 147–8, 157, 165
approach to organization design, 78–9, 105
balanced matrix, 9–11, 26, 28–9
conflict in, 9, 28, 98, 109–28, 133, 135–6, 140, 145
types of, 79–82, 115–22
definition of, 1, 5, 7, 24–7
economizing on human and monetary costs, 145
and elementary structures, 4–7, 48–50
flexible, 10, 161–79
with functional division dimension, 83–4, 102–3
functional division × geographical region matrix, 94–6, 101–3, 115–16, 119–25
functional division × product division matrix, 80–1, 90–2, 94–5, 99–101, 103, 111, 115–16, 118, 120, 123, 125
functional division × product division × geographical region matrix, 92, 94–7, 100, 102–4, 115–16, 118, 121, 123
future of, 215–17
with geographical region dimension, 87, 89–93, 95–9, 101–2, 206–7

matrix structures (cont.)
  history of, 5, 27–8
  innovativeness generated during decision-making, 145–6
  with international division dimension, 85–6
  international division × product division matrix, 85, 205, 216
  lack of theory, 2–3, 75, 217
  literature review, 76–9
  vs. networks, 11, 181–209
  problems of, 28, 75, 109, 136, 202
  with product division dimension, 81, 83–7, 90–2, 95–7, 99–104
  product division × geographical region matrix, 24, 80, 92, 94–5, 102–3, 111, 115, 118–20, 123, 138, 166–7, 205, 207
  project management matrix, 27, 112
  rule-based matrix, 10, 131–59
  speed of decision-making, 144
  structural configuration of, 9–10, 138–9, 158
  thoroughness of evaluation of alternatives, 146
metanational, 199
mode of decision-making, 131–59
Moses, 14
motivation and behavior, 189
multidimensional strategies, 215–17
multidivisional structure, 16–24

N

network designs, 3–4, 31–2, 49, 71–2, 80–2, 113–14, 126, 181–90, 215
  definition of, 184
  situations where they fit less, 190–202
networks. See network designs
non-hierarchical coordination. See information processing, network information processing
number of foreign subsidiaries, 59, 87–8, 91, 95

O

organizational behavior, 30
organizational distance, 49, 53, 80
organization design history, 13–24

P

participative problem solving, 112, 127
power generation and distribution industries, 103
product change, 56–7, 62, 64–5, 68, 71
product diversification, 20–3, 44–6, 48, 54–5, 62, 64–5, 68, 71, 82–4, 91–2, 94–6, 99–101, 105, 204
product diversity. See product diversification
product division structure, 6, 16, 20–1, 44–6, 49–60, 62, 64–7, 71–2, 84–8, 100

Subject Index 239

product modification, 55–6
profit centers, 124, 126–7
punctuated equilibrium theory, 171, 175–6

R
responsibility charts, 140
Roman Catholic Church, 15
rule-based matrix structure
 definition of, 131–6
 situations where it fits, 147–52
 rules, 133–7

S
Sears Roebuck, 16, 22
senior management, role of, 163–4, 168–9, 172–3
size of foreign manufacturing, 58, 62, 64–5, 68, 70, 88–9, 92–4, 105
size of foreign operations, 45, 57–62, 64–5, 68, 70–1, 82, 84–7, 91–2, 94–6, 103, 105
specialization, 4, 14–17, 22, 23, 39, 49, 85, 140, 142, 171, 183, 198, 200–3
strategic orientation
 global strategy, 89–90, 193–5, 205, 210
 international strategy, 89–90, 92–3, 99
 multidomestic strategy, 89, 91, 191, 193, 205

transnational strategy, 89–93, 102, 152, 175, 205, 210
strategy-structure fit
 conceptualization of, 24, 29–31
 for elementary structures, 6, 7, 43–8, 53–66
 for matrix structures, 8, 75–9, 82–106
 for modes of decision-making in a matrix structure, 132–8
strategy-structure-performance fit, 46–8, 98–9
strategy-structure theory
 limitations, 46–8
structured network, 202–3

T
telecommunication industry, 103
tensor structure. *See* matrix structures, functional division × product division × geographical region matrix
Texas Instruments, 149, 177
tight coupling, 191–5, 206–7
transnational MNC, 113, 184

U
uncertainty, 33–5
unity of command, 5, 28, 159

Made in the USA
Coppell, TX
25 January 2023